The Informal Economy

The Informal Economy: Measures, Causes, and Consequences provides a comprehensive account of the economics of informality through the lenses of various economic perspectives.

Although informal economic activity is widespread all around the world, many issues around its nature and consequences remain largely under-explored or unresolved. Most importantly, the evidence presented in the existing literature on informality has failed to generate a consensus on the measurements, causes, and effects of the informal sector among researchers. Most, if not all, of the empirical results are inconclusive or dependent on the nature of the dataset used in the analysis. This book aims to address that gap by exploring different definitions and measures of the informal economy, including different perspectives, then subjecting these measures to a battery of empirical tests to examine the determinants and effects of informality. Through this analysis and an extensive review of the literature, the book explores many of the economic, political, and social factors of the informal economy including the relationship between informality and the tax burden, tax enforcement, and institutional quality.

This key text makes for compulsive reading to scholars and students interested in the informal or shadow economy.

Ceyhun Elgin is a Professor of Economics at Boğaziçi University, Turkey, and a Lecturer in Discipline at Columbia University, USA.

Routledge Frontiers of Political Economy

268 Macroeconomic Measurement Versus Macroeconomic Theory
Merijn Knibbe

269 Hayek's Market Republicanism
The Limits of Liberty
Sean Irving

270 The End of Individualism and the Economy
Emerging Paradigms of Connection and Community
Ann E. Davis

271 Profit, Accumulation and Crisis in Capitalism
Long-term Trends in UK, US, Japan and China, 1855–2018
Minqi Li

272 Global Imbalances and Financial Capitalism
Stock-Flow-Consistent Modelling
Jacques Mazier

273 Markets, Community, and Just Infrastructures
Nancy Neiman

274 The Informal Economy
Measures, Causes, and Consequences
Ceyhun Elgin

275 Understanding Financial Crises
Ensar Yılmaz

For more information about this series, please visit www.routledge.com/books/series/SE0345

The Informal Economy

Measures, Causes, and Consequences

Ceyhun Elgin

Routledge
Taylor & Francis Group
LONDON AND NEW YORK

First published 2021
by Routledge
2 Park Square, Milton Park, Abingdon, Oxon OX14 4RN

and by Routledge
52 Vanderbilt Avenue, New York, NY 10017

Routledge is an imprint of the Taylor & Francis Group, an informa business

British Library Cataloguing-in-Publication Data
A catalogue record for this book is available from the British Library

Library of Congress Cataloging-in-Publication Data

Names: Elgin, Ceyhun, author.
Title: The informal economy: measures, causes, and consequences / Ceyhun Elgin.
Description: Abingdon, Oxon; New York, NY: Routledge, 2020. | Series: Routledge frontiers of political economy | Includes bibliographical references and index.
Subjects: LCSH: Informal sector (Economics) | Labor unions–Organizing.
Classification: LCC HD2341 .E535 2020 (print) | LCC HD2341 (ebook) | DDC 330–dc23
LC record available at https://lccn.loc.gov/2020012360
LC ebook record available at https://lccn.loc.gov/2020012361

ISBN: 978-0-367-28082-6 (hbk)
ISBN: 978-0-429-27493-0 (ebk)

Typeset in Bembo
by codeMantra

To my beloved Akça and Cansu...

Contents

Preface ix

1 Informality: curse or opportunity? 1

2 Definitions of informality 7
2.1 Defining informality 7
2.1.1 Definitions from early descriptive literature 8
2.1.2 Definitions used by national and international institutions 9
2.1.3 Toward a robust definition 10
2.2 State of the art review 11
2.2.1 Informality in the recent literature 11
2.2.2 Future directions in the literature on informality 14

3 Measuring informality 18
3.1 Motivation behind measurement 18
3.2 Existing methods 19
3.2.1 Direct methods 19
3.2.2 Indirect methods 21
3.2.3 Model-based methods 22
3.3 A recent method on the frontier 25
3.3.1 The model 25
3.3.2 Solving the model 27
3.3.3 Calibration and data construction 28
3.3.4 Constructed data set 29
3.3.5 A sectoral model 31
3.4 Comparison of different methods 35
3.4.1 All models considered 35
3.4.2 MIMIC versus DGE 36

4 Size of the informal sector worldwide **41**
4.1 Measures and trends for the global economy 41
4.2 Regional statistics 43
4.3 The informal sector in cities worldwide 45
4.3.1 Simple regression analysis 51
4.4 Forecasts for the near future 53

5 Determinants of informality **57**
5.1 Literature on the determinants of informality 57
5.2 Tax burden 61
5.2.1 A quick look at the plain data 61
5.2.2 A simple model on taxes and informal sector 64
5.2.3 Empirical analysis 77
5.3 Institutional quality 86
5.3.1 A theoretical framework 89
5.4 Other determinants and policy implications 98
5.4.1 Other macroeconomic determinants of informality 98
5.4.2 Implications for policy-makers 99

6 Effects of informality **105**
6.1 Effects on fiscal policy 105
6.1.1 Effects on taxes 105
6.1.2 Effects on public debt 112
6.2 Effects on monetary policy 119
6.2.1 Growth effects of inflation and informal sector 120
6.2.2 Effect on monetary policy through housing markets 128
6.3 Other effects of informality and policy implications 133
6.3.1 Unionization 133
6.3.2 Effects on growth and technology 137
6.3.3 Growth, wage-productivity gap, and informality 145
6.3.4 Pollution 151
6.3.5 Corporate social responsibility 164
6.3.6 Bilateral trade effects 171
6.3.7 Implications for policy-makers 176

7 Concluding remarks **184**

Index 187

Preface

Economics has recently become a science, where most of the profession prefers publishing academic papers over publishing books. Despite this trend, books are still in-demand as they are the ones that explore questions from a broader perspective, present new findings, or summarize the existing ones in a more coherent and disciplined manner. That is why high-quality books in economics are still being published every year. Even though several of these books are on the informal sector, I honestly believe that this book is singled out with its broad scope and comprehensiveness.

Since obtaining my Ph.D. in 2010, I always thought that I should write at least one book in my academic career. Honestly, as I have published over 30 papers on the informal sector, I always had the feeling that this book should have been on the informal sector. However, I would definitely not do this if I was not encouraged by my close friend, colleague, and coauthor Adem Yavuz Elveren. Already having published three books and several book chapters, Adem was the one who literally pushed and encouraged me to undertake such a big project. He also gave several pieces of advice that were extremely helpful while writing the book.

Moreover, as anyone who has ever attempted to write a book would agree, continuous support by friends and family is very important during this process. In this regard, this book would not come into existence if it were not for the invaluable help and support of numerous individuals. First and foremost, I am grateful to my wife and daughter Cansu Yüksel and Akça Elgin for their continuous support and joy. I also like to thank my dear mother, Füsun Elgin, who played a significant role in shaping my education and career. Unfortunately, my dear grandfathers H. Basri Akgiray, M. Cezmi Elgin, my dear father M. Akin Elgin, and my uncle Attila Kurtaran, who always supported me since childhood, could not live to see this, but I am sure they would have been very proud. I am also very thankful to all my coauthors whom I published very interesting research on informality and I also used some pieces of these papers in this book: Dila Asfuroğlu, Serdar Birinci, Kerem Cantekin, Özge Demirci,

Adem Yavuz Elveren, Ayhan Köse, Franzeska Ohnsorge, Gökçer Özgür, Oğuz Öztunalı, Muhammed Burak Sezgin, Friedrich G. Schneider, Hasan Kadir Tosun, Rasim Burak Uras, Shu Yu. Finally, my many thanks go to the economics faculty and department staff at Boston and Columbia University. Both institutions provided me a nurturing workspace, without which I could not complete this book.

1 Informality

Curse or opportunity?

Informality is one of the most widely cited and published topics in the financial and economic pages of emerging market newspapers and magazines. Turkish newspapers generally love to refer to it as a bleeding wound of the economy. This makes sense if one considers the famous circular-flow diagram that economists use in introductory textbooks as it absorbs some of the resources of the formal economy. However, the informal sector is mostly populated by firms and workers that were not able to find opportunities in the formal sector; if they could, most if not all would go formal. Eliminating the informal sector is thus very detrimental to these agents. In Elgin et al. (2013), sponsored by MasterCard Turkey in 2012, my two co-authors and I found that eliminating Turkey's informal sector (approximately 30% of GDP in 2012) would increase the formal sector by a mere 1.67%. While this is only an estimate, it is striking in the sense that one cannot merely add the informal sector on top of the formal one. Most workers, enterprises, and households that engage in informal sector activities do so because they face barriers to participating in the formal sector, so they will not be able to transition to the formal sector if the informal sector shrinks. Therefore, even though the informal sector has several detrimental effects on the wider economy, eliminating it might not benefit all segments of society.

The informal sector also provides an oasis for entrepreneurs (including self-employed) that could otherwise not operate in the formal sector because they mostly lack the resources to work formally. Eliminating the informal sector would mean that these informal entrepreneurs would either go unemployed or work as unskilled workers in the formal sector. Thus, the informal sector may benefit them, as well as for the wider economy, especially when such entrepreneurs eventually join the formal economy after developing their entrepreneurial skills in the informal sector. In this sense, the informal sector may provide an opportunity for entrepreneurs and workers who would otherwise become unemployed in the absence of this sector.

All this being said, working in the informal sector is usually not a very lucrative prospect for employer or worker as it mostly requires working for less than the minimum wage, with little (if any) compliance with labor, health, or environmental standards. Recent studies show that the informal sector work is closely associated with lower maternal, prenatal, and infant health, lower life expectancy, less human capital, less growth, and greater income inequality. Zero or partial social security coverage for informal workers also creates several problems in their lifecycles. Further complicating the issue, there is also a massive asymmetry in terms of the gender composition of the informal and formal sectors in that a substantial fraction of the global female labor force works informally. Finally, informality also creates several problems and difficulties for governments by severely distorting their policies and policy-making processes, especially in countries where the sector is large. However, as seen throughout the book, the relationship of informality with these variables is somewhat complicated and interacts with several other variables. Nevertheless, it should be clear by now why the informal sector may be either a curse or a bleeding wound for an economy.

As is evident from the earlier discussion, there are several different aspects and effects of informality, both positive and unfavorable, which is why the title of this introductory chapter is "Is informality a curse or an opportunity?" I sincerely hope that, by the end of the book, the answer will become more apparent to my readers.

Although informality is widespread globally, economists disagree about its measurement, causes, and effects. While there have been various studies of informality, including the relationship between informality and different factors, such as measures of taxes, law enforcement, institutional quality, and other economic, political, and social factors, many issues regarding its nature and consequences remain largely under-investigated. In addition, most (if not all) empirical results are inconclusive or depend on the nature of the data set used in the analysis. One of the issues behind this lack of consensus, as will be explained in this book, is the difficulty of measuring informality. The different methods to measure the extent of informal economic activity can sometimes produce strikingly different findings. I still remember being interviewed in 2015 by one of the major newspapers in Turkey on the informal economy. After the interview was published the next day, I got an unexpected phone call from the General Director of the Revenue Administration of the Ministry of Finance, who somewhat tensely complained about the Interview, especially about my estimates of the informal sector's size in Turkey.

This book aims to provide a comprehensive account of the economics of informality through the lenses of different economic perspectives. While the existing literature will be extensively reviewed, the scope of the book is not limited to a simple review. Instead, I aim to subject a range of different definitions and measures to a battery of empirical tests to obtain robust results on the determinants and effects of informality. One point to note here is that, as its title suggests, the book focuses on the economics of informality. However, I should acknowledge that there are also vast literatures on informality in other scientific disciplines, including sociology, anthropology, finance, and political sciences. Nevertheless, as an economist, I mostly focus on its economic aspects.

Mainly from a heterodox perspective, Chen (2012) classifies four distinct schools of thought on economic informality: Dualists, Structuralists, Legalists, and Voluntarists. Chen (2012) defines and identifies major studies in each school as follows:

- Dualists locate the informal economy on the fringes of the main economy, whereby it can be an economic resource for the poor, especially in crises; key studies include Hart (1973), ILO (1972), Sethuraman (1976), and Tokman (1978).
- Structuralists see the informal economy as the formal sector's attempt to reduce wages and production costs; key studies include Moser (1978) and Castells and Portes (1989).
- Legalists argue that the informal economy is a reaction to excessive government regulations; key studies include de Soto (1989, 2000).
- Voluntarists argue that some agents choose to operate in the informal economy after weighing the advantages and disadvantages of doing so; a key study is Maloney (2004).

These are not the only schools of thoughts interested in informality, as the interest of both the mainstream and other schools has been growing over time (Hart, 2008).

Research on many aspects of informality is quite recent, especially compared to other subfields within economics. One reason is that, for several reasons, economics has disproportionately focused on issues concerning developed economies. Informality is mostly seen as a developing country phenomenon, although it is also quite large in developed economies. Nevertheless, interest in this phenomenon has been accelerating.

Figure 1.1 illustrates the evolutions of papers containing the terms "informal sector" and "shadow economy" published from 1960 to 2018. The data were obtained from a year-by-year manual search in Google Scholar. The number of papers containing the term "informal sector" fluctuated in single digits or low two digits throughout the 1960s and early 1980s. However, after the publication of the seminal paper by Keith Hart in 1973 (see Hart, 1973), the number of papers jumped to three digits in 1973 before growing exponentially. Use of another frequently used, albeit somewhat less popular term, "shadow economy" also grew rapidly, particularly after the mid-1990s. For 2018 alone, for example, Google Scholar lists 13,900 papers including 'informal sector" and 3,480 papers including "shadow economy".

During the second year of my Ph.D., when I was thinking about several potential research ideas, one of my classmates from Mexico, Mario Solis-Garcia, suggested working jointly on an idea related to informality. Since before admission to his Ph.D. he worked at the Ministry of Finance, he was interested in the subject. Considering that Turkey and Mexico among OECD member economies have the largest informal sectors as a percentage of GDP, such a collaboration was also not very surprising. Having grown up and completed a bachelor's degree in economics in Turkey, I was very much aware of its informal

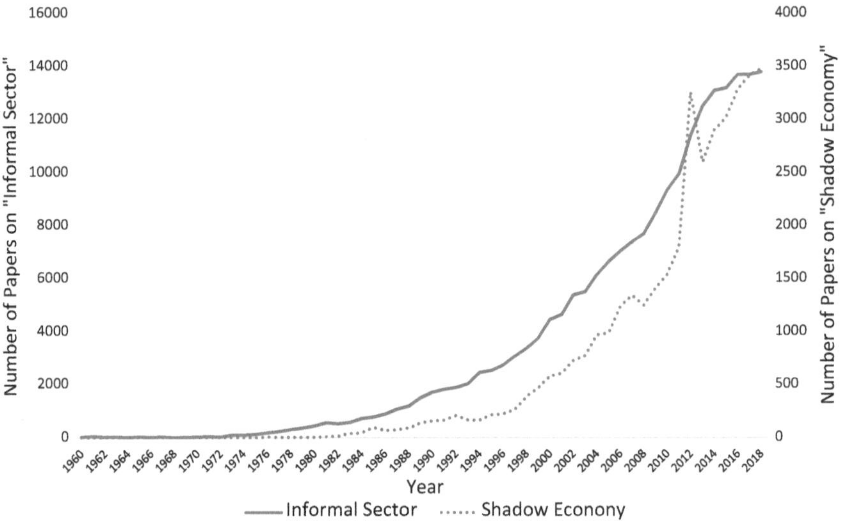

Figure 1.1 Number of papers on "Informal Sector" and "Shadow Economy" over time.

economy. However, I had not considered it a sufficiently important topic to be worth exploring with the tools of modern economics compared to much more *significant* and *essential* issues such as inflation, monetary policy, growth, inequality, and unemployment. Considering that most of the profession, including doctoral candidates, work on economic issues facing developed economies, I was not alone in my undervaluation of the field. I remember that, even after obtaining my Ph.D., publishing several papers, and completing several national and international projects on informality, several of my colleagues at Bogazici University were cynical regarding my work on informality. I remember with sadness comments like, "Again, something on informality?" or "Aren't you bored with the subject?", which exemplified the general stance of the profession toward the field. Thankfully, during my second year in my Ph.D. studies, it did not take me long to realize that I was wrong in undervaluing the field. As soon as I started to delve deeper, I noticed that there are considerable gaps in the literature on informality. The first and most important chapter of my dissertation, which economists choose to call the "job market paper", concerned informality (Elgin, 2015). Although my classmate from Mexico had not written his dissertation on informality, we managed to publish two papers after we graduated (Elgin and Solis-Garcia, 2012, 2015). More importantly, in the past ten years, I have published more than 30 papers, two book chapters, and one encyclopedia entry on informality as well as conducting several national and international scientific projects, including one from the World Bank and one from the European Commission. I am mentioning these to emphasize that the field is still growing (as is also evident from Figure 1.1), and that there are still various unanswered or open questions in the literature. Hopefully, this book will both shed light on several issues regarding informality and motivate some readers to attempt to answer these unanswered questions in the literature.

Finally, I should also acknowledge that this is not the first book on the economics of the informal sector. Leaving aside books focusing on a single country (e.g. Krstic and Schneider, 2015) or a single characteristic of informality (Pickhardt and Prinz, 2012; Schneider and Williams, 2016), at least three books have already been written from a global perspective. These are Chaudhuri and Mukhopadhyay (2010), Schneider and Enste (2013), and Williams (2019). However, there are several key differences between these manuscripts and the current book. First, as explained in Chapters 3 and 4, the current book utilizes the most recently updated version of the largest available data set of informality. Second, this book has been written from a substantially more technical perspective than the above-mentioned books. Third, the current book is the most comprehensive, especially considering the detailed analysis of various determinants and effects of informality presented in Chapters 5 and 6.

The book is organized as follows. Chapter 2,"Definitions of Informality", reviews existing definitions used by economists in both the early and recent literature. The chapter also includes a thorough literature review of different aspects of informality. Chapter 3 provides a comprehensive account of different methods used to measure the extent of informal economic activities while Chapter 4 documents the extent of informal economic activities worldwide, using the most recent estimates of informality. Chapters 5 and 6 discuss the determinants and effects of informality, respectively. Finally, Chapter 7 provides some concluding remarks and suggests future directions in the literature on informality.

References

Castells, M., Portes, A. 1989. World Underneath: The Origins, Dynamics, and Effects of the Informal Economy. In A. Portes, M. Castells, Lauren A. Benton, eds. *The Informal Economy: Studies in Advanced and Less Advanced Developed Countries*. Baltimore, MD: Johns Hopkins University Press.

Chaudhuri, S., Mukhopadhyay, U. 2010. *Revisiting the Informal Sector: A General Equilibrium Approach*. New York: Springer.

Chen, M. A. 2012. *The Informal Economy: Definitions, Theories and Policies*. WIEGO Working Paper No. 1.

de Soto, H. 1989. *The Other Path: The Economic Answer to Terrorism*. New York: Harper-Collins.

de Soto, H. 2000. *The Mystery of Capital: Why Capitalism Triumphs in the West and Fails Everywhere Else*. New York: Basic Books.

Elgin, C. 2015. Informality in a Dynamic Political Framework. *Macroeconomic Dynamics*. 19, 578–617.

Elgin, C., Erzan, R., Kuzubas, T. U. 2013. Comparative Costs of Cash and Credit Card Payments in Turkey (in Turkish). https://newsroom.mastercard.com/eu/files/2015/06/MasterCard-Arastirma-NakitsizYasam-131013.pdf.

Elgin, C., Solis-Garcia, M. 2012. Public Trust, Taxes, and the Informal Sector. *Bogazici Journal Review of Social, Economic and Administrative Studies*. 26 (1), 27–44.

Elgin, C., Solis-Garcia, M. 2015. Tax Enforcement, Technology, and the Informal Sector. *Economic Systems*. 38, 97–120.

Hart, K. 1973. Informal Income Opportunities and Urban Employment in Ghana. *Journal of Modern African Studies*. 11 (1), 61–89.

Hart, K. 2008. *The New Palgrave Dictionary of Economics: Informal Economy*, Second Edition, Eds. Steven N. Durlauf and Lawrence E. Blume. New York: Palgrave Macmillan.

International Labour Office. 1972. *Employment, Incomes and Equality: A Strategy for Increasing Productive Employment in Kenya*. Geneva: ILO.

Krstic, G., Schneider, F. 2015. *Formalizing the Shadow Economy in Serbia: Policy Measures and Growth Effects*. New York: Springer Open.

Maloney, W. F. 2004. Informality Revisited. *World Development*. 32 (7), 1159–1178.

Moser, C. N. 1978. Informal Sector or Petty Commodity Production: Dualism or Independence in Urban Development. *World Development*. 6 (9–10), 1041–1064.

Pickhardt, M., Prinz, A. 2012. *Tax Evasion and the Shadow Economy*. Northampton, MA: Edward Elgar.

Sethuraman, S. V. 1976. The Urban Informal Sector: Concept, Measurement and Policy. *International Labour Review*. 114 (1), 69–81.

Schneider, F., Enste, D. H. 2013. *The Shadow Economy: An International Survey*. Cambridge: Cambridge University Press.

Schneider, F., Williams, C. 2016. *Measuring the Global Shadow Economy: The Prevalence of Informal Work and Labour*. Northampton, MA: Edward Elgar.

Tokman, V. 1978. An Exploration into the Nature of the Informal-Formal Sector Relationship. *World Development*. 6 (9–10), 1065–1075.

Williams, C. C. 2019. *The Informal Economy*. New York: Agenda Publishing.

2 Definitions of informality

2.1 Defining informality

One key issue in research on the informal economy is the definition of what is meant by the term "informal sector". Further complicating the issue, several other terms have been used in the literature to refer to the same phenomenon, including shadow, black informal, second, or hidden economy. In addition to these somewhat interchangeably used terms, several additional concepts have been used to refer at least to one aspect of this phenomenon such as tax morale and tax evasion. These terms generally aim to describe not only the set of activities but also the behavior of consumers, producers, investors, workers, and employers that may escape from official statistics. All these terms have been used generally to characterize an economy that may be ignored or only partially covered in official statistics, consumption, production, and investment, and taking place outside of government regulations or within home production (Elgin et al., 2019).

The informal sector generally produces legal or illegal goods outside of government scrutiny and mostly does not comply with government regulations in the production, consumption, or transaction of these goods (Hart, 2008). As defining informality is, to some extent, by definition a difficult task, a more natural way to define it could be through listing its characteristics. It is generally viewed as a sector which, compared to the formal official economy, is highly (unskilled) labor intensive, less physical and human capital intensive, and less productive. However, it also substitutes for the formal economy both for firms and households. Outside of government scrutiny, it does not comply with government regulations or standards and usually avoids most (if not all) of the applicable taxes. With these characteristics, it provides room for a significant amount of generally unskilled labor while producing substantial value-added, which is mostly (if not totally) absent in official GDP statistics. Notably, among many other complications, this leads to a certain amount of underestimation of total value-added within an economy (Elgin and Oztunali, 2012).

There are different reasons why informal economic activities escape government attention. Some may be omitted from national income statistics because they are entirely illegal; sometimes, they may be hidden from the government because the way they are produced does not fully comply with laws, regulations, or standards, even though the goods and services themselves are legal. Some economic activities can also be omitted because they are conducted domestically rather than by businesses and enterprises. These activities outside the framework of bureaucratic public and private sector establishments can also overlap with each other, which further complicates the task of estimating their extent.

Even though the informal sector is prevalent and poses serious social, cultural, economic, and political challenges globally (especially for developing economies), many issues about its scope, nature, and consequences remain under-explored or unresolved. For example, the evidence presented in the existing literature has failed to generate a consensus among researchers regarding the measurement, determinants, and effects of informality.

There are also many other open questions, including very basic ones, such as whether the definition of informal economy should include specific economic activities (for example, illegal ones), whether taxes are positively correlated with its size, whether it grows during economic booms or recessions, or whether institutional quality and informal economy are substitutes or complementary. One of the main reasons for this lack of consensus is disagreements on its definition. Below, I provide several different definitions from the literature and international organizations. After briefly reviewing these, I consider how a modern and robust definition of informality could be derived from this discussion.

2.1.1 Definitions from early descriptive literature

One of the earliest definitions for the informal sector originates from the definition of the subsistence sector that Lewis (1954) proposed in his seminal work on dual economies. He argued that this sector, as opposed to the modern capitalist sector, basically consists of "that part of the economy which is not using reproducible capital" and includes "the workers on the docks, the young men who rush forward asking to carry your bag as you appear, the jobbing gardener, and the like", for which the marginal product of labor is virtually zero. Obviously, the assumption of zero marginal productivity does not comply with neoclassical economics, whereby the real wages for a profit-maximizing firm are equated to the marginal product of labor in the absence of any distortions and market power. However, other features of this sector, which Lewis characterized as low productivity, low capital intensity, high labor intensity, and low wages, are mostly the features of what modern researchers associate with the informal sector. Nevertheless, the term "informal sector" only became famous much later, not by an economist, but by an anthropologist, Keith Hart, in his seminal paper (Hart, 1973). At the time of its publication, Hart was a lecturer in social anthropology at the University of Manchester. Hart defined informality as a sector with several legal or illegal activities that differ from formal income opportunities across several dimensions. Most importantly, it is not based on wage-earning activities.

Once the concept of the informal sector became popular in the mid-1970s, as evident from Figure 1.1, the number of papers on the concept grew rapidly, along with different proposed or implied definitions. For example, Weeks (1973) characterized it as a "myriad of small, usually owner-operated enterprises using elementary technology" whereas Verlin (1974) defined it as an "impoverished and economically deprived modern subsector". Leys (1973) described it as a sector that relies on indigenous resources, mostly consisting of small family firms, is highly labor intensive, and mostly exploiting adapted technology. According to Bromley (1978), the informal sector is also much easier to enter than the formal sector as it is highly unregulated.

Even in this early literature, there were some criticisms of defining the informal sector as a separate entity from the formal economy. For example, Breman (1976) suggested that, rather than dividing the economy into two separate sectors, one should instead model the entire economy in a fragmented way. Similarly, in a highly cited paper, Mazumdar (1976) provided some support against the dualistic nature of the whole economy. He also listed several microeconomic characteristics of the sector, such as employing predominantly poorly educated and very young or very old workers as well as females, and suggested that informal workers are generally not the primary workers in their households.

Even though there are some variations across these definitions, one common factor is that (except perhaps for Lewis, 1954) most early papers viewed informality as an urban phenomenon. While some saw it as providing a major entry point for workers who had recently migrated from rural to urban areas, others, such as Mazumdar (1976), debunked this claim. Recent data make clear that the informal sector is also highly prevalent in rural areas, especially in the agricultural sector. Therefore, limiting its definition to being an urban phenomenon would ignore a large chunk of it in developing countries, where the rural population and the agricultural sector are still substantial factors.

2.1.2 Definitions used by national and international institutions

Various international institutions, such as the World Bank (WB), the International Monetary Fund (IMF), the International Labour Organization (ILO), the Organisation for Economic Co-operation and Development (OECD), the United Nations Development Programme (UNDP), and the United Nations Conference on Trade and Development (UNCTAD) have conducted research on informality. However, most lack a formal working definition of the informal sector.

One unsurprising exception is the ILO, which conducted a study in Kenya in 1972, financed by the UNDP. Its report, "Employment, Incomes, and Equality: A Strategy for Increasing Productive Employment in Kenya", attracted considerable attention and citations from subsequent researchers. It defined the informal sector as a "range of wage-earners and self-employed persons omitted from national statistics". More importantly, the report rejected characterizations of the sector as limited to marginally productive units; instead, it described it as "economically efficient and profit-making, though small in scale and limited by simple technologies, little capital and lack of links with the formal sector".

In 1993, the 15th International Conference of Labour Statisticians, organized by the ILO, defined the informal sector as a "group of production units comprised of unincorporated enterprises owned by households, including informal own-account enterprises and enterprises of informal employers (typically small and non-registered enterprises)". Notably, this definition was rather limited in scope as it reduced informality to the enterprise level. Eight years later, the 17th International Conference of Labour Statisticians at the ILO broadened this definition by also extending to employment. It defined informal employment as "all remunerative work (i.e. both self-employment and wage employment) that is not registered, regulated, or protected by existing legal or regulatory frameworks, as well as non-remunerative work undertaken in an income-producing enterprise". It also underlined that informal employees lack social security protection and many other benefits available to formal workers. The ILO also differentiated between two similar concepts that are both related to informality but also differ from each other significantly: informal employment and employment outside the formal sector. The former refers to workers employed in at least one informal sector enterprise, ignoring whether the worker is simultaneously employed in a formal job, whereas the latter includes workers employed in the informal sector or in households as paid domestic workers. For most countries, the former definition gives a larger fraction of total employment, although there are exceptions.

The OECD's definition was also in line with the ILO's. It described the informal sector as "consisting of units engaged in the production of goods or services with the primary objective of generating employment and incomes to the persons concerned". These units differ from their formal counterparts by having little substitution between capital and labor inputs, operating on a much smaller scale, and having much more informal labor relations that mostly rely on personal connections rather than contracts and other formalities.

Finally, the statistical agency of the European Union, EUROSTAT, defines the so-called "non-observed economy" as a set of "productive activities that may not be captured in the basic data sources used for compiling national accounts". This very broad definition includes not only the informal economy but also the illegal or underground economy, as well as any activity omitted due to statistical discrepancies or inefficiencies in data collection methods.

2.1.3 Toward a robust definition

As it should be clear by now, defining informality is not easy. Neither early researchers nor international institutions have produced a definition that created a consensus. I believe that any single definition, regardless of its perspective, will inevitably omit one or more features. I also believe that a globally valid definition is impossible because informal sector practices vary across countries and regions. Therefore, rather than supporting a universal definition, I want to focus instead on the characteristics of the sector.

The main characteristics can be listed as follows. (i) It is a sector that produces legal goods and services and escapes most (if not all) government regulations and oversight. This is not only limited to taxes and fees but also includes environmental and labor regulations (including regulations regarding social security, health benefits, and against child labor). In contrast, the production of illegal goods and services is generally considered as comprising the illegal or underground economy. (ii) It is largely (if not totally) omitted from national statistics. Most national statistical agencies try to include at least some informal economic activity within the national income statistics. However, by definition, these are hard to detect and measure, so a significant fraction escapes government scrutiny. (iii) Compared to the formal sector, the informal sector is mostly (unskilled) labor intensive and uses significantly less physical and human capital. (iv) It lacks several social benefits, public subsidies, and (productive) public capital (e.g. infrastructure, contractual enforcement, courts) available to the formal sector.

2.2 State of the art review

2.2.1 Informality in the recent literature

This subsection briefly reviews the existing literature on informality, discussing how informality is modeled within the literature while emphasizing its definition and interpretation. The literature on the measurement, determinants, and effects of informality is discussed separately in later chapters.

I should first mention that the term "informal sector" is popular in various subfields of the economics literature, albeit to differing degrees. A quick search in Google Scholar[1] for the terms "informal sector" along with "microeconomics", "macroeconomics", and "econometrics" yields 3,930, 14,300, and 13,700 papers, respectively, while a search with "informal sector" and "empirical" gives 88,300 results. Searching for "informal sector" with "microeconomic" and "macroeconomic" produces 11,000 and 55,000 results, respectively. Similar numbers result from combining with "tax evasion" instead of "informal sector". This indicates that the informal sector is somewhat more popular in the macro and empirical literature than in microeconomics. While this ignores the relative size of each field, it is still a useful observation.

Apart from measurement, most papers on informality focus on its relationship with different issues affecting the rest of the economy such as business cycles and macroeconomic volatility, fiscal and monetary policy, economic growth, inequality and poverty, redistribution and welfare, financial development, and employment. Theoretical papers typically construct a model economy with two productive sectors, i.e. the formal and informal sectors. A wide range of different models are employed, including two-sector closed or open economy dynamic general equilibrium, overlapping generations, endogenous growth, demand-led growth, or search-matching models.

James Tobin was one of the first economists to the notion of informality in a paper on search and employment models (Tobin, 1972). Generally, search-matching models aim to model frictions in the labor market in a partial equilibrium setting. There are several reasons to believe that these frictions are different in formal and informal labor markets and sectors. For example, Fugazza and Jacques (2004) and Florez (2019) both construct a search-matching model where informal and formal labor markets differ along several dimensions related to taxes and productivity. In a different setting, Chong and Gradstein (2007) base their analysis on productivity differences between the two sectors. Charlot et al. (2016) emphasize the risk that informal workers may be denied benefits such as unemployment compensation. Auriol and Warlters (2005) differentiate the informal sector from the formal sector in terms of the higher entry costs for the latter. Finally, Bosch and Esteban-Pretel (2012) and Meghir et al. (2015), both using two-sector search and matching models to investigate the effect of the informal sector on unemployment, conclude that policies that aim to increase the cost of informality and thereby reduce the size of the informal sector can reduce unemployment.

Several papers focus on tax evasion in the informal sector. One particularly frequently cited paper is Fortin et al. (1997) while Robinson and Torvik (2005) and Keen (2008) are also well-known papers. Newbery (1997) discussed how optimal taxes can be designed for post-socialist transition economies where the informal sector is quite large. Similarly, Cuff et al. (2011) identify optimal policies when there is tax evasion and undocumented workers. Intersecting with these papers, Tumen (2017) investigates how entrepreneurs decide whether to operate formally or informally.

Theoretical studies that focus on the effects of informality, particularly on fiscal policy, often aim to solve for the optimal tax and enforcement policies for a government in the presence of an informal sector. To give some examples, Turnovsky and Basher (2009) build a two-sector model for a developing country context in which the government can choose the tax enforcement level and thereby audit firms. They show that the government faces a trade-off between taxation and auditing. Cerda and Saravia (2013) employ another two-sector model in which firms vary in productivity. They argue that the optimal capital income in this environment tax must be negative, i.e. capital income must be subsidized, while the corporate tax rate should be positive. The sign of the labor income tax, on the other hand, is ambiguous. Finally, Cuff et al. (2011) use a model that features illegal immigration. They conclude that implementing optimal taxation and enforcement policies leads to a wage equalization across the formal and informal sectors.

Other theoretical studies, such as Fernandez and Meza (2014), Restrepo-Echavarria (2014), Mitra (2013), Granda-Carvajal (2012), Busato and Chiarini (2004), and Atesagaoglu and Elgin (2015), model how the informal sector affects business cycles and macroeconomic volatility to reveal the cyclical behavior of macroeconomic indicators. Restrepo-Echavarria (2014), for example, employs a two-sector small open economy model to show that mis-measurement of the informal sector can exaggerate the actual level of consumption volatility as higher than output volatility. This result is valid for most developing countries and even some developed countries. Busato and Chiarini (2004), using a two-sector dynamic general equilibrium model, show that the presence of informal economy explains the internal propagation of shocks better, helps to resolve the employment and productivity volatility puzzles implied by the standard RBC model, and reveals how the informal sector helps to mitigate the effects of recessions.

Regarding the effects of the shadow economy on long-run economic growth, there is no consensus among researchers about whether informality impedes or promotes it. Focusing on the different ways in which informality interacts with economic performance, some authors find supporting evidence for both positions. For example, Sarte (2000) shows that informality is not necessarily an impediment to growth. However, if the bureaucratic rent-seeking behavior encourages people to operate informally because of the costs of property rights protection, economic growth may be reduced. Generally, the microeconomic literature supports a negative relationship between growth and informality (see also Ligthelm, 2011; Elgin and Erturk, 2016). Moreover, according to Atesagaoglu et al. (2017), informality also leads to under-measurement of total factor productivity and its contribution to economic growth. Finally, as investigated in Asfuroglu and Elgin (2016), informality also seems to affect the relationship between growth and inflation.

The informal sector's influence on poverty and inequality is often studied in conjunction with urban-rural migration and trade liberalization. For example, Kar and Marjit (2009) use a two-sector small open economy model to argue that urban income equality and poverty can be mitigated if informal sector wages rise due to trade liberalization. Bhattacharya (2011) uses a three-sector dynamic general equilibrium model to show how rural-urban migration in the presence of informality reduces the Gini coefficient.

Regarding the effects of informality on financial development, Elgin and Uras (2013a) argue that two forces work in opposite directions: on the one hand, tax evasion hinders financial development; on the other hand, a larger informal sector facilitates financial development by easing capacity constraints on the financial sector.

Empirical studies that try to establish links between informality and its potential effects also mainly concentrate on business cycles, poverty, inequality, financial development, public debt, sovereign default, and social policy. Some use macro data for their empirical analysis while others use survey-based micro-level data. Using a Mincerian regression model, Xue et al. (2014) find that a reduction in the share of informal employment reduces income inequality in urban China. Kar and Marjit (2009) apply the Generalized Method of Moments (GMM) estimation to Indian data during the country's trade liberalization period to show that rising informal sector wages reduce the percentage of the population below the poverty line. Other papers investigating the role of informality in redistribution include Bennett (2011) and Ordonez (2014). Another interesting question to ask when exploring the effects of informality is its potential impacts on social policy. Tuesta (2017) uses probit estimations to show that, for Latin American countries, larger informal economies are associated with a lower probability of an individual making contributions to the pension system.

The effect of informality on business cycles and macroeconomic volatility has also been investigated both empirically and theoretically. Mapp and Moore (2014), for example, use bivariate panel regression analysis to show that larger informal economies in the Caribbean are associated with lower output volatility. In contrast, Ferreira-Tiryaki (2008), relying on GMM estimations, argues that countries with larger informal sectors face higher consumption, output, and investment volatility. Finally, using panel regressions for 152 countries, Elgin (2012) concludes that the informal economy is countercyclical while informality amplifies business cycle fluctuations.

As for the effects of informality on fiscal policy, Cicek and Elgin (2011) run estimations using cross-sectional and panel data sets for 78 countries to show that fiscal policy procyclicality is more pronounced in countries with a larger shadow economy. Considering that the optimal fiscal policy should be countercyclical or at least acyclical, this indicates that informality hinders the implementation of optimal fiscal policy designs over the business cycle. More recently, Elgin and Uras (2013b) use different econometric specifications to demonstrate that a larger informal sector is associated with higher public debt and probability of sovereign default. I provide more details on this paper in Chapter 6.

Finally, there are also exotic studies of cultural economics. For example, Rybina (2011) investigates how social norms and ethics relate to digital piracy in post-Soviet transition economies, where informality is highly prevalent. Schneider et al. (2015) find a positive correlation between a country's general religiosity and its informal sector size, although the effect varies across different religions. Somewhat more surprisingly, they also find that the informal sector is generally smaller in countries where the state and the religion are more closely connected.

2.2.2 Future directions in the literature on informality

The brief literature review in the previous subsection demonstrates that research on the informal sector is growing. However, I strongly believe that there are unexamined and undocumented aspects of the sector that will hopefully soon get the attention they deserve.

First, I believe that theoretical contributions both from microeconomic and macroeconomic perspectives will continue, using both existing and new theoretical frameworks such as agent-based computational models and applying experimental methods.

Second, I believe that the informal sector literature will see crucial empirical developments along two different streams. First, better data can be constructed using current approaches. Second, new data can be constructed using novel approaches such as machine learning and big data. Through the development of econometric methodologies, existing data can also be subjected to a larger battery of econometric tests. These new results could shed further light on the determinants and effects of informality.

Finally, another tool that can be used to investigate informality is agent-based modeling. While this has mostly attracted the attention of heterodox economists, it could become a very useful tool to model the complexity of informality.

Note

1 This search has been conducted on October 27, 2019.

References

Asfuroglu, D., Elgin, C. 2016. Growth Effects of Inflation under the Presence of Informality. *Bulletin of Economic Research*. 68 (4), 311–328.

Atesagaoglu, O. E., Elgin, C. 2015. Cyclicality of Labor Wedge and Informal Sector. *Economics Letters*. 136, 141–146.

Atesagaoglu, O. E., Elgin, C., Oztunali, O. 2017. TFP Growth in Turkey Revisited: The Effect of Informal Sector. *Central Bank Review*. 17 (1), 11–17.

Auriol, E., Warlters, M. 2005. Taxation Base in Developing Countries. *Journal of Public Economics*. 89 (4), 625–646.

Bennett, J. 2011. Informal Production and Labour Market Segmentation. *Journal of Institutional and Theoretical Economics*. 167 (4), 686–707.

Bhattacharya, P. C. 2011. Informal Sector, Income Inequality and Economic Development. *Economic Modelling*. 28 (3), 820–830.

Bosch, M., Esteban-Pretel, J. 2012. Job Creation and Job Destruction in the Presence of Informal Markets. *Journal of Development Economics*. 98 (2), 270–286.

Breman, J. 1976. A Dualistic Labour System? A Critique of the Informal Sector Concept: I: The Informal Sector. *Economic and Political Weekly*. 11 (48), 1870–1876.

Bromley, R. 1978. Introduction - The Urban Informal Sector: Why Is It Worth Discussing? *World Development*. 6 (9–10), 1033–1039.

Busato, F., Chiarini, B. 2004. Market and Underground Activities in a Two-Sector Dynamic Equilibrium Model. *Economic Theory*. 234, 863–861.

Cerda, R. A., Saravia, D. 2013. Optimal Taxation with Heterogeneous Firms and Informal Sector. *Journal of Macroeconomics*. 35, 39–61.

Charlot, O., Malherbet F., Ulus, M. 2016. Unemployment Compensation and the Allocation of Labor in Developing Countries. *Journal of Public Economic Theory*. 18 (3), 385–416.

Chong, A., Gradstein, M. 2007. Inequality and Informality. *Journal of Public Economics*. 91 (1–2), 159–179.

Cicek, D., Elgin, C. 2011. Cyclicality of Fiscal Policy and the Shadow Economy. *Empirical Economics*. 413, 725–737.

Cuff, K., Marceau, N., Mongrain, S., Roberts, J. 2011. Optimal Policies with an Informal Sector. *Journal of Public Economics*. 95 (11–12), 1280–1291.

Elgin, C. 2012. Cyclicality of Shadow Economy. *Economic Papers: A Journal of Applied Economics and Policy*. 31 (4), 478–490.

Elgin, C., Erturk, N. F. 2016. Is Informality a Barrier for Convergence? *Economics Bulletin*. 36 (4), 2556–2568.

Elgin, C., Kose, A., Ohnsorge, F., Yu, S. 2019. *Shades of Grey: Measuring the Informal Economy Business Cycles.* World Bank, mimeo.

Elgin, C., Oztunali, O. 2012. *Shadow Economies around the World: Model Based Estimates*. Bogazici University Department of Economics Working Papers, 2012-05.

Elgin, C., Uras, R. B. 2013a. Is Informality a Barrier to Financial Development? *SERIEs: Journal of the Spanish Economic Association*. 4 (3), 309–331.

Elgin, C., Uras, R. B. 2013b. Public Debt, Sovereign Default Risk and Shadow Economy. *Journal of Financial Stability*. 9 (4), 628–640.

Fernandez, A., Meza, F. 2014. Informal Employment and Business Cycles in Emerging Economies: The Case of Mexico. *Review of Economic Dynamics*. 18 (2), 381–405.

Ferreira-Tiryaki, G. 2008. The Informal Economy and Business Cycles. *Journal of Applied Economics*. 11 (1), 91–117.

Florez, L. A. 2019. Job Search Inefficiency and Optimal Policies in the Presence of an Informal Sector. *International Journal of Economic Theory*. 15 (4), 399–429.

Fortin, B., Marceau, N., Savard, L. 1997. Taxation, Wage Controls and the Informal Sector. *Journal of Public Economics*. 66 (2), 293–312.

Fugazza, M., Jacques, J. J. 2004. Labor Market Institutions, Taxation and the Underground Economy. *Journal of Public Economics*. 88 (1–2), 395–418.

Granda-Carvajal, C. 2012. Macroeconomic Implications of the Underground Sector: Challenging the Double Business Cycle Approach. *Economic Analysis and Policy*. 42 (2), 221–236.

Hart, K. 1973. Informal Income Opportunities and Urban Employment in Ghana. *Journal of Modern African Studies*. 11 (1), 61–89.

Hart, K. 2008. *The New Palgrave Dictionary of Economics: Informal Economy*, Second Edition, Eds. Steven N. Durlauf and Lawrence E. Blume. New York: Palgrave Macmillan.

Kar, S., Marjit, S. 2009. Urban Informal Sector and Poverty. *International Review of Economics and Finance*. 18 (4), 631–642.

Keen, M. 2008. VAT, Tariffs, and Withholding: Border Taxes and Informality in Developing Countries. *Journal of Public Economics*. 92 (10–11), 1892–1906.

Lewis, W. A. 1954. Economic Development with Unlimited Supplies of Labour. *The Manchester School*. 22 (2), 139–191.

Leys, C. 1973. Interpreting African Underdevelopment: Reflections on the ILO Report on Employment, Incomes and Equality in Kenya. *African Affairs*, 72, 419–429.

Ligthelm, A. 2011. Survival Analysis of Small Informal Businesses in South Africa, 2007–2010. *Eurasian Economic Review*. 1 (1), 160–179.

Mapp, T., Moore, W. 2014. The Informal Economy and Economic Volatility. *Macroeconomics and Finance in Emerging Market Economies*. 8 (1–2), 185–200.

Mazumdar, D. 1976. The Urban Informal Sector. *World Development*. 4 (8), 655–679.

Meghir, C., Narita, R., Robin, J.-M. 2015. Wages and Informality in Developing Countries. *American Economic Review*. 105 (4), 1509–1546.

Mitra, S. 2013. Informality, Financial Development and Macroeconomic Volatility. *Economics Letters*. 120 (3), 454–457.

Newbery, D. M. 1997. Optimal Tax Rates and Tax Design During Systemic Reform. *Journal of Public Economics*. 63 (2), 177–206.

Ordonez, J. C. L. 2014. Tax Collection, the Informal Sector, and Productivity. *Review of Economic Dynamics*. 17 (2), 262–286.

Restrepo-Echavarria, P. 2014. Macroeconomic Volatility: The Role of the Informal Economy. *European Economic Review*. 70, 454–469.

Robinson, J. A., Torvik, R. 2005. White Elephants. *Journal of Public Economics*. 89 (2–3), 197–210.

Rybina, L. 2011. Music Piracy in Transitional Post-Soviet Economies: Ethics, Legislation, and Expertise. *Eurasian Economic Review*. 1 (1), 3–17.

Sarte, P. D. G. 2000. Informality and Rent-Seeking Bureaucracies in a Model of Long-Run Growth. *Journal of Monetary Economics*. 46 (1), 173–197.

Schneider, F., Linsbauer, K., Heinemann, F. 2015. Religion and the Shadow Economy. *Kyklos*. 68 (1), 111–141.

Tobin, J. 1972. *Note on Search Unemployment and Wage Differentials*. Institute for Development Studies-University of Nairobi, Working Paper No. 71.

Tuesta, D. 2017. Retirement and Labour Markets under the Context of Pension Reform in Latin America. *Economic and Political Studies*. 5 (4), 475–500.

Tumen, S. 2017. Entrepreneurship in the Shadows: Wealth Constraints and Government Policy. *Economics of Transition and Institutional Change*. 25 (2), 239–269.

Turnovsky, S. J., Basher, M. A. 2009. Fiscal Policy and the Structure of Production in a Two-Sector Developing Economy. *Journal of Development Economics*. 88 (2), 205–216.

Verlin, H. H. 1974. The Informal Sector: The Implications of the ILO's Study of Kenya. *African Studies Review*. 17 (1), 205–212.

Weeks, J. 1973. Uneven Sectoral Development and the Role of the State. *IDS Bulletin*. 5 (2–3), 76–82.

Xue, J., Gao, W., Guo, L. 2014. Informal Employment and Its Effect on the Income Distribution in Urban China. *China Economic Review*. 31, 84–93.

3 Measuring informality

3.1 Motivation behind measurement

As I discussed in the second section of the previous chapter, a significant fraction of earlier papers on the informal economy were theoretical, mainly because of the lack of empirically and econometrically usable estimates of informality. Without such estimates, it is impossible to subject informality to proper empirical policy analysis because the lack of data points prevents any statistical or econometric analysis to understand the factors determining the size of the informal economy or to quantify its effects. Similarly, one can also not evaluate the effectiveness of potential policy tools designed to address the sector. Nevertheless, various approaches and methodologies have been suggested, developed, and used in the literature to estimate informal sector size.

By its very definition, estimating the size of the informal economy is very difficult. Most economic data are either directly measured or at least imputed by national governmental or independent non-governmental authorities. Unfortunately, this is not the case for many measures of informality. Except for a few mostly employment-based series, most data sets of informality used in the literature have been constructed by individual researchers or teams and reported as academic publications.

Before examining the different methods used, I should clarify exactly what is being measured. As explained in more detail in later sections of this chapter, these methods actually measure different aspects of the same notion. For example, measuring informal employment requires different assumptions and tools to measuring informal outputs, even though the two concepts are closely related. Similarly, strikingly different approaches are required to measure informality at household or firm level. Finally, informality can be measured at the individual level by measuring attitudes and perceptions toward informal employment, production, or tax evasion. In short, each method must first define informality in its own way before measuring it because definition and measurement are very much related to each other.

3.2 Existing methods

Schneider (2005), Medina and Schneider (2018), and Elgin and Erturk (2019) provide excellent surveys and comparisons of different ways of estimating informal sector size. While I critically review these below, I would refer interested readers to these papers for more extensive surveys of these approaches.

Informal economy estimation methods are generally characterized under three categories that differ in various dimensions, but are all based on the use of several different econometric estimation methods: direct approaches, indirect approaches, and the model approach. I should acknowledge that this categorization is not strict as some methods use hybrid approaches.

3.2.1 Direct methods

As suggested by the term "direct", these methods measure the extent of informality directly, without relying on any assumptions or intermediate steps. Direct approaches are generally based on surveys, questionnaires, interviews, and tax audits of firms and/or households. The data are then used to construct estimates of shadow economy size, generally employing microeconomic or microeconometric methods. Some researchers construct their own data sets from their own household or firm-level surveys whereas others rely on data sets constructed by other researchers or mostly by governmental or non-governmental organizations.

Just labeling a method as direct does not uniquely characterize it as there are several variations depending on what aspect of informality is measured. For example, as discussed in the previous chapter, the International Labour Organization (ILO) publishes data on informality by reporting on informal employment and employment outside the formal sector. While employment outside the formal sector is an enterprise-based concept, informal employment is a more broadly defined, job-based concept. Informal employment comprises all workers in the informal sector and informal workers outside the informal sector. Almost all persons employed in the informal sector are in informal employment. However, not all informal employment is in the informal sector, e.g. unpaid overtime work in the formal sector. Some national statistical agencies also publish household-level data on employment without social security or pension contributions. These measures, constructed from national household surveys, are also interpreted as an indicator of informal employment.

Cantekin and Elgin (2017) is an example of researchers conducting their own survey to obtain indicators of informality. While this survey, given to 1,000 firms in Turkey, included many questions, only a handful of questions were used to measure the extent of informality. One was the ratio of social security payments to wages in each firm. Due to several rules and regulations in the Turkish labor market, the ratio of social security payments to wages should be at least 34.5%. However, 28.89% of the firms (generating 20.02% of the total revenue) fell below this threshold, which indicates that they were engaging in informal economic activities. However, this ratio alone does not provide an exact measure of informality. Two other variables that might yield additional information are the legal category and registration status of each firm. For example, sole proprietorships or limited-liability firms are generally considered more likely to be informal. In this data set, 46.8% of firms fell into this category while two other indicators of informality were paying salaries in cash (40.5%) and not having a bank account for the firm (7.17%).

As these percentages demonstrate, focusing on different aspects of informality yields different estimates of its size. Furthermore, unless the measures are obtained from a governmental survey relying on a full inspection of tax returns of households or firms (which are very hard to obtain in many countries due to strict privacy laws), there is no guarantee that the responses of the survey respondents are truthful. This is especially the case when the firm or the household being surveyed is engaged in activities in the informal sector. Other disadvantages of such direct approaches include difficulties regarding the sample choice, potential selection bias, and measurement errors in interviews and surveys. Finally, direct approaches are mostly used at just one specific time point to conduct surveys or interviews because it is usually too costly and challenging to create time-varying estimates of the informal economy size.

Some direct methods are also used to collect cross-country or panel data. According to Elgin et al. (2019), the most frequently used measure is share of self-employment in total employment (see also Maloney, 2004). As defined by the 1993 International Classification of Status in Employment, self-employed workers include four sub-categories of jobs (as classified in World Development Indicators (WDI) and ILO): employers, own-account workers, members of producers' cooperatives, and contributing family workers. Self-employed workers are those who, working on their own account or with one or a few partners or in a cooperative, hold "self-employment jobs" as defined earlier. As discussed in the previous chapter, when defining informality, two other related measures are informal employment and employment outside the formal sector. These two measures are usually expressed as percentages of total employment (or percentages of non-agricultural employment) to refer to different aspects of informality.

Another example of a direct measure is data on pension coverage, which can be obtained from the WDI. This is defined as the fraction of the labor force that contributes to a retirement pension scheme (Loayza et al., 2010). One advantage of this data series is that it is available as unbalanced annual panel data covering 135 countries from 1990 to 2010 (Elgin et al., 2019). This measure is suitable for analyzing social security issues related to the informal economy.

Two international firm surveys in particular offer reasonably large coverage: the World Bank Enterprise Surveys and Executive Opinion Surveys, both conducted by the World Economic Forum (WEF). The former covers 139 economies from 2006 to 2016 while the latter covers 151 countries over the same period. Both surveys are based on subjective answers by top managers and business owners, who, as business experts, are familiar with their country's business climate. Like labor-related measures, firm surveys have the advantage of being independent of strong assumptions and base-year estimates for calibration. However, they have two drawbacks. First, firm surveys tend to have limited year coverage. Second, since the participants' perceptions do not vary much over time, they lack much time variation. Both drawbacks limit their application in time-series analyses. However, they do shed light on the perceived extent of informality in a country and provide guide for constructing and validating indirect model estimates.

The World Bank Enterprise Surveys compile responses on various topics (including informality) from face-to-face interviews with top managers and business owners in over 130,000 companies in 146 countries. The surveys yield the following measures of informality that have been used in the literature (Elgin et al., 2019; World Bank, 2019): percentage of firms competing against unregistered or informal firms, percentage of firms formally registered when they started operations, (average) number of years that firms operate without formal registration, and percentage of firms identifying the practices of competitors in the informal sector as a significant constraint. These constitute direct measures of specific aspects of informality.

The Executive Opinion Surveys provide a more balanced panel data set, making them more suitable for business cycle analysis. WEF has conducted the survey every year since 1979. In the 2014 edition, more than 13,000 executives in about 145 economies were surveyed. Since 2006, the survey has asked the following question relevant to informality: "In your country, how much economic activity do you estimate to be undeclared or unregistered? (1 = Most economic activity is undeclared or unregistered; 7 = Most economic activity is declared or registered)".

In addition to the firm-level surveys, household surveys can measure the extent of informality in an economy and people's opinions on informal economic activities. The World Value Surveys (WVS) are notable for their country (300,000 respondents from 96 economies) and year coverage while others mainly focus on European countries. In various waves, the WVS has asked respondents whether they can justify cheating on taxes. Responses can range from 1 (never justifiable) to 10 (always justifiable). The average responses at country-year level can be used as a measure of attitudes toward informality (Oviedo et al., 2009).

3.2.2 Indirect methods

Methods in this category usually try to obtain estimates by exploiting various economic relationships under certain assumptions. These can include the differences between postulated hypothesized relationships between variables and their actual realizations. For example, one can focus on the differences between declared income and actual spending, official and actual labor force participation, declared transactions and national income, or electricity consumption and GDP.

One way of conducting estimates in this way relies on utilizing household income-expenditure surveys. For example, it is assumed that respondents report food expenditure truthfully whereas income is generally underreported (Pissarides and Weber, 1989). Using actual estimated values of marginal propensity to food consumption, one can back out the hidden income. This method can also be generalized using macroeconomic-level expenditure and income data.

Another widely used indirect method is the currency demand approach, based on the use of a currency demand function to estimate the size of the shadow economy. Here, the primary assumption is that the informal sector depends more heavily on cash than the formal sector. The method requires estimating a money demand function and making an assumption about the elasticity of money with respect to GDP. If elasticity is not in line with the hypothesized level, then the difference can be attributed to informal sector activities. The Kaufman-Kaliberda electricity consumption method uses a similar approach by first estimating the elasticity of electricity consumption with respect to GDP. Any discrepancy between the hypothesized and actual levels can then be attributed to the presence of informal activities.

Several recently developed econometric methods, such as Bayesian model averaging (Rios, 2019), have been applied to these indirect approaches. The way they are used changes little with respect to their simplifications. These methods are generally criticized for their simplifying and limiting assumptions. They also generally focus on only one aspect or indicator of the shadow economy (using electricity unaccounted for in national income statistics or using more cash than the formal sector), so they neglect many others. Schneider (2005) provides a more extensive review and critique of these approaches while interested readers are also referred to Feige (1979, 2016), Tanzi (1983), Kaufman and Kaliberda (1996), Johnson et al. (1998), and Thomas (1999) for different applications and comparisons of the different methods.

3.2.3 Model-based methods

The many model-based methods generally rely on the use of a theoretical model.

One of the earliest, which builds work by Frey and Weck-Hannemann (1983), is primarily based on a specific structural equation model (SEM) called the multiple-indicators-multiple-causes (MIMIC) model. A dynamic version of this model, named dynamic multiple-indicators-multiple-causes (DYMIMIC), does not differ significantly from the static model. This approach treats the size of the shadow economy as an unobserved latent variable. It consists of two main steps. First, one postulates several time-varying causes and indicators of the informal economy. Second, given these causes and indicators and a specified statistical relationship between them through the unobserved latent variable, one runs a SEM to estimate the coefficients of causes and indicators. This gives an index value of informality at different points in time. This index value can then be applied to a current estimate of the informal sector's size, obtained using another method (e.g. currency demand) to create the full series of informality.

The main aim of the SEM is to examine the relationships among the unobserved variables with respect to the relationships among a set of observed variables using the covariance information of the latter. In particular, the SEM compares a sample covariance matrix, i.e. the covariance matrix of the observed variables, with the parametric structure imposed on it by the hypothesized model. The relationships among the observed variables are described in terms of their covariances, which are assumed to be generated by (a usually smaller number of) unobserved variables. In MIMIC models, the shadow economy is the unobserved variable that is analyzed for its relationship to the observed variables using the covariance matrix of the latter. For this purpose, the unobserved variable is first linked to the observed indicator variables in a factor analytical model, also called a measurement model. Second, the relationships between the unobserved variable and the observed explanatory (causal) variables are specified through a structural model. Thus, a MIMIC model is the simultaneous specification of a factor model and a structural model. The model tests thus the consistency of a structural theory through data, which makes it a confirmatory rather than an exploratory technique. In fact, in a confirmatory factor analysis, a model is constructed in advance. That is, the researcher specifies whether an unobserved (latent) variable or factor influences an observed variable and parameter constraints are often imposed. Thus, economic theory is tested by examining the consistency of actual data with the hypothesized relationships between observed (measured) variables and the unobserved variable. Such a confirmatory factor analysis has two goals: (i) estimating the parameters (coefficients, variances); (ii) assessing the fit of the model. Applying this to the shadow economy research, these two goals entail first measuring the relationships of a set of observed causes and indicators to the shadow economy (latent variable) and second testing if the researcher's theory or the derived hypotheses generally fit the data used.

In summary, the first step in MIMIC model estimation is to confirm the hypothesized relationships between the shadow economy (the latent variable) and its causes and indicators. Once these relationships are identified and the parameters estimated, the MIMIC model results are used to calculate the MIMIC index. However, this analysis provides only relative estimates, not absolute, of the size of the shadow economy. Therefore, an additional procedure, benchmarking or calibration, is required in order to calculate the absolute size of the shadow economy.

According to Elgin and Schneider (2016), two features of the MIMIC approach make it attractive. First, it explicitly considers multiple causes of informal activity and captures multiple outcome indicators of it. It is generally praised for its formalization of the informal economy as the outcome of a multitude of causes like taxes, unemployment, and institutional quality indices. Second, it can estimate informal activity across countries and over time. Indirect approaches, like the currency demand approach or the electricity approach, condense the full range of informal activity across product and factor markets into just one indicator. However, the informal sector shows its effects in various markets, which are captured better in a MIMIC model (Schneider et al., 2010). The data on the causes and indicators of informal activity identified in the literature are mainly annually updatable, macroeconomic panel data. Schneider et al. (2010), for example, produce the highly popular annual cross-country panel estimates, which are updated every year. As long as one has relevant data for indicators and causes, the MIMIC method can be applied to virtually any cross-sectional unit. For example, Wiseman (2013) uses this method to produce state-level panel estimates within the United States.

One issue is that the selection of the causes and indicators is somewhat arbitrary, and changes strikingly from one paper to another. For example, closely following Schneider et al. (2010), Elgin et al. (2019) use government spending as a percentage of GDP, direct taxes as a percentage of overall taxation, the fiscal freedom index, business freedom index, unemployment rate, and GDP per capita as causes and per capita GDP growth rate, labor force participation rate, currency as a ratio of M0 (currency in-circulation) over M1 as indicators. The DYMIMIC method also uses the one-period-lagged informal sector size as another cause of informality. However, I should emphasize that there is no consensus in the literature in the choice of these variables.

The MIMIC approach has also been criticized for being based on the use of certain ad hoc econometric specifications that make it subject to measurement errors. Another shortcoming is that it has no micro-foundations. One of the severest critics of using MIMIC for this purpose is Breusch (2005), who argues that the method is pliable and subjective. Another criticism is that the method lacks an economic theory to guide the estimations. Instead, it relies on a complex estimation strategy. Another problem is that the SEM that it constructs yields a set of index values. For example, if one runs the MIMIC model for Turkey for 1990–2018, it gives an index value for all these years. However, the values are very arbitrary and not necessarily within acceptable ranges, say between 0 and 1 for informal sector size as a percentage of GDP. Therefore, the method needs an estimate, at least for a year, of informal sector size obtained using a different method. Generally, Friedrich Schneider and his co-authors rely on an estimate obtained using the money demand method whereas others use different estimates. Once this estimate is obtained, the growth rate of the index values can be applied to this one single estimate to construct the MIMIC estimates for all years in Turkey. However, the range of the whole series significantly depends on the estimate obtained using another method. Therefore, even though the MIMIC approach is praised for combining different indicators and effects of informality in a single model, the range of the estimates it creates still depends on one existing informal sector estimate using a method based on a single indicator.

MIMIC is not the only model-based method. Recently, there has been growing interest in the measurement of informal sector size, and several macroeconomists and public economists have been developing different methods of measuring it. One relies on using a dynamic general equilibrium (DGE) model, which is generally seen as the workhorse of modern macroeconomics. I will discuss this approach in more detail in the next section.

In summary, like the methods outlined earlier, a theory-based approach relies on the use of ad hoc econometric specifications that make it subject to statistical errors. The estimated coefficients are sensitive to alternative model specifications and sample coverage. These limitations can open MIMIC estimates to manipulation and misrepresentation. Finally, this approach lacks any micro-foundations, that is, it does not rely on microeconomic behavior of households, firms, or other economic agents.

3.3 A recent method on the frontier

In this section, I will discuss a recently developed method that has been increasingly used to estimate the size of the informal sector.

There are several different versions, including Elgin and Oztunali (2012), Orsi et al. (2014), Solis-Garcia and Xie (2018), and Elgin et al. (2019, 2020). Here, I mainly base my discussion on Elgin et al. (2019); however, I also summarize the additional ingredients used by other papers using the DGE model.

The current model relies on a simple two-sector (formal and informal sectors) deterministic dynamic general equilibrium model. Since I want to run the model for as many countries as possible, as opposed to Busato and Chiarini (2004) or Orsi et al. (2014) I do not introduce uncertainty as this would require more observables to calibrate the model. I should also note that the model is mostly adapted from Roca et al. (2001) and Ihrig and Moe (2004).

3.3.1 The model

In the model environment, there is an infinitely lived representative household endowed with $K_0 > 0$ units of productive capital and a total of $H_t > 0$ units of time. The household has access to two productive technologies, denoted *formal* and *shadow*, and maximizes its lifetime utility by solving the following maximization problem:

$$\begin{aligned} \max_{\{C_t, X_t, N_{St}, N_{Ft}\}_{t=0}^{\infty}} \quad & \sum_{t=0}^{\infty} \beta^t U(C_t) \\ \text{s.t.} \quad & C_t + X_t = (1-\tau_t)\theta_{F_t} K_t^{\alpha} N_{Ft}^{1-\alpha} + \theta_{S_t} N_{St}^{\gamma} \\ & K_{t+1} = X_t + (1-\delta)K_t \\ & N_{S_t} + N_{F_t} = H_t. \end{aligned}$$

In the earlier program, $\beta < 1$ is a discount factor. I assume that the instantaneous utility function $U(\cdot)$ is strictly increasing and strictly concave. The first constraint in the maximization problem is the household's resource feasibility constraint. This requires that the amount of consumption C_t and investment X_t should equal the amount produced using the formal and informal technologies. The right-hand side of this resource constraint shows that the formal technology follows a standard Cobb-Douglas specification, where θ_{F_t} is the level of productivity exclusive to the formal sector, K_t is the household's capital stock, and N_{Ft} is the number of hours the household devotes to the formal technology. While a constant elasticity of substitution (CES) function could also be used for production, it would need more data to calibrate its parameters.

In addition, the formal output gets taxed at a rate $\tau_t \in [0, 1]$, whereas the informal sector output is untaxed. The latter can be interpreted as follows: At a cost of zero, the household can attempt to hide the income received from the informal technology and the government cannot enforce payment of taxes on informal output. This might be seen as a limiting assumption as most of the informal sector establishments pay some limited amount of taxes or licensing/registration fees. Therefore, similar to Ihrig and Moe (2004), in an alternative setup one could let the informal sector pay a constant fraction of the taxes paid by the formal sector, i.e. $\rho\tau$, where ρ can be interpreted as a tax or legal enforcement parameter. Nevertheless, in the construction of the informal sector size, one needs variables that vary across time or country for this parameter value ρ. Ihrig and Moe (2004) get around this problem by assuming that ρ can be proxied by the inverse of the growth in money supply, i.e. seigniorage. That is, governments with less ability to enforce taxes would rely more on revenues from money creation. Even though there is definitely a negative relationship between tax enforcement and relying on seigniorage, that relationship may not be as direct as assumed by these authors. In contrast, Orsi et al. (2014), when reporting estimates for Italy, use the fraction of firms audited as a proxy for this parameter. However, this firm-level data series is unavailable for many developing countries. Therefore, like Elgin and Oztunali (2012) or Elgin et al. (2019), I assume that $\rho = 0$. This is also not a game-changer, as Solis-Garcia and Xie (2018) and Elgin et al. (2019) both argue that the results with $\rho > 0$ are qualitatively and quantitatively similar to the benchmark simulation with $\rho = 0$.

In the model, the informal sector technology, which depends only on labor input, takes the form $\theta_{S_t} N_{St}^{\gamma}$, where θ_{S_t} is the level of productivity exclusive to the informal technology, while N_{St} is the amount of time that the household spends in the informal labor market. The literature that uses DGE models to model informality generally assumes that the shadow economy production function only uses labor as an input (see Roca et al., 2001; Busato and Chiarini, 2004; Ihrig and Moe, 2004; Elgin and Oztunali, 2012, 2014; Asfuroglu and Elgin, 2016; Elgin and Erturk, 2016; Elgin and Sezgin, 2017; Solis-Garcia and Xie, 2018; Elgin et al., 2019). However, as indicated by Busato and Chiarini (2004) and Elgin and Oztunali (2012, 2014) one can construct an alternative equivalent model, where the shadow economy also employs physical capital, albeit at a lower intensity. More recently, Orsi et al. (2014) and Solis-Garcia and Xie (2018) use a similar assumption to construct and identify informal sector size in a two-sector dynamic general equilibrium framework. The former study uses both capital and labor in the shadow economy production function; however, for the identification of the shadow economy size it assumes that it is more labor-intensive than the formal sector. The latter study assumes that the shadow economy only uses labor as an input. This assumption that the capital intensity of the shadow economy is smaller than that of the formal sector is also supported by previous empirical findings (see Cantekin and Elgin, 2017; Medina and Schneider, 2018; Wu and Schneider, 2019). Considering all these results, it is safe to assume for the sake of simplicity and without loss of generality that the informal sector technology employs only informal labor.

The rest of the household's problem is standard: The second constraint is the household's law of motion for capital, where $\delta \in [0, 1]$ is a depreciation rate. Finally, the last equation is the household's time constraint.

In this simple model, I assume that the government's policy τ_t is exogenously determined and that tax revenue is used to finance an exogenous stream of government spending G_t. An equilibrium is easy then to define:

Definition 3.3.1. Given the government policy variable tax burden $\{\tau\}$, a competitive equilibrium of the two-sector model is a set of sequences $\{C_t, X_t, K_{t+1}, N_{St}, N_{Ft}, G_t\}_{t=0}^{\infty}$ such that

1 The household's problem is solved by $\{C_t, X_t, K_{t+1}, N_{St}, N_{Ft}\}_{t=0}^{\infty}$.
2 G_t equals $\tau_t \theta_{F_t} K_t^{\alpha} N_{Ft}^{1-\alpha}$.

3.3.2 Solving the model

It is not possible to proceed without assuming specific functional forms for the utility function. Although other forms are possible, for the sake of simplicity, I assume a natural logarithmic utility[1] of consumption. In this case, the household's maximization problem yields the following first-order conditions:

$$\frac{C_{t+1}}{C_t} = \beta[(1-\tau_t)\alpha \frac{Y_{F_{t+1}}}{K_{t+1}} + 1 - \delta], \tag{3.3.1}$$

where $Y_{F_t} = \theta_{F_t} K_t^{\alpha} N_{Ft}^{1-\alpha}$ and

$$\theta_{S_t} \gamma N_{St}^{\gamma-1} = (1-\tau_t)\theta_{F_t}(1-\alpha) K_t^{\alpha} N_{Ft}^{-\alpha}. \tag{3.3.2}$$

The first equation is simply the Euler equation that characterizes the intertemporal tradeoff that the household is facing. The household simply faces a tradeoff between consuming today or saving today for capital and consuming tomorrow. The second characterizing equation is the intra-temporal condition, which represents the tradeoff that the household is facing between supplying one more unit of labor in the formal or informal sector. In equilibrium, by rearranging the Euler equation, one can obtain K_t in terms of N_{Ft}:

$$K_t = N_{F_t}\left[\frac{(1-\tau_t)\theta_{F_t}\alpha}{(1+g_c)/\beta - 1 + \delta}\right]^{\frac{1}{1-\alpha}} \tag{3.3.3}$$

where g_c is the growth rate of consumption in period t, i.e. $1 + g_c = \frac{C_t}{C_{t-1}}$

Moreover, informal labor can now be obtained using the intra-temporal condition as follows:

$$N_{S_t} = \left\{\frac{\gamma\theta_{S_t}}{(1-\tau_t)(1-\alpha)\theta_{F_t}}\left[\frac{(1+g_c)/\beta - 1 + \delta}{\alpha(1-\tau_t)\theta_{F_t}}\right]^{\frac{\alpha}{1-\alpha}}\right\}^{\frac{1}{1-\gamma}} \tag{3.3.4}$$

Given this full characterization of the model, I now can turn to the calibration and how we back out the size of the shadow economy using the model.

3.3.3 Calibration and data construction

The purpose of this section is to back out time-varying estimates of the size of the informal sector as percentage of official GDP in every country for any year t. In the model's terms, this is given by $\frac{\theta_{S_t} N_{S_t}^{\gamma}}{\theta_{F_t} K_t^{\alpha} N_{F_t}^{1-\alpha}}$.

Elgin and Oztunali (2012) proceed with the calibration by assuming, as standard in the real business cycle literature, that $\alpha = 0.36$ and $\delta = 0.08$. However, one of the fundamental macroeconomics data sources, Penn World Tables (PWT) Edition 9.1, recently started to publish data on the labor share, i.e. $1 - \alpha$, and depreciation, δ, varying by country and year. The estimates for this book were constructed using these data series as much as possible. For countries and years for which these values are not reported, I assumed the standard values as indicated earlier.

Moreover, I take the decreasing returns to scale parameter $\gamma = 0.495$ following Ihrig and Moe (2004). Next, I construct the physical capital-stock series $\{K_t\}$ relying on the widely used perpetual inventory method. To do this I obtain the capital stock using the following formulas:

$$K_{t+1} = K_t(1-\delta) + I_t$$

$$\frac{K_{1950}}{Y_{1950}} = \frac{\sum_{i=1950}^{2017}\frac{I_i}{Y_i}}{\delta + g_Y}$$

The first equation is the standard law of motion for capital, where K_t stands for the aggregate capital stock in year t, δ for the depreciation rate of physical capital, and I_t is investment in year t. The data for investment and δ are taken from PWT again. The second equation assumes that the economy is at the steady state in the initial period of analysis which I take as 1950 here. Once the capital stock in 1950 is calculated using the second equation, the first equation allows us to create a capital-stock series for the years between 1950 and 2017.

Once the capital-stock series is constructed one can calibrate β for every country using the Euler equation. While doing that the aggregate consumption data C_t is again obtained from the PWT. Similarly, I obtain the (formal) employment series (N_{F_t}) from PWT as well. Finally, as I assume a balanced budget for the government, τ_t is obtained as the share of government spending in GDP from the same source.

Next, using the specified values for α and δ, the calibrated value of β, and year specific τ_t, N_{F_t}, and K_t, one can use equation (3.3.3) to back out θ_{F_t} for any year t.

The only parameter remaining to be calculated is θ_{S_t}. Here, I assume that θ_{S_t} grows at a rate that is the average of the growth rate of K_t and θ_{F_t}. Notice that the informal sector production function is only a function of the productivity parameter θ_S and labor N_S. As discussed before, this does not necessarily mean that the shadow economy does not employ capital in production as one can interpret the function so that a fixed amount of capital is incorporated in θ_{S_t}. Therefore, the assumption I make regarding the growth of θ_{S_t} is not unrealistic. Having made this assumption regarding the growth rate of θ_{S_t}, I choose $\theta_{S_{2007}}$ to match the shadow economy size in 2007 of the series reported by Schneider et al. (2010) and construct the rest of the θ_{S_t} series using the calculated growth rates.

Finally, I calculate N_{S_t} using equation (3.3.4). Once N_{S_t} is obtained, the size of the shadow economy in a specific year can be easily computed using $\dfrac{\theta_{S_t} N_{S_t}^{\gamma}}{\theta_{F_t} K^{\alpha} N_{F_t}^{1-\alpha}}$ for every year.

3.3.4 Constructed data set

The procedure outlined in the previous subsection allows a data set to be constructed with about 10,800 observations for 161 countries from different regions of the world in an unbalanced panel framework running from 1950 to 2017. The next chapter more thoroughly describes the data set whereas I report some descriptive statistics and present illustrative figures in this chapter.

The first thing to notice is that the 1999–2007 period in this data set has a correlation of 0.97 with the shadow economy data reported by Schneider et al. (2010) and 0.92 with the 1991–2015 part of Medina and Schneider (2018). Notice that these data sets were constructed using the MIMIC method, which is entirely different from the DGE approach discussed here. This suggests that even for such a limited period, the two data sets seem to comove most of the time. Next, to observe the variation of the shadow economy size in a different group of countries over time, we divide the world into six different groups. OECD-EU, Latin American and Caribbean, Post-Socialist (transition), Middle Eastern and North African, sub-Saharan African, and Asian-Oceanian economies. We also report descriptive statistics for the whole data set (denoted by the row labeled "world"). These descriptive group statistics in Table 3.1 are unweighted, that is, I treated each country in a specific group equally. These are group statistics for the 1950–2017 period, except for the Post-Socialist countries, for which the period covered is 1990–2017.

When one calculates the average size of the informal sector for Germany and Luxembourg, which are economies of very different sizes, the unweighted average would simply assume they are of the same size. Therefore, looking at the unweighted series may be a misleading way of calculating the shadow economy size in a group. This is why Table 3.2 shows the descriptive statistics of weighted series for each group of countries. I calculated the weighted series for a group using the following formula: $\frac{\sum_{i=1}^{N} S_i Y_i}{\sum_{i=1}^{N} Y_i}$, where S_i is the size of the shadow economy (as % GDP), Y_i is the GDP in country i, and N is the number of countries in the group. Tables 3.1 and 3.2 indicate several crucial points: First, as ceteris paribus, richer country groups tend to have smaller informal sectors (though the relationship is not totally linear, as reported and explained by Elgin and Oztunali, 2014); once I weight the informal economy size by GDP, both the global and country group averages are significantly reduced. Second, judging from the standard deviations, the size of the shadow economy varies significantly, both between and within groups. Third, Latin American and sub-Saharan economies have significantly larger shadow economies than the other groups, with the OECD-EU group having a significantly smaller shadow economy. Post-Socialist transition economies also have large shadow economies. To understand these variations in different country groups more deeply, one should examine the determinants of shadow economies and how these determinants vary over time. This will be done in the next few chapters.

Table 3.1 Unweighted Informal Sector Size

Region	*Mean*	*Median*	*Minimum*	*Maximum*	*Std. Dev.*
OECD-EU	22.77	20.01	7.82	73.86	11.35
Latin American	46.54	44.83	21.30	105.02	14.32
Post-Socialist	34.42	33.42	14.43	81.69	12.06
MENA	28.95	27.16	13.89	68.88	12.25
Sub-saharan	44.11	41.34	20.76	113.38	12.49
Asia	38.01	36.22	9.50	112.92	17.42
World	36.93	35.70	7.82	113.38	16.37

Table 3.2 GDP-weighted Informal Sector Size

Region	*Mean*	*Median*	*Minimum*	*Maximum*	*Std. Dev.*
OECD-EU	19.93	19.00	15.21	25.03	2.95
Latin American	42.70	40.39	35.01	58.11	6.16
Post-Socialist	33.13	31.70	26.01	56.99	8.80
MENA	28.59	23.69	19.35	59.97	9.79
Sub-saharan	42.56	41.34	34.54	52.19	5.23
Asia	37.90	36.84	20.45	65.58	13.39
World	28.69	28.84	21.43	36.49	4.36

3.3.5 A sectoral model

Clearly, measuring informality, even at a highly aggregate level, is difficult. Therefore, measuring it at a sectoral level is even more daunting. One can conduct more surveys of various sectors, but this would definitely increase the costs. In this regard, Elgin and Sezgin (2017) adopt a novel hybrid approach that basically relies on the DGE method while also including aspects of a survey-based direct method. Below, I outline the model presented in this chapter.

In this model there are heterogeneous firms, denoted by i differing in their productivity levels, A_{it} in period t. There are two types of production technologies available to these firms. The first uses capital and labor as inputs while the other employs only labor, as in the model presented in the previous subsection. The first type of technology is available for formal firms. The profit from using this is taxed at the rate of τ, where ($\tau \in [0, 1]$). The second type of technology is available for informal firms. A firm choosing the informal technology faces a probability of detection by the government that depends on the level of tax enforcement and the number of workers the firm employs. Tax enforcement is again represented by the parameter ($\rho \in [0, 1]$). Employee size is represented by the function $\lambda(l)$, which indicates that possibility of tax evasion is a decreasing function of firm size, as measured by the number of workers in the firm.

The output of a firm in the formal sector is given by $A_{it}f(k_{it}, l_{it})$, whereas the output of a firm in the informal sector is $A_{it}g(l_{it})$. One also needs to assume that both production functions exhibit decreasing returns to scale, so that the firms end up with positive maximized profits in both sectors. Finally, firms rent capital from households at the rate of r_t, and pay w_{it} as wages to their formal sector workers and w_{it}^{inf} to those in the informal sector. Thus, the profit functions can be written as follows:

Formal profits:

$$V_i = \max\ (1 - \tau)\ [A_{it}f(k_{it}, l_{it}) - r_{it}k_{it} - w_{it}l_{it}]$$

Informal profits:

$$V_i^{inf} = \max\ (1 - \rho\lambda(l_{it})\tau)\ [A_{it}g(l_{it}) - w_{it}^{inf}\, l_{it}]$$

Depending on its idiosyncratic productivity level, each firm chooses the sector in which it is going to operate by comparing the maximized profits from each sector. This comparison is made by solving the following problem:

$$\max\{V_{it}, V_{it}^{inf}\} \qquad (3.3.5)$$

The solution to the earlier problem can be characterized by the two propositions below.

Proposition 3.3.1. *As a solution to the earlier problem, there exists a threshold productivity level A_i* such that:*

$$\max\Big[(1-\tau)\big[A_{it}{}^{*}f(k_{it}, l_{it})-r_tk_{it}-w_{it}l_{it}\big]\Big] = \max\Big[(1-\rho\lambda(l_{it})\tau)\big[A_{it}(l_{it})-w_{it}{}^{inf}\,l_{it}\big]\Big]$$

This proposition follows immediately when one inserts the profit maximizing first-order conditions back into the profit equations before comparing the profits of both sectors.

Proposition 3.3.2. *A firm's capital or labor demand depends on which sector it is operating in. That is,*

$$k_{it} = 0 \quad if \quad A_{it} \leq A_t^*$$

On the households' side, the model assumes an infinitely lived representative household maximizing over consumption $\{c_t\}_{t=0}^{\infty}$ and leisure $\{h_t\}_{t=0}^{\infty}$

$$\sum_{i=0}^{\infty} \beta \; U(c_t, h_t) \tag{3.3.6}$$

subject to the following constraints:

$$c_t + i_t + \frac{b_{t+1}^d}{R_t} = r_t K_t + w_t L_t + w_t^{inf} L_t^{inf} + b_t^d$$

$$+ \int_{A_t^*}^{\infty} V_{it} dG(A_{it}) + V_{it}^{inf} G(A_t^*)$$

$$K_{t+1} = i_t + (1 - \delta) K_t$$

and

$$h_t + L_t + L_t^{inf} = \overline{H}$$

Initially, at period 0, the household has a capital stock of $K_0 > 0$ and a government bond stock of b_0. In each period, the household chooses his consumption, leisure, investment, and bond holdings with δ as the assumed depreciation rate. The household rents its capital K_t for a rental rate of r_t and his labor for a wage of w_t if it works in the formal sector and w_t^{inf} for the informal sector. The last two arguments in the budget constraint are the profits received by the household, which are taken after tax from the formal and informal sector firms. Finally, R_t is the interest rate for the stock of government bonds b_t^d.

The government in this model has an exogenous stream of expenditures equal to $\{e_t\}_{t=0}^{\infty}$ and finances these using taxes on profits. However, the only revenue source includes both profits received from the formal firms and income received from fines imposed on detected informal firms. The government's budget constraint is therefore given by the following:

$$\frac{b_{t+1}^s}{R_t} - b_t^s + \tau \int_{A_t^*}^{\infty} V_{it} dG(A_{it}) + \tau \rho \lambda(l_{it}) \; V_{it}^{inf} G(A_t^*) \geq e_t$$

In this environment, the competitive equilibrium is easy to define.

Definition 3.3.2. Given an enforcement level ρ, a competitive equilibrium is sequences of allocations $\{c_t, k_{it}, l_{it}, l_{it}^{inf}, b_t\}_{t=0}^{\infty}$, prices $\{r_t, w_t, w_t^{inf}, R_t\}_{t=0}^{\infty}$, government policy $\{\tau_t, e_t\}_{t=0}^{\infty}$, and threshold productivity $\{A_t^*\}_{t=0}^{\infty}$ such that:

1 Sequences $\{c_t, k_{it}, l_{it}, l_{it}^{inf}, b_t\}_{t=0}^{\infty}$ solve the household's problem.
2 Each firm solves firm's problem (equation 3.3.5), given A_{it}:
3 $\{A_t^*\}_{t=0}^{\infty}$ is determined through the Proposition 3.3.1.
4 The sequences $\{\tau_t, e_t\}_{t=0}^{\infty}$ make the government budget constraint hold every period.
5 Bond, capital, labor, and goods markets are cleared.

For quantitative results, the utility function is assumed to be standard as follows:

$$U = \frac{(c^{\phi_2}(\overline{H} - l)^{1-\phi_2})^{\phi_1}}{\phi_1}$$

The production technology for a formal sector firm is given by

$$Y_{it} = A_{it}\left(k_{it}{}^{\alpha} l_{it}{}^{1-\alpha}\right)^{\theta} \tag{3.3.7}$$

The technology available to informal firms is given by

$$Y_{inf,it} = A_{it}\left(l_{inf,it}^{1-\gamma}\right) \tag{3.3.8}$$

Moreover, $\lambda(l)$, is chosen[2] as follows:

$$\lambda(l) = \sqrt[n]{l}$$

Notice that both production functions exhibit decreasing returns to scale technologies to allow for the existence of positive profits in both sectors. What makes this approach a hybrid one is its attempt to combine this model with survey data. The survey data needed to calibrate the model are taken from a survey conducted in spring 2014 by Cantekin and Elgin (2017).[3] While it contains more than 50 questions, this model uses just a few. These questions enable the necessary parameters to be extracted for the numerical analysis. All the information taken from the survey helps to classify whether the firm operates in the informal or formal sector in a dichotomous way. To use Proposition 3.3.1 and classify firms in either sector, one should first note the answer to the question asking how many employees the firm has. Multiplying this by the average number of hours a worker works in a year in Turkey (1,877 in 2013) gives us each firm's labor size. The capital stock of each firm can then be calculated using the following variables: each firm's revenue, purchases of raw materials and products, rental expenses, and average indicator interest rate for the year in question (Elgin and Sezgin, 2017). Note that the survey used for the study specifically asks: "In 2013, what percentage of your revenue was spent on raw material and product purchases?" and "In 2013, what percentage of your revenue was spent on rent (buildings, land, and/or machinery)?"

Next, to calculate the factor shares, Cantekin and Elgin (2017) use the survey questions about firm expenditures on rent and raw materials, and wages and social benefits. Spending on rent and raw materials represents the investment for physical capital stock while the sum of spending on wages and social benefits represents labor. This allows us to calculate the factor shares at the firm, sector, and economy levels after aggregation. The values of income, capital, and labor, factor shares, and profit maximizing conditions, where marginal productivities are equal to the prices of the factors of production, are then used to back out A_{it} at the firm level. If this level is higher than the threshold, then the firm will choose to operate in the formal sector since its productivity will allow it to generate more profits in the formal than informal sector.

The various parameters that are required for the numerical analysis are chosen based on the results of several previous studies. For the parameters in the utility function, Elgin and Sezgin (2017) use the standard values of $\phi_1 = 1$ and $\phi_2 = 0.75$. β, the discount factor, is chosen to match the average deposit interest rate in Turkey throughout 2013. The depreciation rate δ is chosen to be 0.05, while the total time available for leisure and work, $\overline{H}$, is normalized to 1. The informal sector factor share of labor, γ, and the decreasing to return scale parameter, θ, are calibrated to match the size of the informal sector and informal employment (as a percentage of total non-agricultural employment) in Turkey. The baseline tax rate τ is the average income tax in Turkey, which is about 20%. Finally, the enforcement parameter ρ is taken to be zero in the baseline case.

After calibration with the previously mentioned baseline parameters, we obtain the benchmark estimates for each sector presented in Table 3.3.

Table 3.3 Benchmark Estimates

Sector	*Percentage of Informal Revenue (%)*
Mining and Quarrying	32
Manufacturing	24
Electricity, Gas, Steam, and Air Conditioning Supply	21
Water Supply, Sewerage, Waste Management and Remediation	36
Construction	42
Wholesale and Retail Trade, Repair of Vehicles	31
Transporting and Storage	19
Accommodation and Food Services	56
Information and Communication	22
Financial and Insurance Activities	9
Real Estate Activities	13
Professional, Scientific, and Technical Activities	17
Administrative and Support Service Activities	26
Education	14
Human Health and Social Service Activities	16
Arts, Entertainment, and Recreation	17
TOTAL	28

This shows that the size of the informal economy varies greatly across sectors, although the economy-wide size is at the targeted level of 28%. The highest estimates are obtained for accommodation and food services (56%), construction (42%), water supply and sewerage (36%), and mining-quarrying (32%). Sectors with the lowest informality estimates are financial and insurance activities (9%), education (14%), and human health services (16%). These significant cross-sectoral variations justify our idea of a sectoral analysis and suggest that every sector should be investigated separately when analyzing informality tendencies.

3.4 Comparison of different methods

This section briefly compares the outcomes of the different methods used to estimate informal sector size. Unfortunately, there is no ideal criterion to prefer one over another; however, it is still worth investigating how and why the methods differ from or resemble each other.

3.4.1 All models considered

As should be clear already, the different methods summarized earlier rely on entirely different assumptions and frameworks. Therefore, one should not necessarily expect that they give similar estimates of informality. Indeed, as Figure 3.1 shows, they really don't. This figure, obtained from Elgin (2012a), illustrates the evolution of informal sector size in Turkey (as a percentage of GDP). Every series represents an estimate using a different method from a different academic paper. The methods used are the electricity demand method, money (cash) demand method, and two different MIMIC and DYMIMIC methods with different sets of indicator and causal variables. The figure is really striking and somewhat pessimistic in undermining the efforts spent to develop

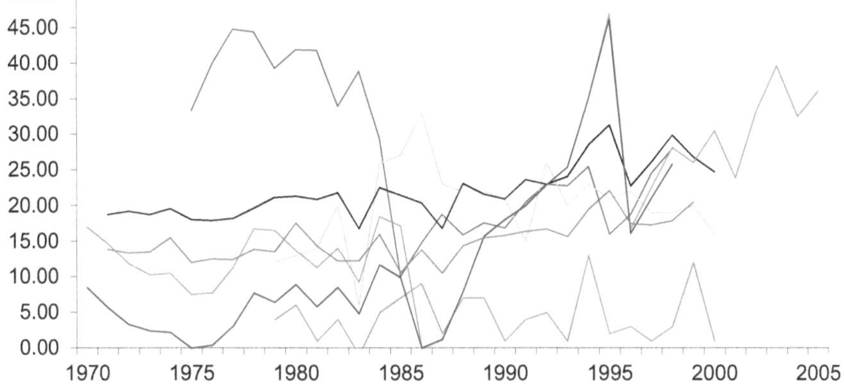

Figure 3.1 Comparison of different methods: informal sector in Turkey.

methodologies to estimate informal sector size. This is because all the series supposedly measure the evolution of the same phenomenon for the same economy. However, some series are negatively correlated with each other and vary strikingly: some exhibit little yearly variation whereas others change drastically and even become negative in certain years. The lack of criteria to determine on which method is better or worse underlines the difficulty of measuring informal economic activity.

3.4.2 MIMIC versus DGE

Several previous researchers have already compared the informal sector size estimates obtained using different methods. Elgin and Schneider (2016) stand out for their comparison of the two largest data sets obtained using MIMIC and DGE. They not only compare the informal sector size estimates for 38 OECD economies but also the driving forces of these estimates as obtained by the two methodologies.

Figure 3.2, obtained from Elgin and Schneider (2016), illustrates the evolution of the average and GDP-weighted informal sector size for OECD economies. The country-by-country data can be found in their paper. When comparing the estimates from the two methodologies, the first observation that one can make is that they are generally comparable in level. This is also evident from the declining trend of both estimates in Figure 3.2.

Although they go in different directions in certain years, such as 2009, considering the short range of the *y*-axis on the figure, one can observe that the

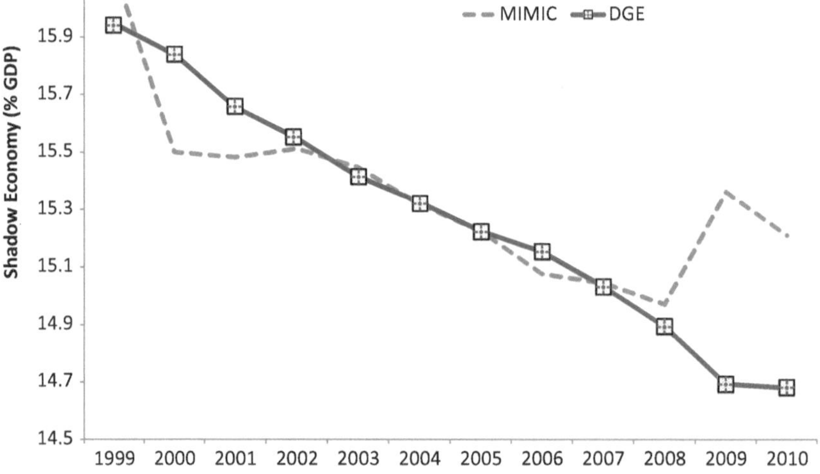

Figure 3.2 Average informal sector size (GDP-weighted) of 38 OECD countries.

estimates are not statistically significantly different from each other. The authors also report that the MIMIC series is less smooth and has a significantly higher standard deviation than the DGE series. Especially, the jump in the MIMIC estimate after 2008 suggests that the countercyclicality of the informal economy (as suggested by Elgin, 2012b) is more evident in the MIMIC series than the DGE one.

While Figure 3.2 reports the average behavior across all countries, there is some variation between specific countries. For most countries, Elgin and Schneider (2016) find that the two series are strongly positively correlated, for example 0.76 for Austria, 0.87 for Turkey, and 0.92 for France. In contrast, it is negative for some countries such as −0.57 for Spain.

The two series are even more different regarding the driving forces of the estimates. For the estimates obtained using the MIMIC model, the percentages of the average driving forces of the informal economy of the 38 OECD countries are personal income tax (13.8%), indirect taxes (14.1%), tax morale (14.5%), unemployment (14.7%), self-employment (14.5%), growth of GDP (14.3%), and the business freedom index (14. 2%). In contrast, according to the estimates constructed using the DGE model, the growth of GDP per capita has by far the largest effect (24.7%), followed by indirect taxes (18.5%), unemployment (18.3%), tax morale (17.1%), personal income tax (11.2%), self-employment (5.8%), and business freedom (4.3%). Overall, the analysis generally shows that even though the two data sets have similar levels and show a declining trend of shadow economy size over the period of analysis, they indicate certain differences with respect to the effects of the causal variables on informal economies.

Another difference between the estimates of the two methods is that MIMIC model estimates vary more than those using DGE. This is because of how the estimates are constructed. The MIMIC approach relies on an SEM with different indicators and causes. Since both can vary strongly through the period of analysis and have a linear effect on the constructed informal sector estimate through the SEM, the estimates are likely to mimic variations in causes and indicators. In contrast, the DGE method produces a stronger decline over the period of analysis. This is because the informal sector production function in the model only employs labor whereas the formal sector production function employs both capital and labor. During capital accumulation, this might create a strong downward trend for informality.

At this point, one important question would be whether any specific factors affect the relative contributions of the causal variables on informal economy size as well as the difference in the relative contributions of the two series used in the paper. To answer this, Elgin and Schneider (2016) conducted a simple regression analysis by regressing the average relative contribution of each driving force on several variables that might be associated with these. The regressors used are capital-output ratio, government spending (as percentage of GDP), GDP per capita (in constant 2005 USD), the bureaucratic quality index, and the democratic accountability index. They find that a larger capital-output ratio is associated with a higher contribution of the growth of GDP per capita and tax morale to informal sector size as measured by the MIMIC approach. However, a higher democratic accountability index (GDP per capita) is associated with a lower contribution of the growth of GDP per capita (tax morale) to informality. Moreover, a larger capital-output ratio and GDP per capita are associated with a larger contribution whereas a larger democratic accountability index is associated with a smaller contribution of the growth of GDP per capita to informality. Similarly, a larger capital-output ratio is associated with a smaller contribution of indirect taxes, and a larger GDP per capita with a smaller contribution of tax morale to informal economies. It is especially worth noting the contribution of capital-output ratio as it plays a key role in DGE estimates. The DGE model assumes that the informal sector does not employ physical capital in production. Therefore, with physical capital accumulation over time, which is one of the major sources of GDP growth, the size of the shadow economy tends to decrease. These results indicate that the differences in the relative contributions of the driving forces are systematic and correlated with certain macroeconomic and institutional characteristics of different countries in their data set.

In addition to Elgin and Schneider (2016), Elgin et al. (2019) also compare different estimates of informality with a comprehensive database of both model-based (DGE and MIMIC) and survey-based estimates. This study also includes employment and perceptual measures of informality in addition to output-based measures. Their main finding is that both the informal output and employment exhibit a declining trend that correlates with similar measures of economic and institutional development.

To summarize, even though the informal sector estimates are constructed after being benchmarked to a specific year of the MIMIC estimate, the evolution of the estimates and the driving forces behind the estimates vary significantly. Except for Elgin et al. (2019), this analysis has not been conducted using estimates based on other methods. However, I would expect the differences to be even more drastic when other methods are compared against each other. It can certainly be said that the literature still needs such comparisons using up-to-date data.

Notes

1 Similar to the production function, a CES function would also work here, but would require more data for calibration.
2 This functional form is chosen to have a probability of detection that increases with the number of employees and is concave in labor. See Elgin and Sezgin (2017) for more details.
3 The cited paper mistakenly mentions this year as 2012.

References

Asfuroglu, D., Elgin, C. 2016. Growth Effects of Inflation under the Presence of Informality. *Bulletin of Economic Research*. 68 (4), 311–328.

Breusch, T. 2005. Estimating the Underground Economy using MIMIC Models, Econometrics 0507003, Econ WPA.

Busato, F., Chiarini, B. 2004. Market and Underground Activities in a Two-Sector Dynamic Equilibrium Model. *Economic Theory*. 234, 863–861.

Cantekin, K., Elgin, C. 2017. Extent and Growth Effects of Informality in Turkey: Evidence from a Firm-Level Survey. *Singapore Economic Review*. 62 (5), 1017–1038.

Elgin, C. 2012a. Taxes and the Informal Sector: An Evaluation and the Case of Turkey. *METU Studies in Development*. 39 (2), 1–22.

Elgin, C. 2012b. Cyclicality of Shadow Economy. *Economic Papers: A Journal of Applied Economics and Policy*. 31 (4), 478–490.

Elgin, C. 2020. Shadow Economies around the World: Evidence from Metropolitan Areas. *Eastern Economic Journal*. 46, 301–322.

Elgin, C., Erturk, N. F. 2016. Is Informality a Barrier for Convergence? *Economics Bulletin*. 36 (4), 2556–2568.

Elgin, C., Erturk, N. F. 2019. Informal Economies around the World: Measures, Determinants and Consequences. *Eurasian Economic Review*. 9 (2), 221–237.

Elgin, C., Kose, A., Ohnsorge, F., Yu, S. 2019. *Shades of Grey: Measuring the Informal Economy Business Cycles*. World Bank, mimeo.

Elgin, C., Oztunali, O. 2012. *Shadow Economies around the World: Model Based Estimates*. Bogazici University Department of Economics Working Papers, 2012-05.

Elgin, C., Oztunali, O. 2014. Institutions, Informal Economy, and Economic Development. *Emerging Markets Finance and Trade*. 50 (4), 145–162.

Elgin, C., Schneider, F. 2016. Shadow Economies in OECD Countries: DGE vs. MIMIC Approaches. *Bogazici Journal*. 30 (1), 51–75.

Elgin, C., Sezgin, M. B. 2017. Sectoral Estimates of Informality: A New Method and An Application to Turkish Economy. *The Developing Economies*. 55 (4), 261–289.

Feige, E. L. 1979. How Big Is the Irregular Economy? *Challenge*. 22 (1), 5–13.

Feige, E. L. 2016. Reflections on the Meaning and Measurement of Unobserved Economies: What Do We Really Know about the "Shadow Economy"? *Journal of Tax Administration*. 2 (1), 1–37.

Frey, B. S., Weck-Hannemann, H. 1983. Estimating the Shadow Economy: A Naive Approach. *Oxford Economic Papers*. 35, 23–44.

Ihrig, J., Moe, K. 2004. Lurking in the Shadows: The Informal Sector and Government Policy. *Journal of Development Economics*. 73, 541–577.

Johnson, S., Kaufmann, D., Zoido-Lobaton, P. 1998. Regulatory Discretion and the Unofficial Economy. *American Economic Review*. 88 (2), 387–439.

Kaufman, D., Kaliberda, A. 1996. *Integrating the Unofficial Economy into the Dynamics of Post-socialist Economies: A Framework of Analysis and Evidence*. World Bank Policy Research Working Paper No. 1691.

Loayza, N., Serven, L., Sugawara, N. 2010. Informality in Latin America and the Caribbean. In N. Loayza and L. Serven, eds. *Business Regulation and Economic Performance*. Washington, DC: World Bank.

Maloney, W. 2004. Informality Revisited. *World Development*. 32 (7), 1159–1178.

Medina, L., Schneider, F. 2018. *Shadow Economies around the World: What Did We Learn Over the Last 20 Years?* IMF Working Paper 18-17.

Orsi, R., Raggi, D., Turino, F. 2014. Size, Trend, and Policy Implications of the Underground Economy. *Review of Economic Dynamics*. 17 (3), 417–436.

Oviedo, A., Thomas, D., Karakurum-Ozdemir, K. 2009. *Economic Informality: Causes, Costs, and Policies: A Literature Survey*. Working Paper 167, World Bank, Washington, DC.

Pissarides, C. A., Weber, G. 1989. An Expenditure-based Estimate of Britain's Black Economy. *Journal of Public Economics*. 39 (1), 17–32.

Rios, V. 2019. *New Evidence on the Size and Drivers of the Shadow Economy in Spain*. Universidad Publica de Navarra, mimeo.

Roca, J. C. C., Moreno, C. D., Sanchez, J. E. G. 2001. Underground Economy and Aggregate Fluctuations. *Spanish Economic Review*. 31, 41–53.

Schneider, F. 2005. Shadow Economies around the World: What Do We Really Know? *European Journal of Political Economy*. 21 (4), 598–642.

Schneider, F., Buehn, A., Montenegro, C. E. 2010. New Estimates for the Shadow Economies All over the World. *International Economic Journal*. 24 (4), 443–461.

Solis-Garcia, M., Xie, Y. 2018. Measuring the Size of the Shadow Economy using a Dynamic General Equilibrium Model with Trends. *Macroeconomic Dynamics*. 56 (C), 258–275.

Tanzi, V. 1983 The Underground Economy in the United States: Annual Estimates, 1930–80. *IMF Staff Papers*. 30 (2), 283–305.

Thomas, J. J. 1999. Quantifying the Black Economy: Measurement without Theory Yet Again? *The Economic Journal*. 109 (456), 381–389.

Wiseman, T. 2013. U.S. Shadow Economies: A State-Level Study. *Constitutional Political Economy*. 24 (4), 310–335.

World Bank. 2019. *Global Economic Prospects 2019 January: Darkening Skies*. Washington, DC: World Bank.

Wu, D. F., Schneider, F. 2019. Nonlinearity between the Shadow Economy and Level of Development. *IMF Working Papers*, 19–48.

4 Size of the informal sector worldwide

4.1 Measures and trends for the global economy

In this section, I review the measures and trends of the informal economy from a global viewpoint. Figures 4.1 and 4.2 present the annual evolution of the globally averaged unweighted and GDP-weighted shadow economy size from 1950 to 2017. The first feature of the two figures is the significant declining trend, which is steadier in Figure 4.2 than in Figure 4.1. This is mainly because richer economies generally tend to have a smaller informal sector. Consequently, when the average is weighted by GDP, these fluctuations are smoothed somewhat. Another feature is that the rate of the decline seems to be decreasing. While this needs deeper investigation, it may hint that the policies that were used in the past to reduce the informal sector may not be optimal anymore.

Figure 4.1 Unweighted informal sector size (% GDP) in the world.

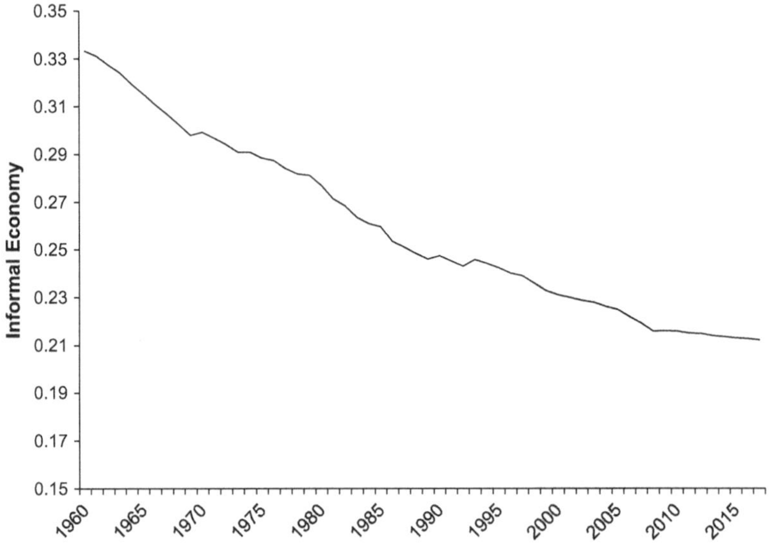

Figure 4.2 Weighted informal sector size (% GDP) in the world.

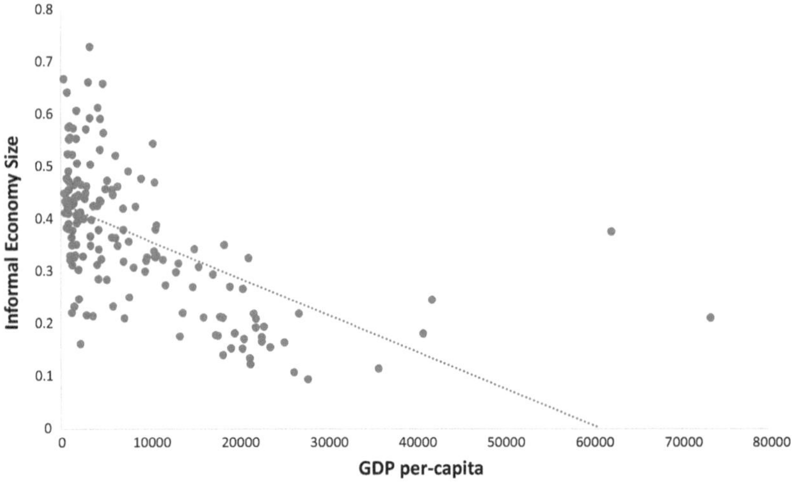

Figure 4.3 Shadow economy in a cross section.

Figure 4.3 shows why there is a significant difference in the variation of the series in Figures 4.1 and 4.2. Richer economies, not surprisingly, tend to have smaller informal sectors. In Figure 4.3, average informal sector size between 1950 and 2017 on the *y*-axis is compared to average real GDP per capita on the *x*-axis, with each dot representing one country. While the linear regression line makes the correlation more visible, the figure also indicates that the relationship

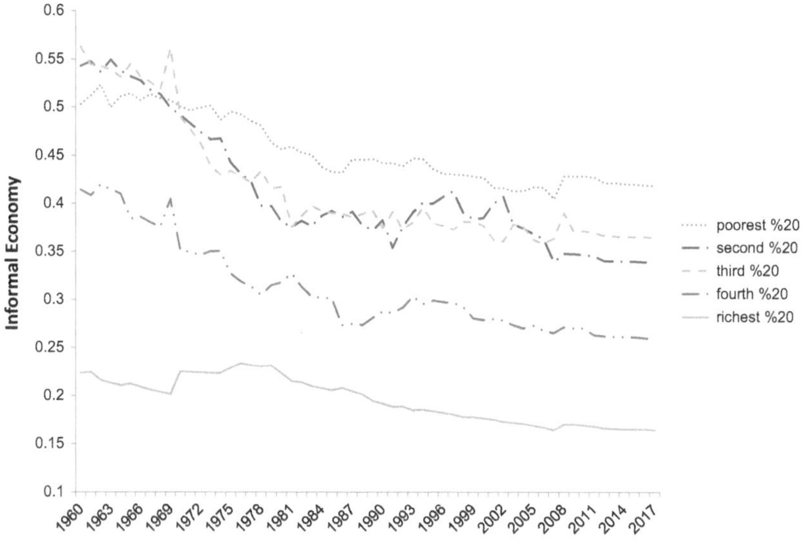

Figure 4.4 Weighted informal sector size (% GDP) in different income groups.

between the two variables may be somewhat non-linear. This non-linearity is even more evident in Figure 4.4, which presents the average informal sector size across different income quintiles. These quintiles are determined according to the real GDP per capita of each country out of 160 countries in the whole data set. For example, the poorest (richest) 20% represent the 32 poorest (richest) countries. One point to note here is that countries move between groups over time as they get richer or poorer than other countries. Therefore, the quantiles do not include the same countries from one year to another. The figure yet again shows that richer countries unsurprisingly tend to have smaller shadow economies. However, this relationship might not be exactly linear, especially during development. While further research is required, this finding may support the informality dimension of the Kuznets curve hypothesis. As it will be discussed in more detail in the next chapter, Elgin and Oztunali (2014) investigate this non-linearity and argue that institutional quality provides the key factor behind this non-linear relationship between GDP per capita and shadow economy size.

4.2 Regional statistics

The comprehensive data set constructed using the dynamic general equilibrium (DGE) method allows us to report the trends of regional averages wide. Tables 4.1 and 4.2 show how the unweighted and weighted informal economy size (as a percentage of GDP) develop in different country groups over time

Table 4.1 Regional Trends (Unweighted Data)

Region	*1960–1970*	*1971–1980*	*1981–1990*	*1991–2000*	*2001–2010*	*2011–2017*
OECD-EU	27.09	23.31	21.13	19.36	17.65	16.50
Latin American	53.54	46.76	43.25	42.69	39.82	38.01
Post-Socialist	–	–	–	36.69	34.52	33.19
MENA	40.27	31.90	26.11	25.51	23.89	23.05
Sub-saharan	51.18	46.13	43.13	42.37	39.28	38.01
Asia	49.35	41.56	36.62	32.63	29.05	28.20

Table 4.2 Regional Trends (GDP-weighted Data)

Region	*1960–1970*	*1971–1980*	*1981–1990*	*1991–2000*	*2001–2010*	*2011–2017*
OECD-EU	22.92	20.26	18.92	17.81	16.48	15.85
Latin American	47.43	41.88	40.02	39.09	36.14	35.07
Post-Socialist	–	–	–	31.56	31.69	33.63
MENA	33.77	24.58	22.89	22.35	20.73	19.67
Sub-saharan	50.36	44.48	40.40	39.91	35.80	34.02
Asia	39.41	34.39	29.63	23.97	19.78	19.58

in approximately ten-year intervals. Both tables reveal a significant and steady decline in the size of the shadow economy for all country groups. As with Figures 4.1 and 4.2, the pace of the decline also changed in the last decade of the 20th century before falling at different rates for different country groups. Moreover, it is also apparent from both tables that the size of the sector varies significantly, both between and within groups. Latin American and sub-Saharan economies have significantly larger informal economies than the other groups of countries while the OECD-EU group has a significantly smaller informal economy. Post-Socialist transition countries also have significant informal economies. This is also the only group where the GDP-weighted average increased over the last two decades. Thus, to understand more deeply the variation in informal sector size in different country groups, one should identify the determinants of shadow economies and how these determinants and their effects change over time.

When examining the yearly changes in the size of the informal sector across different country groups, Elgin and Oztunali (2012) also observed a spike in 2008 for all countries, albeit at different magnitudes. Given the global economic crisis at this time, this could give further support for the hypothesis that the size of the informal economy is countercyclical, as suggested by Roca et al. (2001) and Elgin (2012). However, the degree of countercyclicality is clearly not homogenous across different country groups. Moreover, Elgin and Oztunali (2012) also find that the spike in Asia is much more pronounced when the group series is weighted by GDP. This indicates that the larger economies in Asia experienced the greatest increase in informal economy size due to the 2008 crisis.

4.3 The informal sector in cities worldwide

In this section, I present novel evidence, as reported by Elgin (2020), on the size of the informal sector in different metropolitan areas worldwide. As discussed in Chapter 2, the informal sector has been overwhelmingly defined and viewed as an urban phenomenon since the earliest studies (for example Mazumdar, 1976). Many papers have investigated the relationship between the informal economy and urbanization. Elgin and Oyvat (2013), for example, propose and empirically show that there is an inverted-U relationship between urbanization, as measured by the ratio of the urban population to the total population, and the size of the informal economy.

Similarly, Yuki (2007) argues that rapid urbanization is positively correlated with shadow economy size in economies with initial land inequality whereas the correlation is negative for economies with low land inequality. Motivated by these discussions, in Elgin (2020), to the best of my knowledge for the first time in the literature, I constructed city-level data using an almost identical version of the DGE model outlined in the previous chapter. The model is almost identical to the model presented in the previous chapter, but instead uses various city-level available data for calibration and simulation. The difference is that it uses various city-level data for calibration and simulation while the tax enforcement parameter ρ is assumed to be larger than zero. As in the case of cities the data are constructed for a much smaller number of countries, one can use different proxies for ρ. I therefore assume that formal output gets taxed at a rate $\tau_t \in [0, 1]$, whereas informal output is taxed at a rate of $\rho\tau_t$, where $\rho \geq 0$.

Again, assuming a logarithmic utility of consumption, the household's maximization problem yields the following first-order conditions:

$$\frac{C_{t+1}}{C_t} = \beta[(1-\tau_t)\alpha\frac{Y_{F_{t+1}}}{K_{t+1}} + 1 - \delta], \tag{4.3.1}$$

where $Y_{F_t} = \theta_{F_t} K_t^{\alpha} N_{Ft}^{1-\alpha}$ and

$$(1-\rho\tau)\theta_{S_t}\gamma N_{St}^{\gamma-1} = (1-\tau_t)\theta_{F_t}(1-\alpha)K_t^{\alpha} N_{Ft}^{-\alpha}. \tag{4.3.2}$$

By rearranging the Euler equation, one can obtain K_t in terms of N_{Ft}:

$$K_t = N_{F_t}\left[\frac{(1-\tau_t)\theta_{F_t}\alpha}{(1+g_c)/\beta - 1 + \delta}\right]^{\frac{1}{1-\alpha}}. \tag{4.3.3}$$

where g_c is the growth rate of consumption in period t, that is $1 + g_c = \frac{C_t}{C_{t-1}}$

Moreover, informal labor can be obtained as follows:

$$N_{S_t} = \left\{\frac{\gamma(1-\rho\tau)\theta_{S_t}}{(1-\tau_t)(1-\alpha)\theta_{F_t}}\left[\frac{(1+g_c)/\beta - 1 + \delta}{\alpha(1-\tau_t)\theta_{F_t}}\right]^{\frac{\alpha}{1-\alpha}}\right\}^{\frac{1}{1-\gamma}} \tag{4.3.4}$$

Evidently, the presence of a ρ changes the characterizing equations, only slightly. Next, to back out the informal economy size in a specific city for a specific year t, I proceed as follows: First, I obtain the country-level parameters for the capital share of income, α, and the depreciation rate of physical capital, δ, from Penn World Tables (PWT) 9.1. Both of these parameters are reported in PWT on a country-by-country basis and yearly basis. For the simulation of the model for each country, separately, I use the averages of these parameter series from 2001 to 2017[1] as reported by PWT. These values change by country; however, the average values I use for all countries are $\alpha = 0.40\%$ and $\delta = 4.79\%$, respectively. Next, I take the decreasing returns to scale parameter $\gamma = 0.425$ from Ihrig and Moe (2004); however, I also conduct some sensitivity analyses with respect to this parameter following the benchmark simulation. As a proxy for the enforcement parameter ρ, I use the law and order index of the International Country Risk Guide (ICRG) as follows. This index, which is reported annually for each country, ranges from 0 (low enforcement) to 6 (high enforcement). I simply set $\rho = 0$ when this index takes a value of 0, and 1 when it is equal to its maximum value, that is 6. All the values of ρ between 0 and 1 are calculated as a ratio of the specific law and order index value (calculated as the average from 2001 to 2017) to 6. I then construct the capital-stock series at the city-level $\{K_t\}$ relying on the widely used perpetual inventory method. Specifically, I obtain the capital stock using the following formulas:

$$K_{t+1} = K_t(1 - \delta) + I_t$$

$$\frac{K_{2001}}{Y_{2017}} = \frac{\sum_{i=2001}^{2016} \frac{I_i}{Y_i}}{\delta + g_Y}$$

The first equation is the standard law of motion for capital, where K_t stands for the aggregate capital stock in year t, δ for the depreciation rate of physical capital, and I_t for the amount of investment in year t. Here, I use a different value of δ for each country (where a city is located) from PWT, obtain the data on city-level GDP from OECD-Stat, and construct an aggregate investment series using this city-level GDP series and the country-level investment-to-GDP ratio from PWT. The second equation assumes that the economy is in a steady state in the initial period of analysis which I take as 2001 here. Once the capital stock in 2001 is calculated using the second equation, the first equation allows me to create a capital-stock series for the years between 2001 and 2017. Once the capital-stock series has been constructed for every city and every year, I can then calibrate β for each city using the Euler equation. Here, I obtain the aggregate consumption data C_t by obtaining the product of the city-level GDP series with the consumption share of income from PWT. I also obtain city-level (formal) employment (N_{F_t}) from OECD Stat.[2] Finally, I assume that the government achieves a balanced budget; τ_t is obtained as the share of government spending in GDP similarly from the PWT using country-level data. Next, using the calculated values for α and δ, the calibrated value of β and year-specific τ_t, N_{F_t}, and K_t values, I use equation (5.3.3) to back out θ_{F_t} for any year t.

The only remaining variable to calculate is θ_{S_t}, that is, the informal sector productivity parameter. Here, following Ihrig and Moe (2004), Elgin and Oztunali (2012), and Elgin et al. (2019) I assume that θ_{S_t} grows at a rate which is the weighted average of the growth rate of K_t and θ_{F_t}. Having made this assumption regarding the growth rate of θ_{S_t}, I choose $\theta_{S_{2001}}$ to match informal employment size in 2001 of the series reported by Elgin et al. (2019) for informal employment (as a percentage of formal country-level employment) and construct the rest of the θ_{S_t} series using the calculated growth rates. Finally, I calculate N_{S_t} using equation (4.3.4). Once N_{S_t} is obtained, the size of the shadow economy in a specific year can be easily computed using $\frac{\theta_{S_t} N_{S_t}^{\gamma}}{\theta_{F_t} K^{\alpha} N_{F_t}^{1-\alpha}}$ for every year.

The procedure outlined in the previous section allows us to construct a data set with 969 observations for 57 cities in 31 different countries in a balanced panel framework running from 2001 to 2017. The complete data set (up to 2016, as it was using a previous edition of the PWT) is reported on a city-by-city and year-by-year basis in the appendix to Elgin (2020).

Table 4.3 presents the descriptive statistics[3] of the constructed series in different regions and globally for the whole data set. The unweighted average of the estimates across all 57 cities over 16 years is 15.11% of GDP. However, this varies significantly across cities from different regions. It also varies across cities in the same region. For the two countries with data on more than two cities (Germany and the United States), there is a significant variation across the cities, with within-country standard deviations of 0.87 and 0.27, respectively.

Next, I present illustrative figures and tables to show how the estimates are associated with several variables for which I have city-level data. Table 4.4 reports Spearman rank and pairwise correlations between shadow economy size estimates and different variables: country-level shadow economy size (percentage of GDP), real GDP per capita, population density, youth population (percentage of population below the age of 15), and population. There are certainly other significant possible correlates (determinants or indicators) of informality such as tax burden, monetary base, life expectancy, education or human capital, and institutional quality indices. However, as these series are not available at the city level, they could not be used in these correlation or regression analyses.

Table 4.3 Descriptive Statistics: Shadow Economy Size (%) GDP by Region

Region	*Mean*	*Median*	*Minimum*	*Maximum*	*Std. Dev.*
Global	15.11	14.65	7.92	28.32	5.98
Europe	17.84	16.81	8.15	28.32	5.00
North America	9.11	8.40	7.92	16.04	2.12
Latin America	22.34	23.83	16.45	27.12	3.44
Australia-Asia	14.68	13.34	9.20	23.13	4.90

This table reports summary statistics for the shadow economy size as a percentage of GDP in different regions for the whole data set.

Table 4.4 Correlates of Informality

Spearman Rank Correlations						
Region	*IS*	*Country-IS*	*GDP per cap.*	*Pop. Dens.*	*Youth Pop.*	*Population*
IS	1.00	0.96*	−0.66*	0.29**	−0.47*	−0.22***
Country-IS		1.00	−0.59*	0.26**	−0.44*	−0.20***
GDP per cap.			1.00	−0.28**	0.14	−0.12
Pop. Dens.				1.00	−0.31**	0.40*
Youth Pop.					1.00	0.16
Population						1.00
Pairwise Correlations						
IS	1.00	0.98***	−0.57*	0.26**	−0.40*	−0.13
Country IS		1.00	−0.54*	0.25**	−0.40*	−0.09
GDP per cap.			1.00	−0.25**	0.19	−0.13
Pop. Dens.				1.00	−0.40*	0.71*
Youth Pop.					1.00	−0.11
Population						1.00

IS and Country-IS are the city-level and country-level shadow economy size as a percentage of GDP, respectively. The other variables are population density, percentage of population below the age of 15 years (youth pop.), population (in millions), and real GDP per capita. *, **, and *** indicate significance at 1%, 5%, and 10%, respectively. Except for the Country-IS, all the variables are at the city level.

Table 4.4 shows that the city-level shadow economy size is significantly positively correlated with population density and, unsurprisingly, country-level informal economy size but negatively correlated with GDP per capita and youth population. For population, the Spearman correlation is negative and significant whereas the pairwise correlation is not significant. Since different variables have different units and definitions, Spearman rank correlation, which tests the statistical dependence between the rankings of two data series, is preferred here. It is significant at least to 10% level for all variables.

Using the average data (from 2001 to 2016) for each city, Figure 4.5 plots city-level informal economy size as a percentage of GDP against the natural logarithm of real GDP per capita. As also shown in previous studies, a higher level of development, as measured by the natural logarithm of per capita income, is associated with lower informality.

Figure 4.6 plots the evolutions of two series from 2001 to 2017: the unweighted average global informal economy size (based on yearly simple arithmetic averages of the city-level series) and GDP-weighted averages. The unweighted series declined from about 16% of GDP to less than 15% whereas the GDP-weighted series barely declined while fluctuating much more strongly. It has a standard deviation of 0.80 as opposed to 0.41 for the unweighted series, even though the averages are roughly the same (15.07% versus 15.11%). This may be because the GDP-weighted series also includes fluctuations in GDP (which might be substantial) as well as fluctuations in the informal economy size.

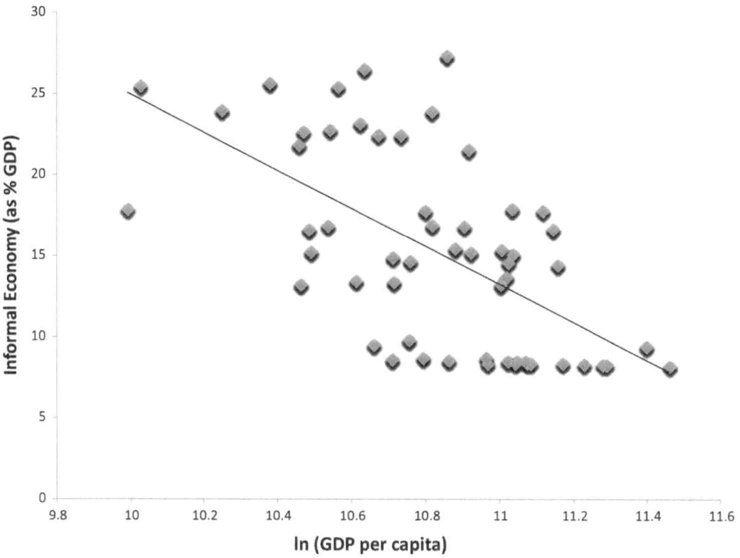

Figure 4.5 Informal economy size (percentage of GDP) versus GDP per capita.

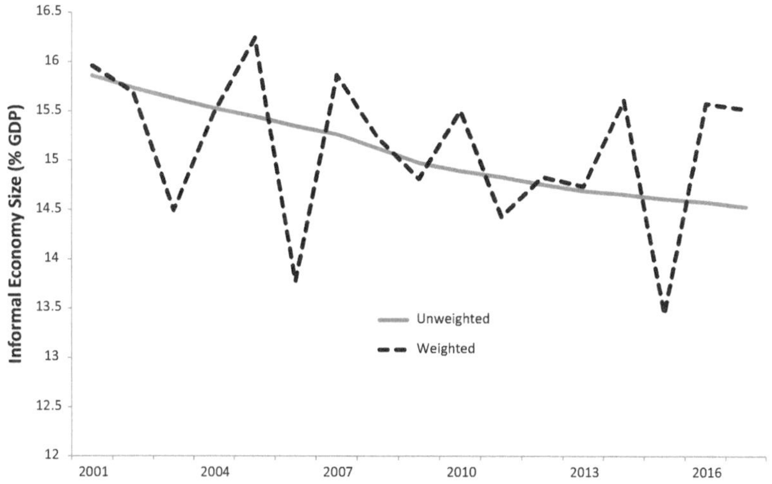

Figure 4.6 Unweighted trend of informal economies in cities.

Contrary to what is being reported here, in Elgin and Oztunali (2012), the global GDP-weighted series was significantly smaller than the unweighted series, possibly because the distribution of the constructed estimates is not symmetric here. This asymmetry is illustrated in Figure 4.7, which plots the frequency distribution for the constructed shadow economy size series and the

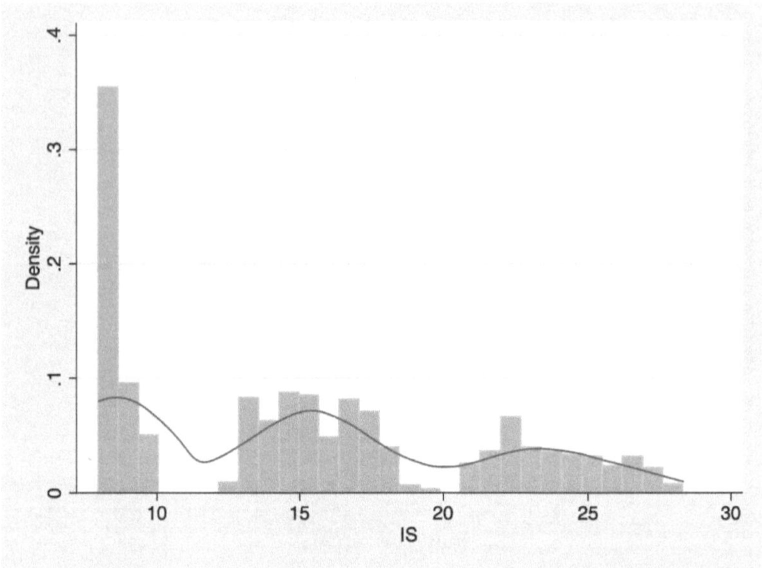

Figure 4.7 Frequency distribution and Kernel density estimate of shadow economy size distribution.

Kernel density estimate of its probability distribution. Due to the lack of data in various emerging markets, the data set asymmetrically includes many cities from the United States, where the informal sector is relatively small. Not surprisingly, this prevents the distribution from being close to normal.

In Elgin (2020), I also present the results of several sensitivity analyses. Note that, among several different parameters of the model, only one of them, γ, is taken to be fixed for each country and year. In the first sensitivity check, I use a different value for γ, which was assumed to be equal to 0.425 in the benchmark analysis, as in Ihrig and Moe (2004). Table 4.5 presents the descriptive statistics for the constructed series in different regions and globally for the whole data set under two different γ values with $\gamma = 0.35$ and $\gamma = 0.50$. The results are largely similar to the benchmark results. Moreover, I also observe that the cross-city or cross-regional rankings are also very similar to the benchmark estimations. Finally, the estimations do not exhibit any non-linearity with respect to a change in γ, that is, increasing γ slightly increases the estimates in a (weakly) monotonic way. The stability of the model is not surprising as the construction of the data is tied to previously reported estimates from 2001 through the determination of $\theta_{S_{2001}}$.

Table 4.6 presents yet another sensitivity check, where $\theta_{S_{2001}}$ is chosen to match the country-level informal employment from Elgin et al. (2019); this table reports simulation results when the country-level informal sector size (as a percentage of GDP) is matched for 2001, as reported by Elgin et al. (2019).

4.3.1 Simple regression analysis

In this subsection, I run several panel fixed-effects regressions to regress the constructed city-level shadow economy size on natural logarithms of GDP per capita, population, population density, and youth population. Rather than finding support for any particular theoretical model, the regression analysis was conducted to determine whether city-level informal sector estimates correlate with specific city-level variables in a meaningful and intuitive manner. Such a regression analysis is very much needed as the significant correlations reported in Table 4.4 may become insignificant after controlling for year, country, and city dummies. Table 4.7 reports the results of four fixed-effects regressions. They are generally in line with the results reported in Table 4.4. Specifically, at the city level, a larger shadow economy size is associated with lower GDP per capita, population, and youth population and higher population density. The negative relationship between GDP per capita and shadow economy size is unsurprising because it is well established in the literature (Johnson et al., 1997). As in

Table 4.5 Descriptive Statistics with Different γ Values

$\gamma = 0.35$	*Region*	*Mean*	*Median*	*Minimum*	*Maximum*	*Std. Dev.*
	Global	15.05	14.65	7.94	28.27	6.00
	Europe	17.79	16.69	8.16	28.28	5.03
	North America	9.09	8.32	7.93	16.00	2.08
	Latin America	22.33	23.76	16.43	27.07	3.44
	Australia-Asia	14.62	13.33	9.20	23.08	4.83
$\gamma = 0.50$	*Region*	*Mean*	*Median*	*Minimum*	*Maximum*	*Std. Dev.*
	Global	15.15	14.70	7.89	28.31	6.0
	Europe	17.92	16.82	8.20	28.32	5.01
	North America	9.17	8.35	7.99	16.06	2.11
	Latin America	22.44	23.80	16.52	27.10	3.47
	Australia-Asia	14.72	13.40	9.26	23.12	4.91

As opposed to the benchmark estimates, where γ was taken to be 0.425, in this table, I report results of two additional simulations with γ reduced to 0.35 and increased to 0.50, respectively.

Table 4.6 Descriptive Statistics with Different Data Matching

$\gamma = 0.35$	*Region*	*Mean*	*Median*	*Minimum*	*Maximum*	*Std. Dev.*
	Global	15.15	14.69	7.97	28.29	6.04
	Europe	17.85	16.73	8.17	28.30	5.02
	North America	9.15	8.37	7.96	16.04	2.07
	Latin America	22.44	23.81	16.47	27.11	3.46
	Australia-Asia	14.72	13.40	9.24	23.12	4.79

As opposed to the benchmark estimates, where $\theta_{S_{2001}}$ is chosen to match the country-level informal employment from Elgin et al. (2019), this table reports simulation results where the country-level informal sector size (as % of GDP) is matched for 2001 as reported in the cited paper.

Table 4.7 Panel Regressions

Dep. Var.: IS				
ln(GDP per capita)	−10.89*	−11.87*	−9.81*	−9.92*
	(1.80)	(1.72)	(1.70)	(1.65)
ln(Population)		2.01*	3.33*	2.03*
		(0.52)	(0.73)	(0.62)
ln(Pop. Dens.)			3.04*	
			(0.93)	
Youth Pop.(% Total)				−0.42**
				(0.21)
R-Squared	0.38	0.46	0.56	0.47
Observations	969	969	969	969
F-statistic (*p*-value)	0.00	0.00	0.00	0.00

All regressions include a constant as well as city, country, and year dummies. Robust standard errors are reported in parentheses. * and ** denote 1% and 5% confidence levels, respectively.

Elgin and Oyvat (2013), shadow economy size is positively correlated with both population and population density. This is because higher population density and population both increase the labor supply and create more room for informal firms, producers, and households. As for the youth population, countries with larger youth or rural populations are generally considered more likely to show higher informality (Loayza et al., 2009). However, a comprehensive literature review on this issue indicates that there is no such robust empirical finding regarding the relationship between youth population ratio and shadow economy size. Moreover, the regressions reported in Table 4.5 show a significant negative correlation between the youth population ratio and shadow economy size only after controlling for population, population density, GDP per capita, and country, city, and year fixed effects. Nevertheless, this is still an interesting finding that needs a more comprehensive explanation that future research may provide.

After obtaining the benchmark estimates of informality, I now turn to comparative static exercises with respect to policy tools. Specifically, I focus on two policy tools present in the model: the tax rate and tax enforcement. In total, I run simulations for four scenarios in addition to the benchmark scenario (S0). The benchmark scenario is used to construct informal sector estimates from 2017, the last year of our data set. The first counterfactual scenario (S1) increases the average tax burden by 10% (for example from 39.36% to 43.30% for Athens, Greece) compared to S0. The second one (S2) instead increases the enforcement parameter by 10% (for example from 0.75 to 0.825 for Athens). The third one (S3) increases both enforcement and the tax burden by 10%. The fourth one (S4) reduces them by 10%, while the fifth one (S5) reduces the tax burden by 10% but increases enforcement by the same amount.

The results of the policy simulations are reported in Table 4.8. S1, S2, and S5 indicate that increasing enforcement and/or reducing taxes reduce shadow

Table 4.8 Shadow Economy Size (percentage of GDP) under Different Policy Scenarios

Region	*S0*	*S1*	*S2*	*S3*	*S4*	*S5*
Tokyo	9.20	9.78	8.24	8.60	9.52	7.96
NYC	7.99	8.74	7.18	7.69	8.28	6.81
Melbourne	12.80	13.98	10.03	11.21	14.11	9.66
Mexico City	24.14	26.00	21.13	23.34	25.00	20.65
London	12.86	13.99	11.25	12.09	13.35	9.99
Rome	25.81	28.29	22.49	24.46	26.99	21.36
Paris	14.56	16.18	12.67	13.73	15.09	11.81
Athens	24.96	27.77	22.27	24.07	25.89	20.97

S0 refers to the benchmark scenario with tax burden and enforcement set as explained in the text. S1 increases the average tax burden by 10% compared to S0. S2 increases the enforcement parameter by 10%; S3 increases both enforcement and the tax burden by 10%; S4 reduces them by 10% and S5 reduces the tax burden by 10% but increases enforcement by the same amount.

economy size while increasing taxes increases shadow economy size. However, S3 and S4 indicate that the results become much more interesting with a mixed policy. Specifically, increasing both taxes and enforcement by 10% compared to the benchmark, as in S3, reduces the shadow economy while S4 has the opposite effect from the opposite policies. The two scenarios indicate that the effect of enforcement outweighs the effect of taxes. Thus, the main message is that enforcement is as important as taxes, so governments should take these findings into consideration to find the optimal policy mix. Ihrig and Moe (2004) and Elgin and Sezgin (2017) reach similar conclusions.

4.4 Forecasts for the near future

This section provides a projection of how the shadow economy could evolve by 2025, based on both existing drivers included in past models and a selection of emerging drivers that may impact future developments. In 2014, I was contracted by the Association of Chartered Certified Accountants to provide such a forecast up to 2025 for a selected number of economies and contribute to a report written by a team (see ACCA, 2017 for the complete report). In this section, I rely on the methodology that I developed for this report to present some forecasts for informal economies over the next few years.

The constructed forecasts for the size of the shadow economy (reported below) again rely on DGE, not only due to its use of micro-foundations or other advantages, but mainly due to its reliance on several observed macroeconomic variables to estimate the size of informal economies. This allows us to construct annual forecasts of the size of informal economies in various countries up to 2025 as there are forecasts of these observed variables constructed by several international institutions.

To back out the size of the informal economy from the model, the forecasts use the earlier described DGE model solution. The values of various observable variables such as consumption, investment, formal output (i.e. GDP), employment, taxes, government expenditures, GDP growth rate are plugged into the model to produce a shadow economy size consistent with the inputs. Data series for all these variables are available for all years up to 2017.

Once the values for the informal sector as a percentage of GDP in a country-by-country and year-by-year basis up to 2017 are constructed, the following econometric regression equation is estimated in a time-series (year-by-year) framework to forecast the informal economy size for country *i*:

$$IS_{i,t} = \beta_0 + \beta_1 IS_{i,t-1} + \sum_{k=2}^{n} \beta_k X_{k_{i,t}} + \epsilon_{i,t}$$

Here, for country *i*, in year *t*, our dependent (left-hand) variable, *IS*, is shadow economy size as a percentage of official GDP. Several variables have been used on the right-hand side (denoted by *X*) to take various determinants of shadow economies into account. These fall into three categories: Institutional Variables, Economic Determinants, and Demographic Variables. The first group includes variables such as Political Stability, Ethnic Tensions, Law and Order, Democratic Accountability, Bureaucratic Quality, and Corruption Control, which represent several dimensions of institutional quality within an economy. Measures for all these variables are available in the ICRG of Political Risk Services. The ICRG reports estimates for these variables up to 2017 and forecasts of all are constructed up to 2025 using an AR (m) model with $m = 2$. That is, all the variables have been forecasted using their first and second lag, as well as their growth rates in the previous ten years. Next, economic determinants are consumption expenditures (as percentage of GDP), investment (as percentage of GDP),real GDP per capita (in thousand USD), unemployment (%), taxes (total tax revenue as percentage of GDP), government expenditures (as percentage of GDP), growth rate of GDP (in %), internet users per thousand people (proxy for technology), and finally, population growth rate (in %), young population to total population ratio (%).

These two groups of variables have been obtained from the World Development Indicators of the World Bank. As with the institutional quality variables, forecasts are constructed up to 2025 using an autoregressive of order m, i.e. AR (m) model, with $m = 2$ for each variable. The constructed forecasts were also statistically compared with those of Oxford Economics, which revealed highly similar paths for the forecasted values. Once the earlier specified econometric regression equation has been run by including all these determinants of shadow economies (within X) the link between these variables and shadow economy size can be established. Specifically, the estimates coefficients for all variables represent the effects of these variables on shadow economy size up to 2017. Next, the forecasted values of the determinants of shadow economies up to 2025 are combined with the estimated coefficients to construct forecasts of shadow economy size.

Table 4.9 Expected Evolution of the Informal Sector (%) GDP

Region	*2019*	*2020*	*2021*	*2022*	*2023*	*2024*	*2025*
Australia	12.11	12.00	11.87	11.75	11.69	11.50	11.47
Azerbaijan	44.12	44.93	45.05	45.01	44.96	45.04	45.02
Brazil	33.03	33.00	32.95	32.99	33.01	32.98	32.97
Bulgaria	27.89	27.80	27.84	27.83	27.81	27.80	27.79
China	9.50	9.45	9.41	9.40	9.40	9.40	9.36
Estonia	25.99	25.89	25.80	25.71	25.69	25.75	25.74
India	17.30	16.90	16.55	16.35	16.30	16.24	16.16
Indonesia	16.06	15.86	15.67	15.50	15.43	15.36	15.33
Italy	25.29	25.31	25.21	25.19	25.21	25.27	25.26
Japan	8.61	8.50	8.30	8.18	8.07	7.96	7.90
Kenya	26.87	26.80	26.75	26.77	26.79	26.80	26.79
Malaysia	26.88	26.00	25.45	25.09	25.12	25.10	25.00
Nigeria	45.03	44.01	43.22	42.65	42.21	41.90	41.70
Pakistan	32.79	33.24	33.35	33.55	33.51	33.49	33.43
Poland	22.14	22.04	21.97	21.94	21.90	21.87	21.85
Russia	37.20	37.15	37.07	37.00	37.09	37.14	37.12
Singapore	10.03	10.21	10.40	10.51	10.62	10.84	10.80
South Africa	23.01	23.19	23.30	23.41	23.54	23.66	23.60
Turkey	25.28	24.41	24.09	23.89	23.70	23.50	23.30
Ukraine	46.24	46.29	46.37	46.90	47.03	47.39	47.40
United Kingdom	11.65	11.56	11.40	11.37	11.32	11.21	11.18
United States	8.01	7.90	7.87	7.82	7.78	7.75	7.72
World (GDP-weighted)	20.94	20.89	20.76	20.69	20.63	20.59	20.53

Overall, the earlier tables indicate that the shadow economy is expected to shrink globally. However, the rate of the decline is not the same in all countries. Indeed, it is forecasted to grow in Azerbaijan, Pakistan, South Africa, and Ukraine. In addition, Bulgaria, Russia, and to some extent Brazil, China, Estonia, and Kenya are forecast to have statistically negligible reductions in shadow economy size. Notice that all these countries in which the informal economy seems to be not declining or stagnating are emerging markets with significant scope to improve their institutional qualities and governance. The main reason for this differential development of shadow economies across countries is the striking difference in the evolution of institutional quality. That is, those countries that can improve their institutional framework in the next few years will benefit most from declining informal economies. Conversely, countries with limited institutional capacity will suffer from large informal economies (Table 4.9).

Notes

1 In Elgin (2020), I only use data up to 2016, whereas the current book uses updated series up to 2017.
2 The link to the metropolitan area database of OECD is https://stats.oecd.org/Index.aspx?DataSetCode=CITIES.
3 See Elgin (2020) for several robustness checks.

References

ACCA, 2017. *Emerging from the Shadows: The Shadow Economy 2025.* ACCA Global. https://www.accaglobal.com/content/dam/ACCA_Global/Technical/Future/pi-shadow-economy.pdf.

Elgin, C. 2012. Cyclicality of Shadow Economy. *Economic Papers: A Journal of Applied Economics and Policy.* 31 (4), 478–490.

Elgin, C. 2020. Shadow Economies around the World: Evidence from Metropolitan Areas. *Eastern Economic Journal.* 46, 301–322.

Elgin, C., Kose, A., Ohnsorge, F., Yu, S. 2019. *Shades of Grey: Measuring the Informal Economy Business Cycles.* World Bank, mimeo.

Elgin, C., Oyvat, C. 2013. Lurking in the Cities: Urbanization and the Informal Economy. *Structural Change and Economic Dynamics.* 27, 36–47.

Elgin, C., Oztunali, O. 2012. *Shadow Economies around the World: Model Based Estimates.* Bogazici University Department of Economics Working Papers, 2012-05.

Elgin, C., Oztunali, O. 2014. Institutions, Informal Economy, and Economic Development. *Emerging Markets Finance and Trade.* 50 (4), 145–162.

Elgin, C., Sezgin, M. B. 2017. Sectoral Estimates of Informality: A New Method and an Application to Turkish Economy. *The Developing Economies.* 55 (4), 261–289.

Ihrig, J., Moe, K. 2004. Lurking in the Shadows: The Informal Sector and Government Policy. *Journal of Development Economics.* 73, 541–577.

Johnson, S., Kaufman, D., Shleifer, A. 1997. The Unofficial Economy in Transition. *Brookings Papers on Economic Activity.* 2, 159–221.

Loayza, N., Serven, L., Sugawara, N. 2009. *Informality in Latin American and the Caribbean.* World Bank Policy Research Working Paper 4888.

Mazumdar, D. 1976. The Urban Informal Sector. *World Development.* 4 (8), 655–679.

Roca, J. C. C., Moreno, C. D., Sanchez, J. E. G. 2001. Underground Economy and Aggregate Fluctuations. *Spanish Economic Review.* 31, 41–53.

Yuki, K. 2007. Urbanization, Informal Sector, and Development. *Journal of Development Economics.* 84 (1), 76–103.

5 Determinants of informality

5.1 Literature on the determinants of informality

As I tried to show in Chapter 2, the microeconomics literature on informality has been primarily concerned with tax evasion. This indicates that taxes are viewed as an important determinant of informality in this literature. This is also why taxation as well as regulation and enforcement or, in broader terms, institutional quality stand out as the most frequently studied determinants of informal economic activity. Araujo and de Souza (2010), Prado (2011), Ulyssea (2010), Ihrig and Moe (2004), and Dessy and Pallage (2003) have all focused on government policy as an important factor in the formation of informality. Araujo and de Souza (2010) address the issue through an evolutionary game theory approach. In their setting, the agents in the economy choose to operate in the formal or informal sector by maximizing their expected pay-offs. They find the optimal level of enforcement and regulatory action that would prevent these agents from being attracted to the informal sector while taking the evolution of labor market conditions into account. Prado (2011) employs a two-sector monopolistic competition model to quantitatively assess how the size of the shadow economy depends on the levels of enforcement and taxation for a given level of regulation. Using a continuous investment model with moral hazard, Ulyssea (2010) finds that different instruments of government policy may have different effects on the level of informality and other economic indicators in a country. More specifically, lowering formal sector entry costs while increasing enforcement reduces informal activity, although higher levels of enforcement may cause welfare losses and unemployment. Ihrig and Moe (2004), adopting a two-sector dynamic general equilibrium framework, argue that it is better to decrease tax rates to prevent welfare losses rather than exercise stricter enforcement to reduce informality. In contrast, Dessy and Pallage (2003) use a heterogeneous agents model with incomplete markets to argue that focusing only on taxation to reduce informality might not always be effective. In their model, the tax revenue collected by the government is used to provide public infrastructure, which raises the productivity of formal firms, whereas informal firms are modeled to be less productive. In this setting, their main finding is that taxation has an ambiguous effect on the size of the informal sector while a fully formalized equilibrium is not affordable for low-income countries.

Another widely studied topic in the literature is trade liberalization as a driving force behind informal economic activity. Using a dynamic extension of the efficiency wage model, Goldberg and Pavcnik (2003) show that the informal sector may grow if trade barriers are removed, as one might expect. However, they argue that this model might be misleading since they do not find substantial supporting empirical evidence from their Latin American data. Paz (2014) analyzes how the formal-informal mix in the labor market changes following an episode of trade liberalization. Applying a small open economy model with heterogeneous firms indicates that the abolition of home import tariffs has an ambiguous effect on informality. In contrast, a decrease in import taxes reduces informal employment in the home country.

Chong and Gradstein (2007), Elgin and Solis-Garcia (2012), and Elgin and Oztunali (2014) have all studied how various aspects of institutional quality in a country affect the prevalence of informal economic activity. Chong and Gradstein (2007) develop a two-sector model with imperfect credit markets to show that the interplay between low institutional quality and high-income inequality results in larger informal economies. Elgin and Oztunali (2014) employ a two-sector dynamic general equilibrium model to argue that higher GDP per capita is associated with a larger informal sector when institutional quality is low and a smaller informal economy when institutional quality is high. Finally, Elgin and Solis-Garcia (2012) find that public trust is a key factor determining the level of informality (see also Elgin and Tosun, 2017). Similarly, D'Hernoncourt and Meon (2012) show that prevalence of trust is associated with smaller informal economies, particularly in developing countries. While taxes are quite important in determining informality tendencies, Elgin (2015) uses cross-country panel data to show that higher taxes are not necessarily associated with a larger informal sector. The paper's theoretical model and empirical analysis show that political stability is an important determinant of the relationship between taxes and informal sector size.

Labor market policies have also been identified as one of the determinants of informal economy size. Bosch and Esteban-Pretel (2012) employ a two-sector search and matching model focusing on five different labor market policies: hiring, firing, payroll taxes, monitoring of the informal sector, and fines against informal firms. They conclude that labor market policies that attempt to reduce the costs associated with formality reduce the share of informality in the economy and decrease unemployment. Florez (2014) focuses on how unemployment benefits, a formal lump sum tax, and a job creation subsidy change the formal-informal mix of the economy. Using a two-sector search and matching model, he suggests that unemployment benefits and job creation subsidies encourage formal employment whereas payroll taxes reduce it.

Other studies have explored how factors like business flexibility, product market policies, and entry costs affect informality choices. Charlot et al. (2015) bring labor and product market imperfections together to study how these conditions influence informality. Using a two-sector search and matching model, the authors infer that product market deregulations can effectively reduce both informal employment and unemployment. Loayza and Rigolini (2011) employ a two-sector small open economy model to show that, in the long run, more informality is associated with less flexible business procedures.

Although financial development can reasonably be viewed as an outcome of informality, it is also studied as one of its determinants. Capasso and Jappelli (2013) argue that if financial development lowers the costs of external funding, then it can reduce the size of the informal sector. In a model where firms make investment decisions either with internal funds that pay lower interest or external funds offering higher returns, financial development reduces tax evasion and hence informality. Blackburn et al. (2012), again making use of a model with financial intermediation and tax evasion, reach similar conclusions to Capasso and Jappelli (2013).

Empirical studies of the factors behind informality may incorporate many variables in their analysis. Some of the most frequently used variables are various aspects of institutional quality such as corruption, legal system indicators, and bureaucratic and regulatory quality, political risk rating, credit market regulations, labor market conditions indicators, urbanization, migration, trade liberalization, fiscal policy indicators, per capita income, and a large number of control variables.

Although a wide range of econometric techniques have been employed in these studies, we most commonly encounter simple ordinary least squares (OLS) regressions, panel regressions, as well as system estimations. In most cases, the dependent variable is the size of the informal sector to formal GDP, share of informal employment, and sometimes probability that a firm operates informally.

From a cross-sectional sample of over 50 countries, Lassen (2007) finds that larger informal sectors are associated with greater ethnic fractionalization and higher corruption. This claim is supported by a review of experimental studies of how people are reluctant to contribute toward a public good if it is enjoyed by other ethnic groups. The likelihood of tax evasion is also increased when public trust is eroded by widespread corruption.

Almeida and Carneiro (2012) investigate the determinants of informal employment in Brazil, focusing especially on labor market conditions. Their findings suggest that stricter labor market regulations and their enforcement reduce self-employment, which, in turn, lowers informal employment. Friedman (2014), employing pooled regressions with a data set of 149 countries, shows that factors like greater political stability, control of corruption, and regulatory quality are associated with smaller informal sectors, which is in line with expectations. However, he finds no robust relationship between the size of the informal sector and voice, accountability, and rule of law in a country.

Dreher and Schneider (2010) use data from 98 countries to reveal the two-way relationship between size of informal sector and corruption.

They hypothesize that corruption and informal economy are substitutes in high-income countries but complement in low-income countries. However, their results obtained from different econometric specifications are not robust. Based on perception-based data on corruption, they fail to support their hypothesis. However, corruption data based on a structural model indicates that corruption and informal economic activity are complementary in low-income countries. Hence, they argue that the relationship between corruption and informality might not be as straightforward as it seems. Torgler and Schneider (2007) show how the political environment has an important influence on the size of the informal sector. Making use of a large panel data set collected from several different sources, they classify the explanatory variables in the following main categories: economic freedom (business regulations, property rights protection, military intervention), institutional quality (political risk rating, corruption, law and order, democratic accountability, government stability), aggregate governance indicators (indexes of governance, voice and accountability, regulatory quality), willingness to pay taxes and control variables (income per capita, population, trade volume, linguistic fractionalization). The fixed-effect (FE) estimations indicate that improving various aspects of institutional quality, governance, and tax morale helps to limit the size of the informal sector. They especially emphasize the moral dimension as one of main determinants of informality.

According to Colombo et al. (2016), during banking crises, the informal sector expands to act as a buffer against losses in official economy. This is also closely related to the countercyclicality of informal sector size, as documented by Elgin (2012).

Using three different proxies for the size of the informal sector for over 100 countries, Elgin and Oyvat (2013) argue that urbanization and share of urban informality have an inverted U-shaped relationship. That is, informality initially grows along with urbanization whereas in later stages of urbanization, the urban informal sector shrinks. This conclusion bears a strong resemblance to the Kuznets' hypothesis.

Another potential determinant of informality that has been discussed both theoretically and empirically is trade liberalization. Bosch et al. (2012), using the general method of moments and OLS estimation, show that tariffs have rather ambiguous effects in Brazil even though import penetration has a significant impact on the share of informal employment. In contrast, their estimation results suggest that constitutional changes concerning labor market conditions, such as unionization and hiring/firing costs, have a sizeable effect on the allocation of labor across the formal and informal sectors as opposed to trade liberalization indicators.

Finally, discussed in the first half of this section, fiscal policy is a crucial determinant of informality. Johnson et al. (1997) is one of the many empirical studies that focus on fiscal policy in relation to corruption. Specifically, they challenge the claim that higher taxes lead to large informal sectors while corruption is also associated with greater informality. The main finding from their estimations is that higher levels of corruption and less strict regulation seem to account for large informal sector sizes across the small sub-group of countries used in the study. However, this relationship becomes less apparent for a larger sample of countries.

5.2 Tax burden

In this section, I first present several surprising observations from the data and then use the model from Elgin (2015) to illustrate a theoretical framework that relates taxes to informality. Finally, I present more detailed econometric results to illustrate that the models are generally in line with the data. Elgin and Solis-Garcia (2012) are also related to the results presented here. However, in that model, taxes serve more as effects than determinants. Therefore, a full discussion of that model is given in the next chapter.

5.2.1 A quick look at the plain data

Considering that informality and tax evasion have been frequently used interchangeably to refer to the same phenomenon, one would expect to see a positive correlation between taxation level and the size of the informal sector. However, this assumption is not generally supported by empirical studies. This assumption seems reasonable when one thinks of the informal sector as a place where people lurk to evade taxes: if taxes are higher, more people will tend to evade them. However, several empirical studies surprisingly associate higher tax rates with a relatively smaller informal economy. These include Johnson et al. (1997), Friedman et al. (2000), Torgler and Schneider (2007), Elgin and Solis-Garcia (2015), Elgin (2015), and Aruoba (2018).

Tax is certainly a somewhat vague concept as it may involve various taxes, ranging from different types of income to consumption taxes, or federal/national to local taxes. As most tax rates also depend on income or consumption level, it is also important to distinguish between statutory taxes and average effective taxes. It is also important here to emphasize the distinction between the overall tax burden and various statutory tax rates. Tax burden is defined as the ratio of total tax revenues to GDP. One might suspect that the negative relationship between the tax burden and the informal sector may simply arise because a larger informal economy implies a smaller tax base, hence a lower tax revenue. However, considering that only imperfect estimates of the informal economy are included in national income calculations, a larger informal economy also implies a lower official GDP. Moreover, as the empirical analysis presented below clearly shows, this negative relationship is also evident between various statutory tax rates and the size of the informal sector.

There is a clear negative relationship between informal sector size and tax burden, corporate tax rate, average labor income tax rate, or top marginal income tax rate. Figures 5.1 and 5.2 show this relationship for a cross-section of 160 economies in 2017 for informal sector size (as percentage of GDP) against

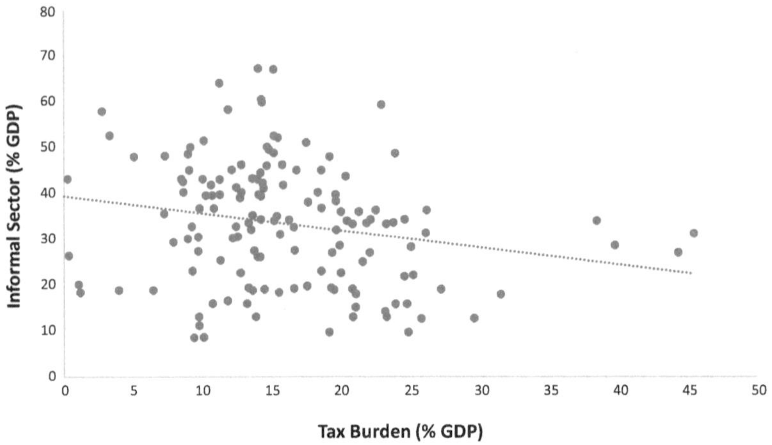

Figure 5.1 Informal sector versus tax burden.

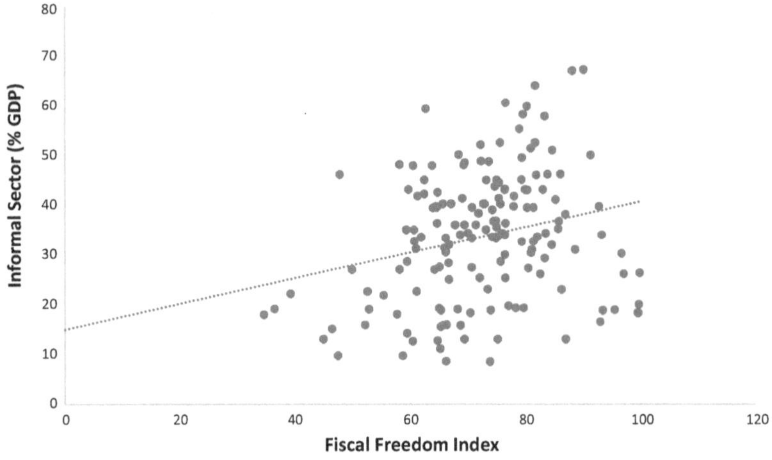

Figure 5.2 Informal sector versus fiscal freedom index.

the tax burden (percentage of GDP) and the fiscal freedom index. The former is interpreted as a measure of the actual average tax rate for an economy whereas the fiscal freedom index, constructed and published by the Heritage Foundation, is a decreasing function of statutory taxes. These two figures are not presented as part of a complete econometric analysis; instead, they demonstrate the clear negative correlation between taxes and informal sector size.

In contrast to the empirical analyses outlined earlier, a common result in the few models dealing with the informal sector is a positive relationship between tax rate and informal sector size. These include Rauch (1991), Loayza (1996), Fortin et al. (1997), Ihrig and Moe (2004), Busato and Chiarini (2004), and Amaral and Quintin (2006). This result seems intuitive because higher tax rates may create incentives for people to avoid them, and one way of doing this is by participating in the informal sector. Keeping taxes exogenous and not letting the informal sector pay any taxes (or letting it pay a smaller fraction than the formal sector), this result is also immediate in a two-sector neoclassical growth model with formal and informal sectors, where the variation in taxes is exogenous. In this regard, existing theoretical frameworks cannot account for the surprising negative relationship between tax rates and the size of the informal sector.

Some of these empirical papers indicating a negative relationship between tax rates and the informal sector deserve more discussion as they are more closely related to this study.

Although Johnson et al. (1997) and Johnson et al. (1998) use different sets of countries in their empirical analyses, they both conclude that tax rates are negatively correlated with the size of the informal sector. Johnson et al. (1997) also provide a very simple model in which the only two stable equilibria of the model feature a totally formal and totally informal economy. However, contrary to their empirical findings, their model implies a positive relationship between tax rates and informal sector size. Johnson et al. (1998) claim that the administration of taxes and regulatory discretion both play key roles in this result. Once they take composite indices of both tax rates and quality of tax administrations into account, they find that these indices are positively correlated with the size of the informal sector. However, the quality indices they use are largely based on subjective evaluations of certain experts and institutions, rendering them prone to measurement errors and endogeneity issues. Friedman et al. (2000) suggest that several institutional factors may cause the positive correlation such as corruption and bureaucratic quality. They find that a one-point increase in tax rates reduces the share of the unofficial economy by 9.1%. Although controlling for several variables and instrumenting on others reduce this by half, the negative tax coefficient remains significant. They conclude that this is probably because higher tax rates generate revenue that provides productivity. This, in turn, enhances public goods, creates a strong legal environment, and reduces corruption. However, they only consider the production side of the economy, so their highly stylized partial equilibrium model only focuses on the corruption part of the story. Aruoba (2018) develops a general equilibrium model in which the key factor creating variation in taxes and the size of the shadow economy is quality of institutions, specifically the degree of tax auditing by the government.

Elgin (2015) presents a novel theoretical and empirical model to address the somewhat contradictory findings in the literature with respect to the relationship between taxes and informal sector size. Below, I present a simplified version of this model and elaborate on the results derived from it.

5.2.2 A simple model on taxes and informal sector

The theoretical model in Elgin (2015) is essentially a simple two-sector growth model which consists of a unit measure of households and a government. In this model, households can divide their labor endowment between two sectors, formal and informal, to produce the same good. Specifically, given k_1, $\{r_t, w_t, \tau_{k_t}, \tau_{n_t}\}_{t=1}^{\infty}$, a stand-in household maximizes the following discounted utility from consumption.

$$\sum_{t=1}^{\infty} \beta^{t-1} U(c_t)$$

subject to the following budget constraint:

$$c_t + k_{t+1} - (1 - \delta_k)k_t = r_t k_t(1 - \tau_{k_t}) + w_{ft} n_{ft}(1 - \tau_{n_t}) + y_{it}(n_{it})$$

and time constraint

$$n_{ft} + n_{it} = 1$$

where the household spends n_{ft} time in the formal labor market, and n_{it} in the informal labor market. Labor and capital income in the formal sector are taxed at rates τ_{k_t} and τ_{n_t}, respectively. The utility function is assumed to be strictly increasing, concave, and twice-continuously differentiable. Moreover r_t and w_{ft} stand for the rental rate of capital and formal wage rate, respectively. $y_{it}(n_{it})$ represents the informal sector income. Finally, δ_k is the depreciation rate for private capital.

One can obtain the following first-order conditions at an interior solution of the consumer's problem:

$$-U_{c_t} + \beta U_{c_{t+1}}(1 - \tau_{k_{t+1}})r_{t+1} = 0$$

$$U_{c_t}(1 - \tau_{n_t})w_{ft} - U_{c_t}w_{it} = 0,$$

where w_{it} stands for the wage rate in the informal sector.

In line with the definitions made earlier, the informal sector is generally viewed as a highly labor-intensive, small-scale sector that cannot utilize public capital as much or as easily as the formal sector.

Motivated from the definition of informality, I assume that each firm in the informal sector produces according to the following decreasing returns to scale technology:

$$y_{it} = f_2(n_{it})$$

On the other hand, the technology for each firm in the formal sector is given by

$$y_{ft} = f_1(k_t, n_{ft}, G_t)$$

Here, G_t stands for the productive public capital.

Notice that the informal sector uses only labor as an input. One possible justification for this constraint could be that firms in the informal sector use significantly less capital due to lack of access to external finance (Amaral and Quintin, 2006) while public capital complements private capital (Aschauer, 1989).

The source of uncertainty in the economy arises from the existence of two political parties, party 1 and party 2, which can be in power at any $t \geq 0$. I define the state of incumbency at any period t as $z_t \in \mathcal{Z}_t = \{1, 2\}$. I then assume that the uncertainty follows a Markov process, i.e. at the end of each period, the incumbent political party stays in the office with an exogenous probability of ρ or loses the office to the other party with probability $1 - \rho$, i.e. $Pr(z_{t+1} = i|z_t = j) = \Pi_{ij} = 1 - \rho$ and $Pr(z_{t+1} = i|z_t = i) = \Pi_{ii} = \rho$, for $i, j \in \{1, 2\}$

One can interpret $1 - \rho$ as the measure of the degree of political turnover. Alternatively, ρ can be interpreted as the degree of political stability or probability of reelection in a democratic country.

I also assume that the incumbent balances the government budget in each period. The budget has two potential sources of revenue: labor and capital income taxes from the formal economy. The incumbent party also chooses how much of this revenue to spend on productive public investment G_{t+1} versus office rent S_t. The latter can thus be interpreted as nonproductive public spending, office rent, or embezzlement. For this reason, it is party specific and can only be benefited from when in office. Hence, the government budget is given by

$$r_t K_t \tau_{k_t} + w_{ft} N_{ft} \tau_{n_t} = S_t + G_{t+1} - (1 - \delta_g) G_t$$

where δ_g is the depreciation rate of public capital, and K_t and N_{ft} are the aggregate private capital and formal labor, respectively.

I further assume that the objective functions of the two political parties are symmetric, i.e. the period utility of the incumbent party $i \in \{1, 2\}$ is given by

$$U(C_t) + U^g(S_t)$$

whereas the period utility of the opposition party is simply $U(C_t)$.

Finally, I define the aggregate resource constraint of this economy as follows:

$$C_t + K_{t+1} + S_t + G_{t+1} = Y_{ft} + Y_{it} + (1 - \delta_k) K_t + (1 - \delta_g) G_t$$

Here, Y_{ft} and Y_{it} stand for aggregate formal and informal output, respectively.

Definition 5.2.1. For a given government policy $\prod = \{\tau_{k_t}, \tau_{n_t}, S_t, G_{t+1}\}_{t=1}^{\infty}$ and k_1, G_1, a competitive equilibrium for this economy is an allocation vector for households $\{c_t, k_{t+1}, n_{ft}, n_{it}\}_{t=1}^{\infty}$ and a price vector $\{r_t, w_{ft}, w_{it}\}_{t=1}^{\infty}$ such that

1 Given prices and government policy, the allocation vector of households solves the households' problem.
2 Prices satisfy $r_t = \frac{\partial Y_{ft}}{\partial K_t}$, $w_{ft} = \frac{\partial Y_{ft}}{\partial N_{ft}}$, and $w_{it} = \frac{\partial Y_{it}}{\partial N_{it}}$
3 The government budget constraint is satisfied.
4 The aggregate resource constraint holds.

Before presenting the results for the general environment, I first discuss the Markov-perfect equilibrium in a simple finite-period economy. The finite horizon allows me to obtain certain crucial analytical results under some specific simplifying assumptions.

For this subsection, I make the following assumptions regarding the form of the utility and production functions, and the depreciation rates of private and public capital:

Assumption 1. $U(C_t) = \alpha_c \log(C_t)$ and $U^g(S_t) = \alpha_s \log(S_t)$, where $\alpha_c + \alpha_s = 1$

Assumption 2. $Y_{ft} = F_1(K_t, N_{ft}, G_t) = K^\gamma N_{ft}^{1-\gamma}(\frac{G_t}{K_t})^\gamma$ and $Y_{it} = F_2(N_{it}) = N_{it}^{1-\gamma}$

Assumption 3. $\delta_k = \delta_g = 1$

Notice that in this setup the formal sector production function exhibits constant returns to scale at both individual and aggregate levels. The assumption that the powers of K and $\frac{G}{K}$ in the formal sector production function are the same is quite limiting, albeit necessary to obtain an analytical solution. However, notice that this is not equivalent to assuming the absence of K, because the household must still choose a positive amount of K in the steady state to have positive amount of formal output. Nevertheless, I will relax this assumption later on in the numerical analysis. Barro and Sala-i Martin (1992) argue that the way that G enters the formal sector production function with congestion reflects public goods that are rival but not excludable for the formal sector firms. However, since the informal sector cannot utilize these public goods in this setting, this assumption makes G excludable for the informal sector.

Let us assume for now that the economy only lasts for T periods and $T = 2$. Below I consider the symmetric Markov-perfect equilibrium (SMPE) in this environment. By definition, in a Markov-perfect equilibrium, households and the government base their decisions only on the current state variables, in this case the aggregate private and public capital stock at the beginning of each period. The timing of choices in this setup is as follows: In the first period, the incumbent, after observing G_1 and K_1 (which are initially given), chooses S_1, G_2, τ_{n_1}, and τ_{k_1} subject to the government budget constraint, taking the following as given:

1 Households maximize utility subject to their budget constraints and markets are competitive.
2 The policy implemented by the government in period 2, which is a function of K_2 and G_2.
3 The exogenous probability of keeping the office in period 2 is ρ.

In the second period the government in office observes K_2 and G_2 and chooses τ_{n_2}, τ_{k_2}, and S_2, taking as given that households maximize utility. I further assume that the incumbent lacks commitment, even if it had been in power in the previous period which implies that the government in period 2 will not internalize how its actions affected the decisions made in period 1. Finally, using the timing described earlier, I solve the model by backward induction. The results can be summarized by the following proposition:

Proposition 5.2.1. *Under assumptions 1–3 and for $\alpha_s > 0$, $\rho > 0$ SMPE allocations of the first period have the following features:*

1. *The tax rate on formal labor income is zero in both periods.*
2. *The tax burden falls on capital in both periods.*
3. *As the probability of reelection increases, productive public investment increases more than the first-period office rent falls, i.e. the tax burden in the first period also increases.*
4. *A4. As the probability of reelection increases, productive public investment increases more than the first-period office rent falls, i.e. the tax burden in the first period also increases..*
5. *An increase in the probability of reelection reduces the amount of labor spent in the informal sector for the second period.*
6. *An increase in the probability of reelection reduces the size of the informal sector in the second period.*

Proof. I will solve the model by backward induction starting from the second period:

Since period 2 is the final period, households do not invest in private capital and consume all of their income. Similarly, the government does not invest in the public capital either. Therefore, from the budget constraint we can write $C_2 = Y_{f2} + Y_{i2} - S_2$. Moreover, the labor and capital taxes can be obtained as functions of N_{f2} and S_2 only using $(1-\tau_{n2})w_{f2} = w_{i2}$ and $\tau_{k2} = \frac{S_2}{\gamma Y_{f2}} - \tau_{n2}w_{f2}$. Now, for any given G_2 and K_2, the problem of the incumbent in period 2 can be written as, choosing S_2 and N_{f2} to maximize

$$U(Y_{f2} + Y_{i2} - S_2) + U^g(S_2)$$

Under assumption 1, the first-order conditions with respect to S_2 and N_{f2}, respectively, are:

$$U_{c2} = U_{s2}$$

$$U_{c2}(w_{f2} - w_{i2}) = 0$$

Comparing the second equation here with the Euler equation from the consumer's problem, I obtain $\tau_{n2} = 0$, i.e. all the tax burden falls on K_2. Now, the first equation, together with assumption 1 implies that consumption and office rent in the second period are constant fractions of total output, i.e. $C_2 = \alpha_c Y_2$ and $S_2 = \alpha_s Y_2$. Moreover, from the earlier second first-order condition and assumption 2, I obtain $\frac{N_{i2}}{N_{f2}} = G_2^{-1}$. Hence all period 2 allocations can be defined as a function of G_2 only.

Next, using the Euler equation I obtain $K_2 = m_1(Y_1 - G_2 - S_1)$, where m_1 is an increasing function of G_2. From the resource constraint of period 1, it follows that $C_1 = (1 - m_1)(Y_1 - G_2 - S_1)$. Next, I consider the maximization problem of the first-period incumbent: Given some initial K_1, G_1, and the probability of reelection ρ, the first-period incumbent chooses S_1, G_2, and N_{f1} to maximize

$$U(C_1) + U^g(S_1) + \beta\{\rho[U(C_1) + U^g(S_2)] + (1 - \rho)U(C_2)\}$$

or equivalently

$$U(C_1) + U^g(S_1) + \beta U(C_2) + \beta\rho U^g(S_2)$$

subject to the following constraints:

$$C_1 = (1 - m_1)(Y_1 - G_2 - S_1)$$

$$K_2 = m_1(Y_1 - G_2 - S_1)$$

$$C_2 = \alpha_c Y_2$$

$$S_2 = \alpha_s Y_2$$

This objective function clearly shows the effect of ρ. Increasing ρ affects the marginal rate of substitution between tomorrow's office rent and current office rent, and current private consumption and tomorrow's private consumption. Notice that C_2 and S_2 are functions of G_2 only. Now, combining the first-order conditions with respect to S_1 and N_{f1} yields:

$$U^g_{S1}(w_{f1} - w_{i1}) = 0$$

This implies that $\tau_{n1} = 0$. Hence, the burden of taxation again falls entirely on capital. However, the period 1 incumbent cannot avoid the distortion created by period 2 capital tax, which changes the margin between private consumption and office rent in period 1 (i.e. $U_{C1} \neq U^g_{S1}$). Specifically, the first-order condition with respect to S_1 implies:

$$U^g_{S1} = (1 - m_1)U_{C1}$$

This shows that a higher G_2 makes S_1 more expensive.

With assumption 1, regarding the form of the utility functions one can also obtain

$$S_1 = \alpha_s(Y_1 - G_2)$$

This equation shows that, given K_1, G_1 which since $\tau_{n1} = 0$ directly determine N_{f1} and N_{i1}, an increase in G_2 implies a reduction in S_1. Moreover, the reduction S_1 is less than the increase in G_2, because $\alpha_s < 1$.

Finally, the first-order condition with respect to G_2 allows us to express G_2 as a function of the initially given K_1, G_1, and all other parameters, including ρ. Specifically,

$$(\alpha_c + \rho\alpha_s)\gamma = [G_2(\gamma - \alpha_s) - \alpha_s]f(G_2)$$

where $f(G_2)$ is an increasing function of G_2, provided that $\alpha_s < \gamma$. Thus, the earlier equation implies that increasing ρ increases G_2 and hence by the equation defining S_1 reduces S_1. Moreover, since $\alpha_s < 1$, the increase in G_2 is more than the reduction in S_1 causing the tax burden of the first period to increase. Since the capital tax is the only tax instrument used by the government, this means that τ_{k1} increases due to an increase in ρ.

Notice that the results of the two-period model can be somewhat misleading for the desired results of this section. This is because the finite-period model implicitly assumes that $T = 2$ is the final period, in which there is neither private nor public investment. Obviously, such a period does not exist for an infinite horizon economy. In addition, for a two-period economy, some of the first-period allocations generally depend on the initial state variables, namely K_1 and G_1. Nevertheless, the two-period model still provides some helpful insights for understanding the main mechanism of the model as these remain valid for the results of the infinite horizon economy.

According to Proposition 5.2.1, the tax rate on formal labor in both periods is equal to zero so the burden of taxation falls on capital. The labor tax in period 2 is equal to zero because the incumbent in period 2 faces a static problem. Furthermore, due to the existence of an informal sector, the tax on formal labor income is distortionary. In contrast, the capital income tax is not distortionary since the capital of the second period has already been invested. Hence, the burden of taxation falls completely on capital. However, the tax rate on capital in period 2 depends on the value of α_s, and $\tau_{k_2} < 1$ if only if α_s is sufficiently low. Otherwise, $K_2 = 0$ and the economy shuts down in period 2. Therefore, an interior solution requires α_s to be small enough. Now, under this assumption, the economy is at the first-best ($U_{c2} = U_{s2}$) in period 2, because the only tax instrument used, capital tax, is non-distortionary. Therefore, both S_2 and C_2 are constant fractions of the second-period total output. Next, using this result, assumption 2 and equation 2, I can express S_2, C_2, N_{f2}, and N_{i2} as functions of G_2 only. More specifically, one can also obtain N_{f2} as an increasing function of G_2.

Having derived all the second-period allocations as a function of G_2 only, I can now define the problem of the incumbent in the first period. Of course, ρ plays an important role here, because from the first period's perspective, whether the first-period incumbent will enjoy office rent in the second period or not depends on the value of ρ. Thus, ρ increases the weight of the office rent of the second period in the first-period incumbent's utility function. Therefore, as the probability of reelection, i.e. ρ, increases, the marginal rate of substitution between current office rent and future office rent and the marginal rate of substitution between current private consumption and future office rent change in favor of the future office rent. This lets the current incumbent decrease the current office rent and increase the tax rate on current capital to reduce current private consumption. With more tax revenue at hand, the incumbent invests more on the productive public investment. Notice that the labor tax in the first period is also equal to zero and the burden of taxation falls on capital again. However, the government in the first period additionally faces an intertemporal distortion created by the capital tax in the second period. This distorts the margin between private consumption and office rent in the first period.

For the last two statements, one might wonder what happens to the formal and informal sector labor in the first period. This depends on the first period's stock of private and public capital, K_1 and G_1, and the labor tax rate. Since K_1 and G_1 are exogenously given and $\tau_{n_1} = 0$, formal and informal labor in the first period together with formal and informal output are fixed. However, formal and informal labor of the second period are functions of the second-period public capital, which is an increasing function of ρ. Thus, as the probability of reelection increases, so do the formal sector labor and the formal sector output in the second period, which, in turn, reduces the relative size of the informal sector in the second period.

The two-period economy with the simplifying assumptions can be generalized to an arbitrary T period economy. Moreover, letting $T \to \infty$, I can state the following result for the equilibrium of the infinite horizon economy as the limit of the finite horizon economy described earlier:

Proposition 5.2.2. *For small enough α_s and assuming that the assumptions 1, 2, and 3 hold, there exists an interior Markov-perfect equilibrium of the infinite horizon economy that is the limit of the Markov-perfect equilibrium of the finite horizon economy, in which the steady state statistics feature:* $\tau_n = 0$, $\tau_k > 0$, $\frac{\partial \tau_k}{\partial \rho} > 0$, $\frac{\partial (G/Y)}{\partial \rho} > 0$, $\frac{\partial (S/Y)}{\partial \rho} < 0$, $\frac{\partial (G+S)/Y}{\partial \rho} > 0$, $\frac{\partial (Y_i/Y_f)}{\partial \rho} < 0$

where $Y = Y_i + Y_f$. T

Proposition 5.2.2 is actually an extension of the previous one. I refer interested readers to Elgin (2015) for the proof. Intuitively, it simply states that the key results of the two-period environment extend to an infinite horizon environment. Notice that the steady state features a labor tax rate equal to zero. However, the tax rate on formal labor can be easily made positive by making the current capital tax also distortionary. One way of doing this is extending the model with endogenous capital utilization by allowing households to choose the amount of private capital to be utilized in the formal sector production function. This way, without changing the desired result of the negative correlation between the tax burden and the informal sector size, one can have both positive capital and labor taxes in the steady state. Notice that with both propositions at hand, I have an environment in which both the relative size of the informal sector and the tax burden depend on the exogenous probability of reelection. An increase in this probability also increases the tax burden while reducing the size of the informal sector, exactly as observed in the data.

Even though the earlier model assumes that households do not value leisure, it can easily be extended to include leisure in the utility function without changing the main results, most importantly the relationship between the tax burden and the size of the informal sector. To this end, the following assumption can be made regarding preferences:

Assumption 4. $U(C_t, \ell_t) = \alpha_c \log(C_t) + \alpha_\ell \log(L_t)$ and $U^g(S_t) = \alpha_s \log(S_t)$, where $\alpha_c + \alpha_\ell + \alpha_s = 1$

Notice that L_t stands for aggregate leisure. In this environment, I can state the following theorem:

Proposition 5.2.3. *For small enough α_s and under assumptions 2, 3, and 4 there exists an interior Markov-perfect equilibrium of the infinite horizon economy in the earlier described environment in which the steady state statistics feature the following:* $\tau_n < 0, \quad \tau_k > 0, \quad \frac{\partial(G/Y)}{\partial \rho} > 0, \frac{\partial(S/Y)}{\partial \rho} < 0, \frac{\partial(G+S)/Y}{\partial \rho} > 0, \frac{\partial Y_i/Y_f}{\partial \rho} < 0$

This proof is simply an extension of Proposition 5.2.2. The proof is presented in Elgin (2015). One problem of the environment with leisure is that the tax on formal labor, which was zero in the previous environment, becomes negative. Consequently, in equilibrium, there is a labor subsidy that turns out to be a decreasing function of ρ. The idea here is that the incumbent uses the labor subsidy to correct part of the distortion created by the capital tax. One way of having a positive labor tax is to introduce endogenous capital utilization a la Martin (2010). However, because none of these complications involve any qualitative changes in the main results, they are excluded from this text.

The equilibrium concept employed here is the same as that in Klein and Rios-Rull (2003) or, more recently, Martin (2010). The key assumption is that the government does not commit to any of its future policy choices. In each period, the government acts first by choosing current period policies. The equilibrium is called Markov-perfect since the government's choices depend only on the value of the current period's state, which in this case is just the aggregate private and public capital stocks. In addition, I only consider equilibria where policy depends differentially on private and public capital stock. In other words, I assume that the policy functions are differentiable with respect to the state variables. Finally, after the government has moved, the private sector chooses its current period action.

Consider the two first-order conditions of the problem of the household and notice that in a Markov-perfect equilibrium, the government follows a set of policy functions that are only functions of public and private capital today. After setting $\varsigma = (K, G)$ to be the vector of state variables,[1] let me define $G' = \Gamma(\varsigma)$, $\tau_k = \Theta_k(\varsigma)$, and $\tau_n = \Theta_n(\varsigma)$ to be these objects. Households will understand that in equilibrium government follows policy functions Γ, Θ_k, and Θ_n; thus, the first-order conditions of the private sector yield stationary decision rules for private capital tomorrow and labor in the formal sector today that only depend on the private and public capital stock today. Calling them $\mathcal{K}(\varsigma)$, and $\mathcal{N}_f(\varsigma)$, respectively, I can write the two household first-order conditions in a more compact form as follows:

$$\eta(\varsigma, \varsigma', \mathcal{K}(\varsigma'), \Gamma(\varsigma'), \mathcal{N}_f, \mathcal{N}_f(\varsigma'), \tau_k, \Theta_K(\varsigma'), \tau_n, \Theta_n(\varsigma')) = 0 \tag{5.2.1}$$

$$\varphi(\varsigma, \varsigma', \mathcal{N}_f, \tau_n, \tau_k) = 0 \tag{5.2.2}$$

The earlier two equations characterize household behavior for the current period for any arbitrary policy of the current government given that the government follows Θ_K, Θ_n, and Γ and thus implements $\mathcal{K}$ and $\mathcal{N}_f$.

Moreover, I can define the following aggregate functions for the office rent and private consumption:

$$\mathcal{S}(\varsigma) = rK\tau_k + wN_f\tau_n - G' + (1 - \delta_g)G \tag{5.2.3}$$

$$\mathcal{C}(\varsigma) = rK(1 - \tau_k) + wN_f(1 - \tau_n) + Y_i - K' + (1 - \delta_k)K \tag{5.2.4}$$

Now, given the perception that government follows some policy Γ, Θ_K, and Θ_n which, in turn, induces household and government behavior given by $\mathcal{K}(\varsigma)$, and $\mathcal{N}_f(\varsigma)$, I can write the problem of the current incumbent party as follows:

$$\begin{aligned} V(\varsigma) = \max\nolimits_{\{K', G', N_f, \tau_k, \tau_n\}} \; & U(\mathcal{C}(\varsigma)) + U^g(\mathcal{S}(\varsigma)) + \beta\{\rho V(\varsigma') \\ & + (1 - \rho)W(\varsigma')\} \end{aligned} \tag{5.2.5}$$

subject to equations (5.2.1), (5.2.2), (5.2.3), and (5.2.4).

Notice also that

$$W(\varsigma) = U(\mathcal{C}^*) + \beta\{\rho W(\varsigma'^*) + (1 - \rho)V(\varsigma'^*)\} \tag{5.2.6}$$

is the value function of the current opposition party where C^* and $\varsigma'^* = (K'^*, G'^*)$ are consumption, tomorrow's private and public capital, respectively, chosen by the incumbent.

I restrict my focus on (differentiable) interior SMPE of the earlier described game. This leads to the following definition of a politico-economic equilibrium:

Definition 5.2.2. An interior SMPE is defined by two value functions $W(\varsigma)$ and $V(\varsigma)$ and policy functions, $\mathcal{K}$, Γ Θ_k Θ_n, $\mathcal{N}_f$ such that for all $K \in (0, \bar{K}]$ and for all $G \in (0, \bar{G}]$, where $K^* = \mathcal{K}(K^*, G^*) < \bar{K}$ and $G^* = \Gamma(K^*, G^*) < \bar{G}$ and given the Markov chain regulating the probability of reelection ρ the following conditions are satisfied:

1 Given the value functions $W(\varsigma)$ and $V(\varsigma)$, policy functions $\mathcal{K}$, Γ Θ_k Θ_n, $\mathcal{N}_f$ solve the government maximization problem for the variables K', G', τ_k, τ_n, and N_f, respectively.

2 Given the policy functions $\mathcal{K}$, Γ Θ_k Θ_n, $\mathcal{N}_f$ value functions $W(\varsigma)$ and $V(\varsigma)$ satisfy the functional equations in (5.2.5) and (5.2.6).
3 Policy functions are differentiable in both of their arguments.

Moreover, the following proposition fully characterizes the symmetric (interior) differentiable Markov-perfect equilibrium in this economy:

Proposition 5.2.4. *The interior symmetric differentiable Markov-perfect equilibrium (interior) is a set of smooth functions* $\{\Theta_n, \Theta_k, \mathcal{K}, \Gamma, \mathcal{N}_f\}$, *that for all* $K \in (0, \bar{K}]$ *and* $G \in (0, \bar{G}]$ *satisfy equations* (1) *and* (2), *together with the following equations:*

$$\Theta_n = 0$$

$$\begin{aligned}
&-U_c + \lambda F_1 + \beta[\rho U_{s'}[Y^{f'}_{K'} + 1 - \delta_k]] + \beta(1-\rho) \\
&\Bigg\{U'_{c'}\{[1-\gamma\tau_{k'}]Y^{f'}_{K'} - \mathcal{K}'_{K'} + 1 - \delta_k\} + \beta\frac{\mathcal{K}'_{K'}}{1-\rho}\left[\rho\frac{U_{c'} - \lambda' F'_1}{\beta}\right. \\
&+ (1-2\rho)U_{c''}\left[Y^{f''}_{K''} + 1 - \delta_k\right]\Bigg] + \beta\frac{\Gamma'_{K'}}{1-\rho}\left[\rho\frac{U_{s'} - \lambda' F'_2}{\beta}\right. \\
&+ (1-2\rho)U_{s''}\left[Y^{f''}_{G''} + 1 - \delta_g\right]\Bigg] + \lambda' F'_3\Bigg\} = 0
\end{aligned}$$

$$\begin{aligned}
&-U_s + \lambda F_2 + \beta[\rho U_{s'}[Y^{f'}_{G'} + 1 - \delta_g]] + \beta(1-\rho) \\
&\Bigg\{U'_{c'}\{[1-\gamma\tau_{k'}]Y^{f'}_{G'} - \mathcal{K}'_{G'}\} + \beta\frac{\mathcal{K}'_{G'}}{1-\rho}\left[\rho\frac{U_{c'} - \lambda' F'_1}{\beta}\right. \\
&+ (1-2\rho)U_{c''}\left[Y^{f''}_{K''} + 1 - \delta_k\right]\Bigg] + \beta\frac{\Gamma'_{G'}}{1-\rho}\left[\rho\frac{U_{s'} - \lambda' F'_2}{\beta}\right. \\
&+ (1-2\rho)U_{s''}\left[Y^{f''}_{G''} + 1 - \delta_g\right]\Bigg] + \lambda' F'_4\Bigg\} = 0
\end{aligned}$$

The first equation given earlier simply states that all the burden of taxation in this environment falls on capital. The other two equations are the generalized Euler equations characterizing the Markov-perfect equilibrium. They show two simple things and are very intuitive: For example, the second one shows the tradeoff that the incumbent political party faces by investing one more unit of public capital today. Investing one more unit of public capital G_{t+1} today directly reduces S_t by one unit. That is why the second equation starts with the term $-U_s$. It also distorts the Euler equation of the households which is represented by the term λF_2. However, depending on the value of ρ it brings benefits tomorrow and thereafter. These benefits are represented by the terms after β. With probability ρ, the incumbent of today stays in office and continues to enjoy the office rent, which is represented by the term $\beta[\rho U_{s'}[Y^{f'}_{G'} + 1 - \delta_g]]$. Notice that the term in the bracket refers to the extra office rent effect of one additional unit of public investment today. On the other hand, the incumbent loses the power with probability $1 - \rho$. The first term within the large curly brackets refers to the additional present value of discounted utility of the today's incumbent in this case. Even if the incumbent loses the power, there are still benefits from additional public investment today, which manifest themselves as extra gains from formal sector output (enjoyed by today's incumbent despite losing office) Moreover, the current incumbent can still affect the decisions of the next period's government. This is because the current incumbent plays as a Stackelberg leader against the next period's incumbent. This incumbency advantage of the current incumbent is represented by the last three terms in the curly bracket which is a continuation value of the decision made by the incumbent today. Similarly, the first equation illustrates the tradeoff the incumbent faces by investing one more unit of private capital today. All the discussion for the second equation given earlier also applies to the first one.

Numerical analysis

In order to proceed with the numerical analysis, I keep assumption 1; however, I also relax assumption 2 to the following:

Assumption 5. $Y_{ft} = K^{\gamma} N_{ft}^{1-\gamma} (\frac{G_t}{K_t})^{\mu}$ and $Y_{it} = F(N_{it}) = N_{it}^{\phi}$

This class of dynamic policy games may feature both differentiable and non-differentiable Markov-perfect equilibria. However, I restrict my attention only to the differentiable Markov-perfect equilibrium and numerically calculate the steady state statistics of this economy. I describe the relevant computational algorithm in appendix C of Elgin (2015).

The parameterization of the baseline economy is standard. The capital share, as standard in the RBC literature, is assumed to be equal to $\gamma = 0.36$. Moreover, I assume that $\beta = 0.96$.

To determine the depreciation rates of private capital δ_k and public capital δ_g, I follow Baier and Glomm (2001) and Elgin (2015) to jointly match the average capital-output ratio from my data set (2.27) and the public investment-to-output ratio (0.04). This procedure implies a depreciation rate of about 0.07 on private physical capital and a depreciation rate of about 0.10 on public capital. Finally, I take $\mu = 0.15$ from Eicher and Turnovsky (2000) which also use the same functional form for production function in an optimal taxation environment similar to this chapter. However, to check the sensitivity of my results with respect to this non-standard parameter I will also conduct two simulations using different values of μ.

Now, the only remaining parameters are α_s in the utility function and ϕ in the informal sector production function. Regarding the calibration of these two parameters, I conduct two exercises. In the first one, I choose their values to match average informal sector size (8.40%) and tax burden (24.40%) in the United States for the period 1999–2017. (The calibrated values are 0.06 and 0.35, respectively.) In the second exercise, I calibrate α_s and ϕ to match the average size of the tax burden (18.09%) and the informal sector size (33.88%) in my data set. The calibrated values in the second exercise are $\alpha_s = 0.11$ and $\phi = 0.45$. Having calibrated these two parameters, I take the probability of reelection data given by Brender and Drazen (2008) for 58 countries, feed their series for all 58 countries into the model as ρ to obtain the generated series of relevant endogenous variables in the steady state, i.e. tax burden $\frac{r_t K_t \tau_{k_t}}{Y_t}$, the relative size of the informal sector $\frac{Y_i}{Y_f}$, public capital-output ratio G/Y, and the office rent-output ratio S/Y.

Quantitative results and experiments

Figure 5.3 plots two relationships between informal sector size and the tax burden. Panel A compares the behavior of the model against the US data using the calibrated values of α_s and ϕ. The model series clearly passes through the US data and also can account for the negative relationship between informal sector size and taxes. However, it does not match the correlation so well between these two variables in the cross-country setting. Panel B plots the same relationship using values of α_s and ϕ to match the average values of informal sector size and the tax burden. The model can clearly account both for the sign and magnitude of the correlation between these two variables. Using the same series, Figure 5.4 compares the linear regression lines drawn for the actual data and for the model generated data. The slopes are so similar that two lines almost overlap.

In Figures 5.5 and 5.6, using the calibrated values for α_s and ϕ, I plot certain endogenous variables of interest against various values of ρ to reveal mechanism behind the model's crucial result. As Figure 5.5a shows, increasing ρ reduces the size of the informal sector while Figure 5.5b shows that it increases the tax burden. However, as Figure 5.6a and b shows, the two components of government spending go in opposite directions. As the probability of reelection increases, the public capital-output ratio goes up whereas the office rent-output ratio goes down.

Figure 5.7 presents the sensitivity analysis with respect to the choice of μ. Here, in addition to the benchmark simulation with $\mu = 0.15$ (middle line), I run two additional simulations with $\mu = 0.25$ (lower line) and $\mu = 0.05$ (upper line). In both cases, the model can still match the negative correlation between informal sector size and the tax burden, which indicates that the model's performance is generally robust to the choice of μ. Because the simulated series of the other variables does not change significantly with different values of μ, I do not include these simulations due to space constraints.

Figure 5.8 presents another sensitivity check with respect to the informal sector production function. Remember, that I have so far assumed that the

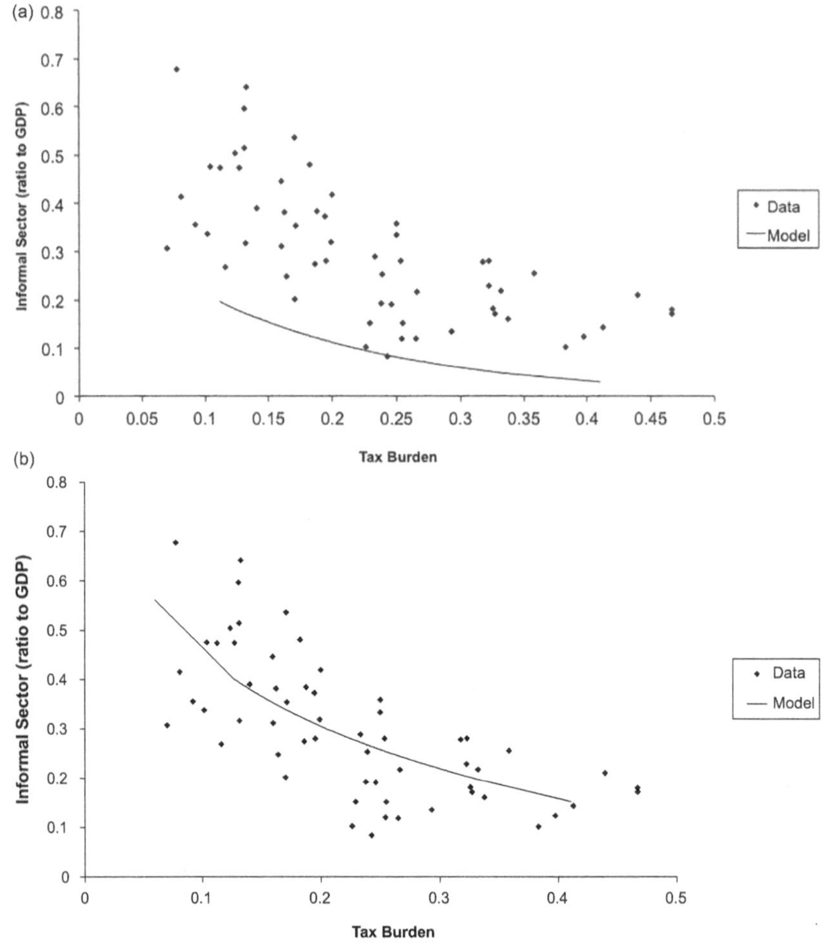

Figure 5.3 Informal sector versus tax burden: model versus data. (a) Calibrating to the United States. (b) Calibrating to the world average.

informal sector does not employ private or public capital. Here, I relax this assumption and assume that $Y_{it} = K_{it}^{\gamma_i} N_{it}^{\phi} (\frac{G_t}{K_{it}})^{\mu_i}$. For this specific exercise, I assume $\gamma_i = 0.25$, $\mu = 0.10$. These values ensure that the shares of private and public capital in the informal sector are less than those in the formal sector. I then use the same procedure as earlier to calibrate α_s and ϕ to match the average values of informal sector size and the tax burden in the data. Figure 5.8 plots informal sector size versus tax burden using these values. Here, the solid line represents the benchmark while the dashed line represents the simulation corresponding to the sensitivity check. As expected, the results are quantitatively similar to the benchmark case like in the previous sensitivity check.

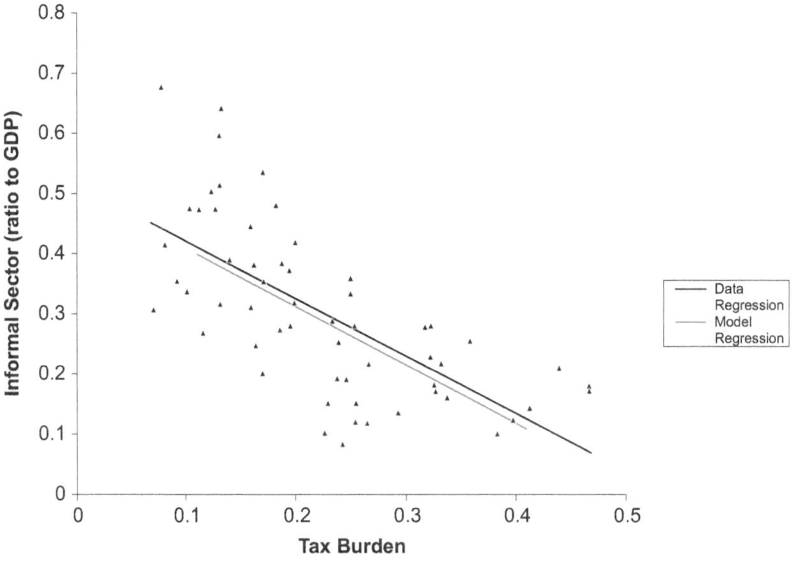

Figure 5.4 Informal sector versus tax burden: model and data regressions.

5.2.3 Empirical analysis

In this subsection, I present empirical evidence testing the main results of the model presented in the previous section. While these results rest on those presented in Elgin (2015), I use updated data sets to report results from the most recently available data. More specifically, in contrast to Elgin (2015), where I used the panel data set for 1999–2017 from Schneider et al. (2010), here I use the most recent panel data on informality from Elgin et al. (2019). In what follows, I first describe the data set, then discuss the econometric methodology, and finally present the estimation results.

In the econometric estimations, I use four measures of taxes to check the robustness of the analysis: first, the tax burden data from the IMF's Government Finance Statistics (GFS) data; second, taxes on income, profits, and capital gains (as percentage of GDP) from the World Development Indicators; third, the fiscal freedom index of the Heritage Foundation, a composite index comprising the top tax rate on individual income, the top tax rate on corporate income, and total tax revenue as a percentage of GDP; fourth, data on top marginal income tax rates from the Fraser Institute. The regression results reported here are mainly based on the GFS tax burden data; however, the results do not change if one uses other types of taxation data from the four sources listed here.

I use two measures of political turnover: first, the political stability index, a composite measure of government unity, legislative strength, and popular support from the International Country Risk Guide (ICRG); second,

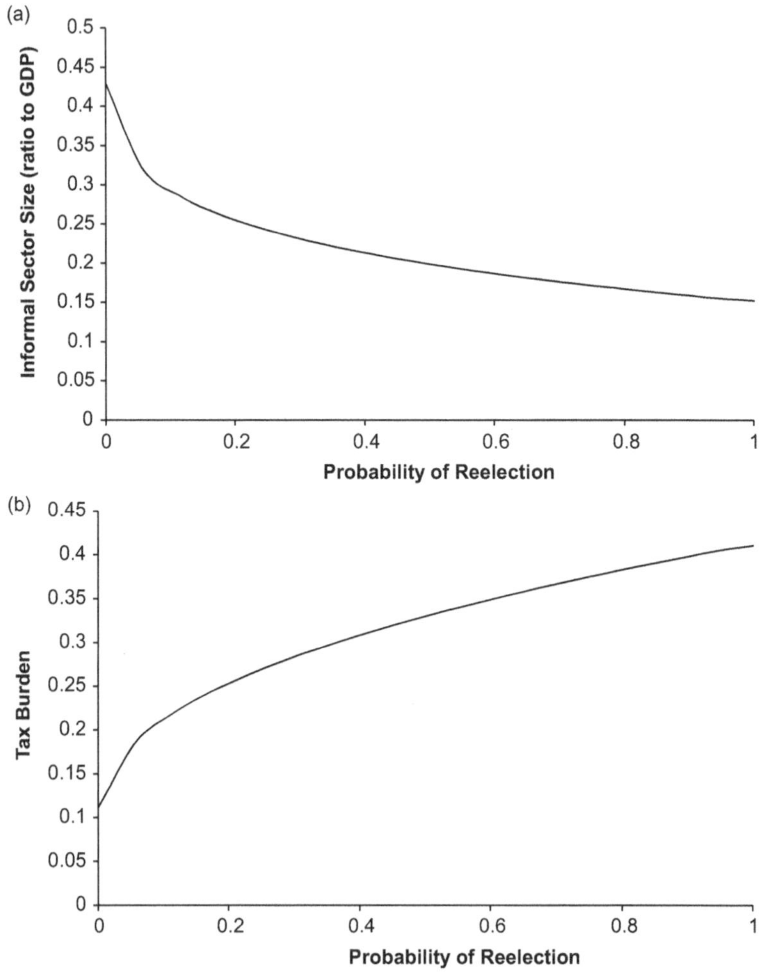

Figure 5.5 (a)Informal sector versus probability of reelection. (b) Tax burden versus probability of reelection.

the probability of reelection index developed by Brender and Drazen (2008) using election data from a significant number of countries. The probability of reelection database is available for 58 countries of the 160 countries in my informal sector data set.[2] It is also only cross-sectional whereas the ICRG political stability index is a yearly panel for 141 countries for any year after 1984.

In the regression analysis I also use several control variables such as GDP per capita, growth of GDP, capital-output ratio and measures of law and order, corruption, bureaucratic quality, and democratic accountability. I take the data for GDP per capita, growth and capital-output ratio[3] from the most-recent

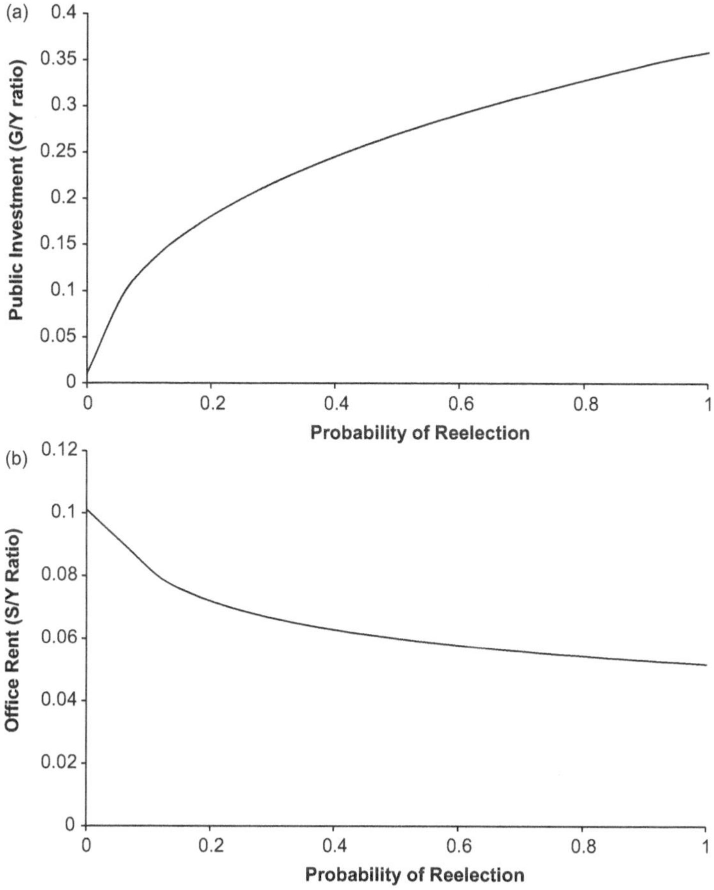

Figure 5.6 (a) Public investment versus probability of reelection. (b) Office rent versus probability of reelection.

version of the Penn World Tables (PWT). For measures of institutional quality, I use data from the ICRG.

I present descriptive statistics of all the variables in Table 5.1.

To check the robustness of the negative relationship between taxes and informality, I run a number of regressions using different sets explanatory variables and econometric specifications.

In the static panel data analysis with FE the estimated equations are of the following form:

$$IS_{i,t} = \beta_0 + \beta_1 tax_{i,t} + \sum_{k=2}^{n} \beta_k X_{k_{i,t}} + \theta_i + \gamma_t + \epsilon_{i,t}$$

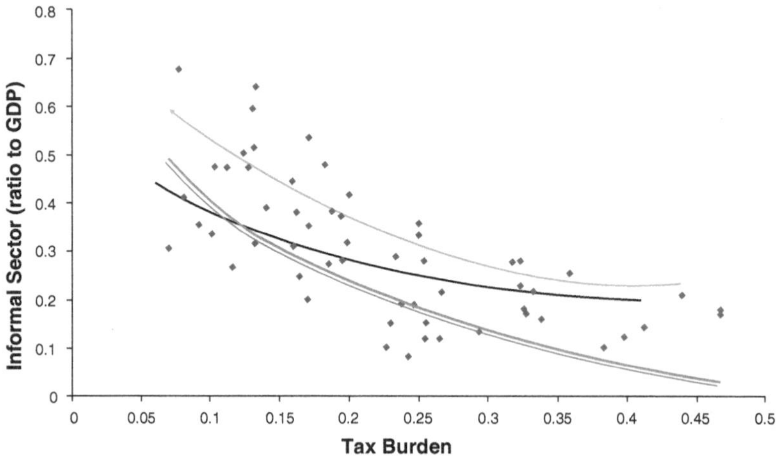

Figure 5.7 Informal sector versus tax burden: robustness checks 1.

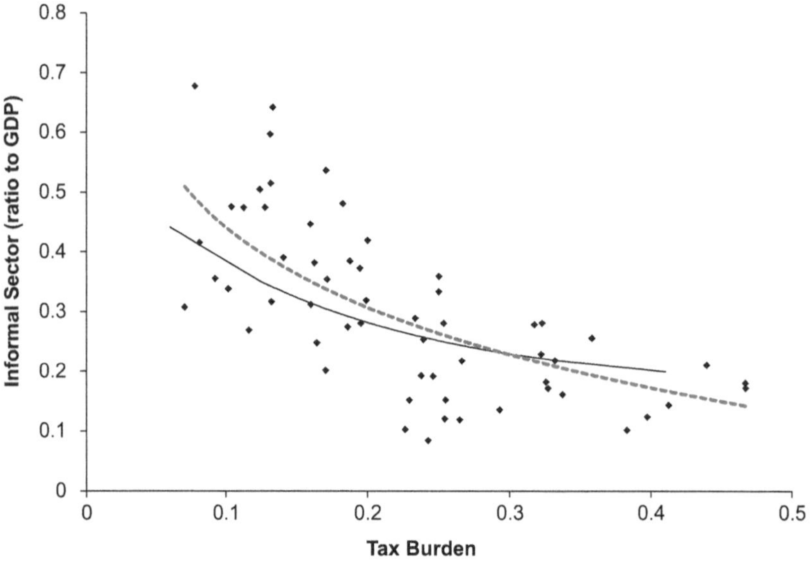

Figure 5.8 Informal sector versus tax burden: robustness checks 2.

where $X_{k_{i,t}}$ are the other explanatory variables in addition to taxes and θ_i, γ_t are the country and period FE, respectively. Moreover $IS_{i,t}$ is the size of the informal sector relative to GDP and $tax_{i,t}$ is the tax rate. In addition to the FE estimator, I will also run regressions using three additional estimators. These are the OLS, the instrumental variable (IV) estimator using the method

Table 5.1 Summary Statistics

	Mean	*Std. Dev.*	*Minimum*	*Maximum*
Tax Burden (in %)	18.09	7.18	0.84	53.21
Fiscal Freedom Index	72.11	15.79	33.09	99.9
Informal Sector Size (in %)	33.88	12.67	7.78	68.80
Political Stability Index	9.05	0.99	6.88	11.20
Probability of Reelection	0.37	0.33	0.00	1.00
GDP per capita (PPP in thousand $)	12.21	13.90	0.17	76.09
Law and Order Index	3.77	1.37	0.50	6.00
Bureaucratic Quality Index	2.30	1.09	0.00	4.00
Corruption Index	2.69	1.17	0.00	6.00
Democracy	4.00	1.59	0.00	6.00
Capital-Output Ratio	2.27	1.97	0.85	5.72
Growth of GDP (%)	3.09	3.37	−4.41	12.32

These are cross-sectional summary statistics of the panel averages. All the variables except the probability of reelection are for 141 countries. For probability of reelection I have data for only 58 countries.

of Anderson and Hsiao (1982) with clustered standard errors and finally the generalized method of moments (GMM) estimator a la Arellano and Bond (1991) in which I use lagged independent variables as instruments for the levels of these variables. In these regressions, I expect the estimate of β_1 to be significantly negative.

I also run regressions using measures of political turnover on the right-hand side. In these cases I estimate the following equation with an interaction term for political stability and taxes on the right-hand side:

$$IS_{i,t} = \beta_0 + \beta_1 tax_{i,t} + \beta_2 tax_{i,t} pols_{i,t} \sum_{k=3}^{n} \beta_k X_{k_{i,t}} + \theta_i + \gamma_t + \epsilon_{i,t}$$

In this specification, when using the panel political stability series, I again conduct estimations with the four different estimators listed earlier in the panel data setting. However, when I use the cross-country probability of reelection series, then I simply run an OLS regression with heteroskedasticity consistent standard errors. Given the results of the theoretical model of the previous section, in the regressions with political stability, I expect the estimates of β_1 and β_2 to be positive and negative, respectively. That is, after controlling for political stability, I predict that the effect of taxes on informality interacts with political stability. More specifically, with higher political stability, the correlation between informal sector size and tax burden becomes negative.

Tables 5.2 and 5.3 report the results of the benchmark estimation, using, respectively, the tax burden series and the FFI index as the relevant independent variable. I first run OLS, FE, IV, and GMM regressions with tax burden, GDP per capita, and the three institutional quality indices on the right-hand side of the regression equation. I then add democratic accountability, growth of GDP, capital-output ratio, and lagged informal sector size to the right-hand side. As

Table 5.2 Informal Sector and Tax Burden

Dep. var.: IS								
	OLS	*FE*	*IV*	*GMM*	*OLS*	*FE*	*IV*	*GMM*
Tax	−0.35*	−0.40**	−0.27**	−0.29**	−0.30*	−0.44*	−0.18**	−0.18**
	(3.11)	(2.23)	(2.18)	(2.34)	(2.16)	(2.96)	(2.09)	(2.14)
GDP	−0.02**	−0.02*	−0.02*	−0.02*	−0.02*	−0.02*	−0.02*	−0.02*
	(2.28)	(2.21)	(2.77)	(2.44)	(2.99)	(3.01)	(2.99)	(2.84)
Law	−0.70*	−0.59*	−0.58*	−0.52*	−0.53*	−0.61*	−0.57*	−0.55*
	(3.90)	(3.70)	(3.34)	(3.18)	(3.71)	(3.08)	(3.16)	(3.31)
Bureaucracy	−1.02**	−0.99	−0.85	−0.70	−0.99	−0.91	−0.84	−0.83***
	(1.95)	(1.07)	(1.53)	(1.42)	(0.98)	(1.03)	(0.92)	(1.77)
Corruption	−0.80**	−0.91**	−0.65*	−0.69*	−0.08**	−0.89*	−0.75*	−0.71*
	(2.03)	(2.11)	(2.98)	(2.09)	(2.51)	(2.72)	(2.87)	(2.90)
Democracy					−0.19	−0.55	−0.72	0.77
					(0.41)	(0.42)	(0.48)	(0.51)
Capital					−1.87*	−1.77*	−2.07*	−1.93*
					(2.90)	(3.15)	(3.18)	(3.21)
Growth					0.21	0.18	0.16	0.80***
					(0.89)	(0.99)	(0.30)	(1.78)
IS(−1)					0.40*	0.19	0.68	1.20**
					(3.11)	(1.20)	(1.18)	(1.99)
R-sq	0.51	0.54			0.67	0.61		
Obs.	2469	2469	2328	2328	2328	2328	2189	2189
J-Test				0.24				0.17
AR(2)-Test				0.49				0.45

Absolute values of the robust *t*-statistics are reported in parentheses. *, **, and *** denote 1%, 5%, and 10% confidence levels, respectively. In all regressions a constant is also included but not reported.

both tables show, there is a statistically significant association between higher taxes (actual or statutory)[4] and a smaller informal sector in all specifications. Likewise, higher levels of GDP per capita, law and order, corruption control, and capital-output ratio are all significantly associated with a smaller informal sector.

Table 5.4 reports the estimation results with political stability using panel data from 141 countries. Given the panel nature of this series, I run regressions with four different panel specifications. As expected, the estimate of the coefficient of the tax burden is positive; however because it interacts with political stability, the correlation between tax burden and informal sector size is generally negative with higher levels of political stability. In Elgin (2015), I also report various robustness checks of these benchmark results in which I run regressions with stratified data sets.

Table 5.5 complements Table 5.4, but for 58 countries with available cross-country probability of reelection data. The first two columns report the results from the cross-sectional regressions on the probability of reelection series. The next eight columns report the panel regressions on political stability for the 58-country subset.

Table 5.3 Informal Sector and Fiscal Freedom

Dep. var.: IS								
	OLS	*FE*	*IV*	*GMM*	*OLS*	*FE*	*IV*	*GMM*
FFI	0.22*	0.23**	0.18*	0.14*	0.16*	0.16*	0.13*	0.11*
	(2.91)	(2.04)	(2.92)	(2.86)	(2.78)	(2.90)	(2.87)	(2.88)
GDP	−0.02**	−0.02**	−0.02*	−0.02**	−0.02*	−0.02*	−0.02*	−0.02*
	(2.21)	(2.18)	(2.78)	(2.19)	(2.79)	(2.91)	(2.86)	(2.90)
Law	−0.73*	−0.53*	−0.57*	−0.53*	−0.58*	−0.58*	−0.54*	−0.54*
	(4.01)	(3.73)	(3.26)	(3.15)	(3.69)	(3.06)	(3.10)	(3.19)
Bureaucracy	−1.10**	−0.94	−0.84	−0.73	−1.01	−0.95	−0.88	−0.79
	(1.98)	(1.13)	(1.61)	(1.45)	(0.96)	(1.02)	(0.94)	(1.59)
Corruption	−0.89**	−0.90**	−0.69*	−0.77*	−0.93**	−0.88*	−0.74*	−0.75*
	(1.94)	(2.11)	(2.94)	(3.02)	(2.24)	(2.93)	(3.02)	(3.01)
Democracy					−0.16	−0.58	−0.80	0.80
					(0.38)	(0.45)	(0.43)	(0.50)
Capital					−1.83*	−1.71*	−2.20*	−2.05*
					(2.95)	(3.26)	(3.28)	(3.20)
Growth					0.17	0.18	0.15	0.79
					(0.86)	(0.95)	(0.32)	(1.63)
IS(−1)					0.39*	0.16	0.78	1.15**
					(3.1)	(1.21)	(1.19)	(2.02)
R-sq	0.40	0.44			0.51	0.58		
Obs.	2469	2469	2328	2328	2328	2328	2189	2189
J-Test				0.20				0.28
AR(2)-Test				0.27				0.25

Robust *t*-statistics are reported in parentheses. * and ** denote 1% and 5% confidence levels, respectively. In all regressions a constant is also included but not reported.

Finally, I also report the regression results for the behavior of key variables in the model with respect to political stability. The estimations here aim to test whether political frictions play an important role in the composition and level of public finance. The estimations investigate the role of political stability as the key friction. That is, if political stability is higher, which means that the incumbent is more certain of staying in office, the government will direct more tax revenues toward productive public investment and less toward wasteful government spending, specifically office rent and corrupt activities. Therefore, although the overall tax rate will increase with higher political stability, the change in the composition of public spending will make the formal sector more attractive for households. Based on this hypothesis, greater political stability (or probability of reelection) is associated with lower corruption, higher productive government spending, a larger tax burden, and a smaller shadow economy. The final set of regressions provides some empirical evidence supporting these predictions.

The results are presented in Tables 5.6 and 5.7. First column, "OLS", reports the cross-sectional regression results with probability of reelection as the measure of political stability. Subsequent columns use the ICRG's political

Table 5.4 Regressions with Political Stability

Dep. var.: IS								
	OLS	*FE*	*IV*	*GMM*	*OLS*	*FE*	*IV*	*GMM*
Tax	0.07**	0.11**	0.08**	0.16*	0.05**	0.12**	0.08**	0.12*
	(1.98)	(2.14)	(2.01)	(2.99)	(2.06)	(2.04)	(2.07)	(2.98)
Pols.	−2.01**	−2.05**	−2.12**	2.11**	−2.00**	−2.05**	−2.32**	−2.20**
	(2.07)	(2.20)	(1.96)	(1.93)	(1.97)	(2.10)	(2.11)	(2.11)
Pols.·Tax	−0.04*	−0.05*	−0.05*	−0.07*	−0.07*	−0.08*	−0.07*	−0.09*
	(4.03)	(3.44)	(3.29)	(3.88)	(2.99)	(3.12)	(3.18)	(3.20)
GDP	−0.01***	−0.01***	−0.01	−0.01	−0.01	−0.01	−0.01	−0.01
	(1.79)	(1.79)	(1.61)	(1.61)	(1.52)	(1.07)	(1.19)	(1.14)
Law	−0.70*	−0.42*	−0.46*	−0.51*	−0.50*	−0.44*	−0.51*	−0.50*
	(3.75)	(3.69)	(3.11)	(2.98)	(3.03)	(3.81)	(2.90)	(3.04)
Bureaucracy	−0.89	−0.67	−0.72	−0.74	−0.83	−0.82	−0.82	−0.52
	(1.51)	(1.29)	(1.21)	(1.12)	(0.88)	(0.87)	(0.91)	(0.94)
Corruption	−1.02**	−0.83**	−0.75*	−0.72*	−1.00*	−0.94*	−0.82*	−0.77*
	(2.39)	(2.46)	(3.30)	(3.27)	(2.97)	(2.99)	(3.11)	(3.28)
Democracy					−0.70	−0.55	−0.62	0.71
					(0.44)	(0.42)	(0.55)	(0.57)
Capital					−2.05*	−2.02*	−2.09*	−2.25*
					(3.79)	(3.75)	(3.90)	(3.88)
Growth					0.05	0.04	0.02	0.01
					(0.24)	(0.20)	(0.24)	(0.21)
IS(−1)					0.32**	0.54	0.85***	0.94***
					(2.40)	(1.62)	(1.87)	(1.86)
R-sq	0.50	0.51			0.64	0.59		
Obs.	2469	2469	2328	2328	2328	2328	2189	2189
J-Test				0.27				0.23
AR(2)-Test				0.26				0.20

Robust standard errors are in parentheses. *, **, and *** denote 1%, 5%, and 10% confidence levels, respectively. In all regressions a constant is also included but not reported.

stability index in a panel data framework. The second and third columns only use the 58-country subset of this panel whereas subsequent columns use the 141-country data with different econometric specifications.

Table 5.6 presents the estimation results using the tax burden as the dependent variable. These support the hypothesis regarding the positive relationship between the tax burden and political stability (or probability of reelection). The lower panel of Table 5.7 reports the estimated relationship between corruption and political stability. The results support the hypothesized negative relationship, i.e. a higher level of political stability increases the control of corruption index (i.e. reduces corruption). Moreover, as reported in the upper panel of Table 5.7, political stability is positively correlated with GDP per capita. Finally, the lower panel of Table 5.7 reports the regression of public investment[5] (as ratio to GDP) on political stability. There is a positive correlation between these two variables, in line with the theoretical model.

Table 5.5 Probability of Reelection versus Political Stability for 58 Countries

Dep. var.: IS	*OLS*	*OLS*	*OLS*	*FE*	*IV*	*GMM*	*OLS*	*FE*	*IV*	*GMM*
Tax	0.08*	0.09*	0.13*	0.13*	0.13*	0.14*	0.11*	0.14*	0.11**	0.10*
	(2.98)	(2.99)	(3.00)	(3.02)	(3.16)	(3.11)	(3.15)	(2.90)	(2.81)	(3.05)
Reelect.	−0.12**	−0.13**								
	(2.03)	(2.11)								
Reelect.·Tax	−0.27*	−0.27*								
	(3.82)	(3.19)								
Pols.			−1.76**	−1.48**	−1.59**	−1.69**	−2.01**	1.53**	1.64**	1.70**
			(2.13)	(1.96)	(1.95)	(2.01)	(2.09)	(2.03)	(2.05)	(2.19)
Pols.·Tax			−0.09*	−0.08*	−0.11*	−0.10*	−0.07*	0.08*	0.09*	0.11*
			(3.73)	(2.96)	(3.04)	(3.02)	(2.98)	(3.10)	(3.20)	(3.11)
GDP	−0.01	−0.03	−0.02**	−0.02**	−0.02**	−0.02**	−0.01**	−0.02**	−0.02**	−0.02***
	(0.62)	(0.65)	(2.06)	(1.99)	(2.00)	(2.03)	(2.03)	(2.01)	(2.02)	(1.77)
Law	−0.95	−0.97	−0.92**	−0.72**	−0.75**	−0.76**	−0.78**	−0.75**	−0.78**	−0.71**
	(1.32)	(1.21)	(2.27)	(2.03)	(2.01)	(2.01)	(2.01)	(2.01)	(2.04)	(2.11)
Bureaucracy	−0.12	−0.21	−0.47	−0.49	−0.69	−0.72	−0.65	−0.70	−0.71	−0.75
	(0.87)	(0.65)	(0.80)	(0.84)	(0.76)	(0.82)	(0.78)	(0.82)	(0.94)	(0.88)
Corruption	−0.41	−0.42***	−0.39	−0.30	−0.33	−0.45	−0.20	−0.32	−0.31	−0.32
	(1.51)	(1.88)	(0.87)	(0.81)	(0.90)	(0.94)	(0.57)	(0.59)	(0.73)	(0.81)
Democracy	−0.02	−0.06					−0.09	−0.11	−0.07	−0.08
	(0.11)	(0.14)					(0.21)	(0.32)	(0.28)	(0.23)
Capital		−1.18*					−2.00*	−2.01*	−2.10*	−1.90*
		(2.99)					(2.98)	(3.03)	(3.00)	(3.19)
Growth		−0.08					−0.06	−0.07	−0.06	−0.05
		(0.33)					(0.16)	(0.15)	(0.18)	(0.11)
IS(−1)							0.35*	0.31*	0.33*	0.40*
							(3.32)	(3.20)	(3.17)	(3.21)
R-sq	0.45	0.54	0.50	0.53			0.52	0.55		
Obs.	58	58	1102	1102	1044	1044	986	986	986	986
J-Test						0.23				0.19
AR(2)-Test						0.20				0.21

Robust standard errors are in parentheses. *, **, and *** denote 1%, 5%, and 10% confidence levels, respectively. In all regressions a constant is also included but not reported.

Table 5.6 Further Regressions of Other Variables

Dep. Var: Tax Burden								
	OLS	*OLS (58)*	*FE (58)*	*OLS*	*FE*	*FE*	*GMM*	*IV*
Pols.		2.33*	2.82*	4.61**	3.98*	3.91**	4.01*	3.17*
		(3.19)	(3.29)	(2.10)	(4.20)	(2.09)	(3.99)	(3.41)
Reelect.	15.30*							
	(3.21)							
Tax (−1)						0.82*	0.82*	0.73*
						(2.97)	(3.02)	(3.118)
R-squared	0.15	0.22	0.34	0.22	0.31	0.40		
Observations	58	1102	1102	2469	2469	2328	2189	2189
Hansen J-Test							0.16	
AR(2) Test							0.20	
Dep. Var: Corruption								
	OLS	*OLS (58)*	*FE (58)*	*OLS*	*FE*	*FE*	*GMM*	*IV*
Pols.		0.33**	0.32**	0.40**	0.41*	0.420	0.39**	0.38**
		(2.21)	(2.26)	(2.10)	(3.32)	(2.99)	(2.09)	(2.11)
Reelect.	3.61*							
	(3.69)							
Corruption(−1)						0.72*	0.63*	0.60*
						(3.98)	(3.90)	(3.18)
R-squared	0.15	0.14	0.20	0.23	0.28	0.31		
Observations	58	1102	1102	2469	2469	2328	2189	2189
Hansen J-Test							0.14	
AR(2) Test							0.15	

Robust standard errors are in parentheses. * and ** denote 1% and 5% confidence levels, respectively. In all regressions a constant is also included but not reported.

5.3 Institutional quality

This section analyzes the behavior of the informal sector and its interaction with institutional quality as an economy develops. I therefore investigate the validity of this conjecture both theoretically and empirically. Theoretically, I wish to develop a model of the informal economy to investigate the relationship between GDP per capita and informal economy size. Specifically, I try to find whether there is a straightforward negative relationship between informal economy size and economic progress as measured by GDP per capita,[6] or whether this negative relationship is conditional on the introduction of additional dimensions related to development such as the quality of institutions. The two-sector dynamic general equilibrium model that I construct for this purpose indicates that institutional quality strongly interacts with the relationship between GDP per capita and informal economy size. Specifically, higher GDP per capita levels are associated with larger informal sectors in countries with low institutional quality whereas the size of the informal sector is negatively associated with GDP per capita in countries where institutional quality is high.

Table 5.7 Further Regressions of Other Variables

Dep. Var: GDP per capita	*OLS*	*OLS (58)*	*FE (58)*	*OLS*	*FE*	*FE*	*GMM*	*IV*
Pols.		17.21*	17.88*	18.86*	19.16*	20.02*	18.34*	18.27*
		(3.90)	(3.89)	(4.03)	(4.02)	(3.97)	(4.11)	(4.23)
Reelect.	9.40*							
	(4.02)							
GDP(−1)						0.30*	0.34*	0.37*
						(4.08)	(5.11)	(5.23)
R-squared	0.18	0.21	0.30	0.32	0.36			
Observations	58	1102	1102	2469	2469	2328	2189	2189
Hansen J-Test							0.20	
AR(2) Test							0.23	

Dep. Variable: Pub.Inv.	*OLS*	*OLS (58)*	*FE (58)*	*OLS*	*FE*	*FE*	*GMM*	*IV*
Pols.		4.98**	3.08**	3.00**	2.56**	2.50**	2.71**	2.34**
		(2.13)	(2.05)	(2.09)	(2.12)	(2.11)	(2.14)	(2.11)
Reelect.	6.85**							
	(2.10)							
Pub. Inv.(−1)						0.28***	0.31*	0.32**
						(1.79)	(1.01)	(2.20)
R-squared	0.09	0.11	0.14	0.18	0.20	0.22		
Observations	58	1102	1102	2469	2469	2328	2189	2189
Hansen J-Test							0.26	
AR(2) Test							0.30	

Robust standard errors are in parentheses. *, **, and *** denote 1%, 5%, and 10% confidence levels, respectively. In all regressions a constant is also included but not reported.

I also study the relationship between the size of the informal economy, GDP per capita, and various indicators of the institutional environment empirically. We should first note that empirical studies on informality are rare because of limited data availability since informality is hard to measure by definition. The largest data set in the literature, constructed by Buehn and Schneider (2012a), includes 162 countries for just nine years (from 1999 to 2007). However, institutional quality, which is one of the central components of my empirical analysis, does not vary much over a short time horizon as nine years. Toexamine the evolution of the shadow economy over the longer course of development, particularly taking its relationship with institutions into account, Elgin and Oztunali (2014) draw on the longer series of shadow economy estimates from Elgin and Oztunali (2012). This includes 161 countries from 1950 to 2009. Using panel data estimation techniques, I investigate how the size of the shadow economy changes during economic development with varying institutional quality. My results indicate that institutional quality strongly interacts with the relationship between economic development and informal economy size as suggested by my theoretical model. In this section, I present the theoretical model of Elgin and Oztunali (2014), but supplemented by an empirical analysis using more recent data from Elgin et al. (2019).

The literature has explored to some extent the effects of the informal economy on economic progress, instead of the reverse mechanism studied in this section. Using firm-level data, Raj (2011), Byiers (2009), and Taymaz (2009) find large productivity differences between formal and informal firms in favor of formal firms, and conclude that the low productivity levels of the informal firms are an obstacle to growth. On the other hand, according to La Porta and Scleifer (2014), while highly productive formal firms are more responsible for economic growth, informal firms provide livelihoods for the poor despite facing eventual extinction. Bah (2011) makes a similar point. Aside from the low productivity argument, Gatti and Honorati (2008) and Caro et al. (2012) find that higher levels of informality in various forms are associated with less access to credit, which is an important determinant of economic performance.

Various papers have studied the effects of the institutional environment on informal economy size. Torgler and Schneider (2007, 2009) and Aruoba (2018) find negative relationships between measures of institutional quality and informal sector size. Johnson et al. (1998) report that the effectiveness of government officials' discretion in the functioning of the regulatory system is a main determinant of informal economy size. Similarly, Feld and Schneider (2010) focus on the effects of the design of tax policies and state regulation. Regarding fiscal policy, Buehn et al. (2013) show that fiscal decentralization is a key determinant of informality. However, in contrast to the common argument that higher taxes induce informality, Friedman et al. (2000) find that the level of informality is mainly positively associated with over-regulation and corruption while Singh et al. (2012) find a negative relationship between the rule of law and the size of the informal economy. Regarding political determinants of informality, Schneider and Teobaldelli (2012) report that the degree of direct democracy is negatively associated with shadow economy size while Buehn and Schneider (2012b) find that corruption and the shadow economy are complements rather than substitutes.

Somewhat more closely related to the results presented in this section, Dell'Anno (2010) shows that institutional quality is one of the key indicators of informality in Latin American economies. He also finds evidence of an inverted-U relationship between human development and informal economy size.

While this section is broadly related to the findings summarized earlier, it makes a significant contribution to the literature because it is also distinct in several ways. First, along with Elgin and Oztunali (2014), it is one of the few attempts to use a dynamic general equilibrium framework to investigate the relationship between informal economy size, GDP per capita, and quality of institutions. Second, most empirical research only focuses on a few countries over a limited time (5–10 years). However, the results reported here are based on the largest data set to date. Finally, this is the first study apart from Elgin and Oztunali (2014) to identify, both theoretically and empirically, a relationship between informal economy size, institutional quality, and GDP per capita.

5.3.1 A theoretical framework

In Elgin and Oztunali (2014) we considered a two-sector dynamic general equilibrium model with formal and informal sectors. In this environment, the representative household solves the following infinite horizon utility maximization problem:

$$\max_{\{C_t, K_{t+1}, N_{It}, N_{Ft}\}_{t=0}^{\infty}} \quad \sum_{t=0}^{\infty} \beta^t [\log(C_t) + \phi \log(T - N_{It} - N_{Ft})]$$

$$\text{subject to} \quad C_t + K_{t+1} - (1-\delta)K_t = (1-\tau)\theta_F K_t^{\alpha} N_{Ft}^{1-\alpha} + (1-\rho\tau)\theta_I N_{It}^{\gamma}$$

In the earlier specification, the representative household makes consumption and investment decisions in each period, and allocates labor to formal and informal sectors. To do this, it derives utility from consumption, denoted by C_t, and from leisure which is denoted by $T - N_{It} - N_{Ft}$. K_t stands for physical capital, δ for depreciation of physical capital, T for total time endowment, and ϕ for the weight given to leisure in the household's utility function. The first term on the right-hand side is the income from formal sector production net of taxes τ, while the second term is the income from informal sector production. Here, θ_I and θ_F stand for the total factor productivities (TFP) of the informal and formal sectors, respectively. N_{Ft} stands for labor devoted to the formal sector while N_{It} denotes labor devoted to the informal sector. Taxes are not enforced to the same degree across both sectors. The degree of tax enforcement in the informal sector is denoted by ρ where $\rho \in [0, 1]$. The sum of taxes collected from both sectors is equal to the government spending G_t which is thrown away. Note that endogenizing the government's decision in an optimal taxation framework would not change the results qualitatively (see Elgin and Solis-Garcia, 2012; Elgin, 2015).

Given this environment, I can define the competitive equilibrium as follows:

Definition 5.3.1. Given the government policy variables $\{\tau, \rho\}$, an equilibrium of this two-sector model is a set of sequences $\{C_t, , l_t, K_{t+1}, N_{It}, N_{Ft}, G_t\}_{t=0}^{\infty}$ such that

1 The representative household chooses $\{C_t, l_t, K_{t+1}, N_{It}, N_{Ft}\}_{t=0}^{\infty}$ to maximize life-time utility.
2 G_t equals $\tau\theta_F K_t^{\alpha} N_{Ft}^{1-\alpha} + \rho\tau\theta_I N_{It}^{\gamma}$ and is thrown away.

Characterization

Given the definition of the competitive equilibrium, the model's first-order conditions can be manipulated to obtain the following:

$$\frac{C_{t+1}}{C_t} = \beta[(1-\tau)\theta_F \alpha K_{t+1}^{\alpha-1} N_{Ft+1}^{1-\alpha} + 1 - \delta]$$

$$(1-\tau)\theta_F(1-\alpha)K_t^{\alpha} N_{Ft}^{-\alpha} = (1-\rho\tau)\theta_I \gamma N_{It}^{\gamma-1}$$

The first equation is the standard Euler equation while the second equation represents the condition that the net marginal products of labor in both sectors should be equal at the optimum. Imposing the steady state on the two equations given previously produces the following expression, which characterizes the steady state informal and formal labor:

$$N_I = \left\{ \frac{(1-\rho\tau)\gamma\theta_I}{(1-\tau)(1-\alpha)\theta_F} \left[\frac{1/\beta - 1 + \delta}{\alpha(1-\tau)\theta_F} \right]^{\frac{\alpha}{1-\alpha}} \right\}^{\frac{1}{1-\gamma}}$$

$$N_F = \frac{(T - N_I)\gamma(1-\rho\tau)\theta_I N_I^{\gamma-1} - \phi(1-\rho\tau)\theta_I N_I^{\gamma}}{\gamma(1-\rho\tau)\theta_I N_I^{\gamma-1} + \phi[(1-\tau)\theta_F(\frac{\alpha(1-\tau)\theta_F}{1/\beta-1+\delta})^{\frac{\alpha}{1-\alpha}} - \delta(\frac{\alpha(1-\tau)\theta_F}{1/\beta-1+\delta})^{\frac{1}{1-\alpha}}]}$$

Notice that, given these equations, every variable of the model at the steady state can now be expressed as functions of the exogenous parameters. With all these variables at hand, one can also express the informal economy as % of GDP, i.e. $\frac{\theta_I N_{It}^{\gamma}}{\theta_F K_t^{\alpha} N_{Ft}^{1-\alpha}}$.

As the expressions are extremely rich in terms of their parameters, it is not possible to obtain a further analytical result with respect to the relationship between informal economy size and GDP per capita (i.e. formal output). I therefore present the results of the numerical simulations using the model-generated series in the next section.

Numerical analysis

This section provides some numerical comparative-statics results regarding the size of the informal economy. Specifically, I intend to see how informal economy size as % of GDP, i.e. $\frac{\theta_I N_{It}^{\gamma}}{\theta_F K_t^{\alpha} N_{Ft}^{1-\alpha}}$ changes when GDP per capita $\theta_F K_t^{\alpha} N_{Ft}^{1-\alpha}$ varies. As there is no population growth in the model GDP and GDP per capita do not differ. However, notice that both informal and formal outputs are endogenous in the model. This means that one needs to create a variation in at least one parameter of the model to create some variation in these two variables. I achieve this by varying two specific non-standard parameters of the model to represent institutional quality within the economy.

Choosing the right values for parameters is critical for the numerical simulation of a model. Here, I follow Ihrig and Moe (2004) to set $\alpha = 0.33$,

$T = 100$, $\beta = 0.97$, $\gamma = 0.495$, and $\delta = 0.08$. I calibrate $\phi = 0.10$ to match the average informal economy size (as a percentage of GDP) in the data set obtained from Elgin et al. (2019). Finally, to vary institutional quality, I initially fix the formal sector TFP parameter θ_F and the tax enforcement parameter ρ at numeraire and assume that $\theta_I = 6$. Setting this value for the informal sector TFP parameter is in line with various studies using firm-level data.

To mimic an economic environment with decreasing institutional quality, in every step of the simulation, I reduce ρ by 10% in grids from 1 to 0, and increase $\frac{\theta_I}{\theta_F}$ by 10% in grids of 0.6. This corresponds to an economy with deteriorating institutions in which the degree of tax enforcement falls while the informal sector TFP parameter increases relative to the formal sector one. Remembering the forms of the production functions, as I do not have government spending as an input in the functions, increasing the ratio of TFPs can be interpreted as reducing the quality of government spending, which is a further indicator of institutional quality.[7] Similarly, to mimic an economic environment with improving institutional quality, in every step of the simulation, I increase ρ by 10% while keeping $\frac{\theta_I}{\theta_F}$ constant. I use the ratio of TFPs in both sectors and the level of tax enforcement proxies for institutional quality, such that a higher value for the ratio of θ_F to θ_I and ρ is equivalent to an environment with better institutions. This assumption has been used by Blanchard Wolfers (1999), Crafts and Kaiser (2004), and Charles (2011) among many others.

Panel A of Figure 5.9 plots the size of the informal economy as a percentage of formal output against deteriorating institutional quality. Panel B plots the same series against improving institutional quality. The simulations indicate that the relationship between informal economy size and GDP per capita strongly interacts with institutional quality. That is, economic growth fails to reduce informality if institutions are poor; instead, the informal economy continues to grow alongside the formal one.

Having numerically simulated the model, the next section reports the empirical analysis to determine whether the model's results are empirically supported by panel and cross-country regressions. Specifically, the empirical analysis aims to show that a higher level of GDP per capita is associated with

1 a larger informal economy size when the level of institutional quality is low,
2 a smaller informal economy size when the level of institutional quality is high.

Empirical analysis

The empirical analysis aims to provide support for the theory that institutional quality strongly interacts with GDP per capita in the latter's relationship with informal economy size.

In the benchmark analysis, I estimate the regression equation below using the FE estimator. For these estimations, I use the FE estimator as the Hausman test

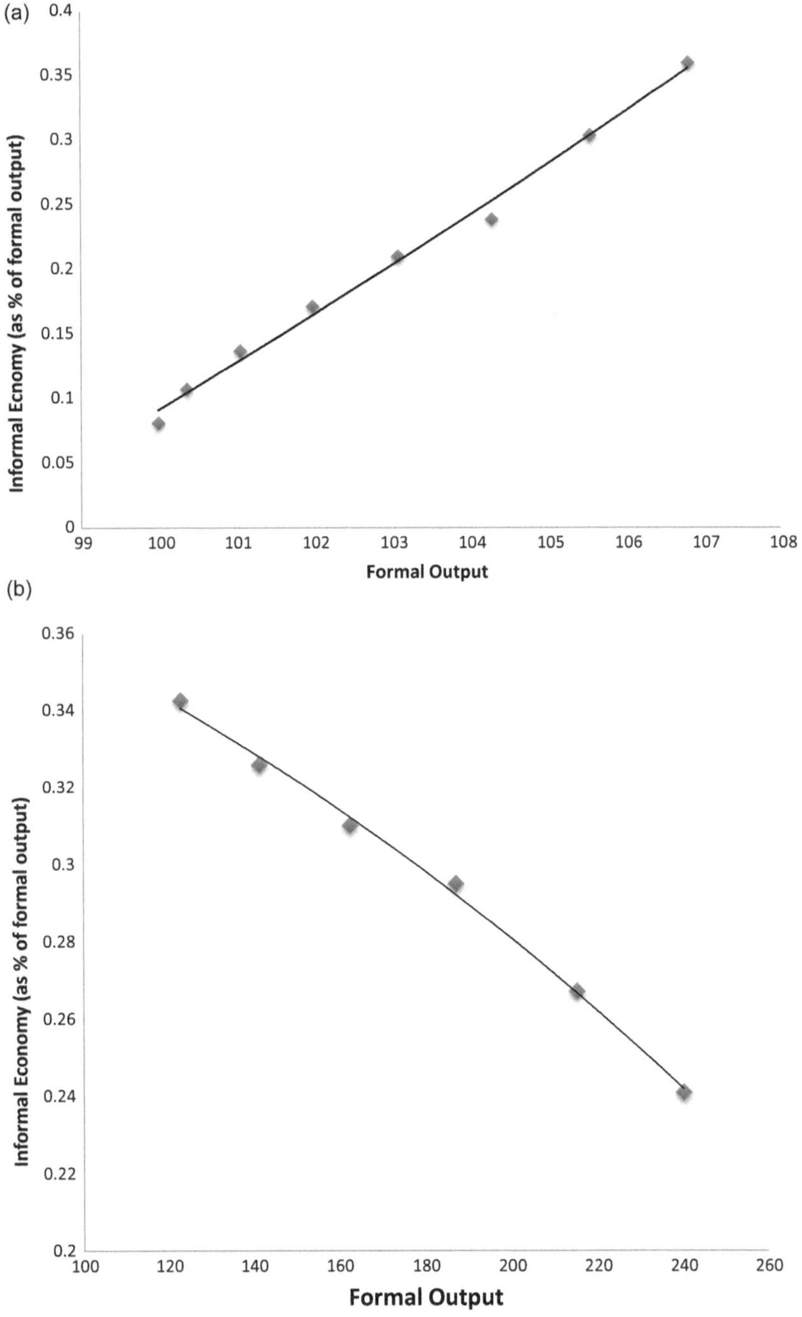

Figure 5.9 (a) Low institutional quality. (b) High institutional quality.

favors this specific estimator. However, to capture persistence and potentially mean-reverting dynamics in informal sector size, I also use the GMM estimator of Arellano and Bond (1991), with qualitatively similar results. The results are also strikingly similar for estimations using OLS and IV estimations. The regression equation is as follows:

$$IS_{i,t} = \sigma_0 + \sigma_1 GDP_{i,t} + \sigma_2 GDP_{i,t} \cdot Inst_{i,t} + \sum_{k=3}^{n} \alpha_k X_{ki,t} + \mu_i + \gamma_t + \epsilon_{i,t}$$

Here, $IS_{i,t}$ is the informal economy size as a percentage of GDP in country i in year t while GDP denotes GDP per capita. $X_{k_{i,t}}$ represents the other explanatory variables used as controls while μ_i, γ_t are the country and period FE, respectively, and $\epsilon_{i,t}$ denotes the error term. In the regressions, I am specifically interested in the estimated coefficients of σ_1 and σ_2, with the former showing the direct relationship between informal economy size and GDP per capita when institutional quality is held constant; the latter represents the interaction of institutional quality with this relationship. Given the earlier theoretical analysis, the estimated coefficients of σ_1 and σ_2 should be positive and negative, respectively.

As explained earlier, I use the informal sector panel data of Elgin et al. (2019) for 1950–2017 for 160 countries. Considering the length of the time series, I use this data set for the informal economy size. The GDP per capita series comes from PWT 9.1. The control variables are trade openness (defined as the ratio of the sum of exports and imports to GDP), government spending (as percentage of GDP), capital-output ratio, and growth of GDP per capita. These variables are also drawn from the PWT. To measure institutional quality, I use three institutional quality indices from the ICRG: corruption control, law and order, and bureaucratic quality. This choice stems from the conjecture that informality is mostly affected by these dimensions of institutional quality. Elgin (2010) and Elgin and Solis-Garcia (2012) exemplify the use of these indices for related environments. Moreover, these indices are also the closest proxies for their theoretical counterparts ($\frac{\theta_F}{\theta_I}$ and ρ) in the previous section. They are obtained from the ICRG and the rest of the variables are from PWT 9.1. Unfortunately, the institutional quality indices are only available after 1984 and only for 141 countries. Therefore, the data set for this analysis is restricted to 141 countries from 1984 to 2017.

Table 5.8 provides descriptive statistics for all the variables used in the empirical analysis.

Panels A and B of Figure 5.10 show the interaction of institutional quality with GDP per capita. To plot these two figures, a variable was created, named Institutions, defined as the weighted average of the three institutional quality indices in the regressions. The data set is then divided into two parts based on the average value of this new variable. Figure 5.10a and b plots informal economy size against GDP per capita for countries below (above) the mean of this institutional quality variable. The two panels strikingly resemble panels A

Table 5.8 Complete Data Set Summary Statistics

	Mean	*Std. Dev.*	*Minimum*	*Maximum*
Informal Economy (% GDP)	33.88	12.67	7.78	68.80
GDP per capita (thousand USD)	12.21	13.90	0.17	76.09
Trade Openness (% GDP)	76.86	41.10	8.29	401.09
Government Spending (Govt. sp.) (% GDP)	12.11	8.09	1.29	51.10
Capital-Output Ratio	2.27	1.97	0.85	5.72
Growth (%)	3.09	3.37	−4.41	12.32
Corruption Control	2.69	1.17	0.00	6.00
Law and Order	3.77	1.37	0.50	6.00
Bureaucratic Quality	2.30	1.09	0.00	4.00

and B of Figure 5.9, which shows the model simulations. This indicates that the model mimics the plain correlations in the data remarkably well.

Estimation results

Table 5.9 reports the first batch of regression results with all the annual[8] data for 141 countries from 1984 to 2017. Out of nine regression results, eight use the FE estimator while the last uses the IV estimator. The first five regressions include a variable named "Inst", defined as the average of the three institutional quality measures. The next three regressions include the three estimates of institutional quality separately while the IV regression uses "Inst".

As Elgin and Oztunali (2014) found, the estimated coefficients of GDP per capita and the interaction term are positive and negative, respectively. There is no qualitative change in the results from using the interaction term (GDP · Inst.) of the institutions variable or the interaction terms with the three institutional quality variables separately. Moreover, other than institutional quality, higher GDP growth rate and capital-output ratio are robustly associated with a smaller informal economy. This is not surprising as higher capital intensity and growth rate should attract firms and households to the formal economy. On the other hand, trade openness and government spending are positively associated with informal economy size in most regressions. With greater trade openness, formal enterprises may link their activities to the informal sector to reduce costs and increase labor flexibility. Accordingly, openness can be viewed as a proxy for the external subordination of the informal sector to the formal sector. Higher government spending, possibly along with higher taxes, may crowd out investment and capital intensity, thereby producing a larger informal economy.

Further robustness checks

In the first robustness check, I run regressions for different time periods and countries. To this end, Table 5.10 reports two sets of regressions with FE, IV, GMM, and OLS regressions for both subsets. First, I only use data from the 30 OECD countries in our sample with data for every year between 1984 and

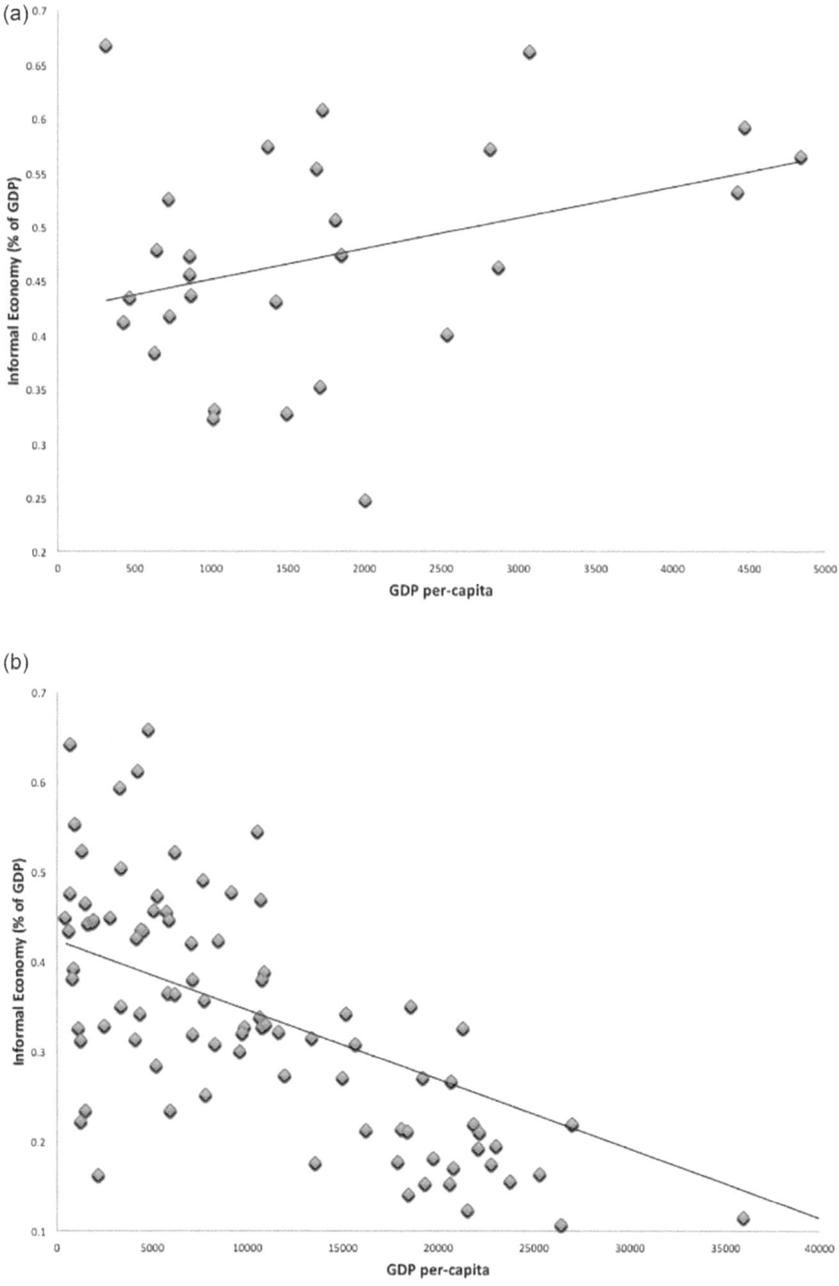

Figure 5.10 (a) Low institutional quality. (b) High institutional quality.

Table 5.9 Informality versus GDP per capita: FE Estimations

Informality									
	(1)	*(2)*	*(3)*	*(4)*	*(5)*	*(6)*	*(7)*	*(8)*	*(IV)*
GDP	0.51*	0.48*	0.49*	0.45*	0.46*	0.26*	0.24*	0.26*	0.32*
	(2.99)	(2.97)	(2.87)	(3.01)	(3.11)	(3.20)	(2.51)	(2.88)	(2.76)
GDP · Inst.	−0.12*	−0.12*	−0.11*	−0.11*	−0.11*				−0.14*
	(6.11)	(6.09)	(6.13)	(6.20)	(6.11)				(4.88)
Inst	0.15	0.24	0.27	0.28	0.36	0.11.	0.40	0.12	0.10
	(0.91)	(0.94)	(0.72)	(0.79)	(0.77)	(1.12)	(0.61)	(0.41)	(0.25)
Openness		0.02*	0.02*	0.02*	0.02*	0.03*	0.02*	0.02*	0.02**
		(3.01)	(3.08)	(3.19)	(3.12)	(3.07)	(3.04)	(2.99)	(1.92)
Govt. Sp.			0.03	0.06*	0.09*	0.09*	0.09*	0.10*	0.12*
			(1.32)	(2.89)	(2.76)	(3.01)	(3.09)	(3.13)	(3.09)
Capital				−3.01*	−3.02*	−3.31*	−3.29*	−3.27*	−3.00*
				(3.66)	(3.61)	(3.85)	(3.96)	(3.82)	(3.12)
Growth					−11.37*	−12.05*	−13.10*	−13.39*	−10.08*
					(4.16)	(4.09)	(4.01)	(3.89)	(2.98)
GDP · Law						−0.33*			
						(3.89)			
GDP · Corr.							−0.37*		
							(4.23)		
GDP ·Bur.								−0.18*	
								(5.98)	
R-squared	0.44	0.44	0.45	0.50	0.51	0.19	0.51	0.52	0.30
Observations	4790	4790	4790	4730	4730	4730	4730	4730	4589
F-Test	0.00	0.00	0.00	0.00	0.00	0.00	0.00	0.00	
J-Test									0.19
AR (2)-Test									0.37

All panel regressions include a country fixed effect and year dummies. Absolute values of robust *t*-statistics are reported in parentheses. * denotes 1% confidence level. IV refers to instrumental variable regression.

2017. For the second subset, I use data from the complete data set for every year between 1992 and 2017 for which there is data for all the countries in the analysis. As Table 5.10 shows, the results are robust to this stratification of the data set.

Elgin and Oztunali (2014) included further robustness checks using data for informal sector size based on multiple-indicators-multiple-causes (MIMIC) rather than dynamic general equilibrium (DGE), as well as different institutional quality measures from other sources. However, I do not replicate these here to save space. Interested readers are referred to the cited paper.

Summarizing the empirical results

I showed earlier that higher GDP per capita is associated with larger informal sectors in countries with low institutional quality whereas the informal sector shrinks as GDP per capita increases in countries where institutional quality is high.

Table 5.10 Informality versus GDP per capita: FE Estimations (All Years) – Different Periods and Countries

Informality								
	OECD: 1984–2017				*All: 1992–2017*			
	FE	*IV*	*GMM*	*OLS*	*FE*	*IV*	*GMM*	*OLS*
GDP	0.21*	0.20*	0.23**	0.20*	0.61*	0.59*	0.51*	0.68*
	(2.90)	(2.96)	(2.02)	(2.98)	(3.33)	(3.39)	(3.07)	(3.11)
GDP · Inst.	−0.15*	−0.16*	−0.17*	−0.19*	−0.12*	−0.13*	−0.14*	−0.15*
	(3.65)	(3.61)	(3.59)	(3.51)	(3.99)	(3.98)	(3.57)	(3.61)
Inst	0.10	0.14	0.26	0.95	0.21	0.23	0.05	0.06
	(0.39)	(0.30)	(0.71)	(1.29)	(1.14)	(0.89)	(0.91)	(1.00)
Openness	−0.02**	−0.02**	−0.01*	−0.01*	0.02*	0.02*	0.02*	0.02**
	(2.05)	(2.11)	(2.88)	(2.91)	(3.11)	(3.31)	(3.19)	(2.12)
Govt. Sp.	0.04	0.07	0.02	0.06	0.10*	0.09*	0.11*	0.12*
	(0.22)	(0.29)	(0.32)	(0.31)	(2.79)	(3.07)	(3.55)	(3.29)
Capital	−1.78*	−2.00*	−2.10*	−2.12*	−2.99*	−3.02*	−3.09*	−3.12*
	(2.92)	(3.091	(2.97)	(3.19)	(3.12)	(3.70)	(3.74)	(3.62)
Growth	−4.39*	−4.11*	−3.65*	−3.11*	−3.02*	−4.39*	−4.59*	−7.84*
	(3.30)	(3.17)	(3.22)	(3.01)	(4.09)	(4.10)	(4.*1)	(4.52)
L. Informality			0.76*				0.92*	
			(3.61)				(3.88)	
R-squared	0.46	0.49		0.41	0.44	0.40	0	0.43
Observations	1020	990	960	30	3661	3520	3379	141
F-Test	0.00			0.00	0.00			0.00
J-Test		0.22	0.23			0.20	0.29	
AR (2)-Test		0.20	0.30		0.20	0.37		

All panel regressions include a country fixed effect and year dummies. Absolute values of robust *t*-statistics are reported in parentheses. * and ** denote 1% and 5% confidence levels, respectively. FE, IV, GMM, and OLS refer to fixed-effects, instrumental variable, generalized method of moments, and ordinary least squares regressions, respectively.

One immediate question this raises is how important the quantitative influence of the quality of institutions on the shadow economy is while keeping the level of GDP per capita constant. Specifically, we want to understand the quantitative effect of varying institutional quality. Table 5.11 reports the percent change in informal economy size (relative to its mean) in relation to a one-standard-deviation change in each institutional quality measure (corruption control, law and order, and bureaucratic quality). Table 5.11 reports the IV estimates with all the independent variables on the right-hand side of the regressions.

For example, a one-standard-deviation increase in the corruption control index (meaning higher institutional quality) is associated with an 8.18% reduction in the informal economy for an average OECD member. While the effect of institutional quality varies for different indices, Table 5.11 clearly shows that informal sector size not only produces statistically significant coefficients but also has economically significant effects on the default risk measures. Unsurprisingly, the effect of institutions is smaller for OECD countries

Table 5.11 Quantifying Effect of Institutions on Informality (1984–2017)

Variable	*Corruption*	*Law and Order*	*Bur. Qual.*
OECD	8.18	9.01	7.71
Latin America	15.82	18.61	12.90
Asia	13.01	15.82	9.77
MENA	9.74	10.90	9.03

because institutions are likely to play a larger role if there is greater room for improvement, i.e. when institutional quality is low initially. Quantitatively, the most striking effect is in Latin America while there are also significant effects in Asian and Middle East and North Africa (MENA) countries.

5.4 Other determinants and policy implications

5.4.1 Other macroeconomic determinants of informality

Even though they are the two main ones, taxes and institutional quality are not the only determinants of informality as various other variables can affect informal sector size to some degree. While economic theory and applied econometric methods can shed light on these determinants, it is hard to identify the precise nature of these determinants and quantitative effects.

The primary reason for this difficulty is that many determinants are endogenous when used as explanatory variables in a regression when informal sector size regressed on them. One could get around this problem in the presence of truly exogenous IVs, i.e. related to these potential determinants of informality but not directly to informal sector size. Unfortunately, such variables are extremely difficult if not impossible to find. Therefore, most studies that claim to identify the determinants of informality can only establish correlations rather than produce causal arguments. Nevertheless, this does not mean they are unhelpful for identifying the correlates of informality.

Leaving these difficulties aside, the standard MIMIC models generally consider several so-called causal variables of informality such as personal income tax, indirect taxes, tax morale, unemployment, self-employment, GDP growth, and business freedom. In MIMIC models, informal sector size is positively correlated with the two tax measures, and unemployment and self-employment whereas it is negatively correlated with tax morale, GDP growth, and business freedom.

In addition to the MIMIC variables, other studies have identified different determinants. However, these determinants and their effects vary from one country or period to another. Therefore, different studies using different data sets from different countries and time periods generally end up with different results.

Ruge (2010), for example, evaluates several determinants using a data set of 11 latent variables and 58 indicators from 35 countries. He finds that the following factors all reduce informal sector size, albeit to varying degrees: higher wealth and development levels (measured by an index comprising GDP per capita, the human development index, and the Gini coefficient), a better administrative system (measured by several institutional quality variables), lower taxes and social security payments (measured by several tax measures and tax morale), higher tax complexity and surveillance (including various variables related to fiscal issues), and the extent of labor market regulations (including unemployment, wages, and regulatory variables). Using data from the Baltic economies, Putnins and Sauka (2011) find that important determinants of informality include trust in government and the tax system, and firm age and sector.

Neck et al. (2012) similarly link complexity of the tax system to the size of the informal sector. They also provide some evidence that work hour limits increase informality. Manolas et al. (2013) use panel data for 19 economies from 2003 to 2008 to show that major determinants of informality include the quality of governance, the regulatory framework in product, labor, and credit markets, and the tax burden in terms of the direct cost for entrepreneurial activity and the cost of compliance with the tax administration framework. Using a database of 38 economies from 1991 to 2008, Acosta-Gonzalez et al. (2014) evaluate the effects of 274 potential determinants in various econometric model combinations. Their results indicate that the major determinants are taxes on capital gains of individuals, corporate taxes on income, profits and capital gains, domestic credit, bank secrecy, ethnic fractionalization, urban population, globalization, corruption, and the socialist legal origin of the country.

Using cross-sectional data from 118 economies, Dell'Anno (2016) finds that income inequality generally reduces GDP, so informal sector size as a percentage of GDP is reduced. Finally, Goel and Nelson (2016) try to establish a consensus regarding the determinants of informality using three cross-national informality measures. They report that bureaucratic complexity, tax complexity, and business startup costs are the most robust determinants.

5.4.2 Implications for policy-makers

The main purpose of this chapter was to identify potential determinants of informality. Economists working on informality are generally interested in doing so in order to develop policy recommendations to present to policy-makers.

If policy-makers are truly interested in dealing with informality, they must have a firm understanding of its relationship with its determinants. The major reason for this is that the informal sector is endogenous, that is, there is no way for policy-makers to develop tools that can directly change informal sector size. Policy-makers should therefore primarily focus on changing these determinants so as to indirectly address the issues related to informality.

Various potential determinants have been identified in the literature, with tax-related being among the most important. Tax levels, particularly for certain kinds of taxes, and the complexity and the efficiency of the tax system seem to be crucial. One positive message from these findings is that taxes are generally easier to control for policy-makers. While this certainly does not imply that writing a tax code is an easy task, governments can more easily and quickly change taxes than affect other determinants of informality that can only be modified in the long run.

The second most important group of determinants are those related to institutional quality, including political stability, public trust, tax morale, bureaucratic quality, and corruption control. Unfortunately, improving institutional quality and influencing people's perceptions about the government and the tax system are much more difficult in the short run, as reputation is a highly lagged variable.

Notes

1 Also to save some space I define $\varsigma' = (K', G')$.
2 In this paper the authors construct a series of probability of reelection in a narrow sample of 58 democratic countries over the period from 1960 to 2000.
3 I constructed the capital-stock series using the perpetual inventory method and investment series from Penn World Tables.
4 Notice that the fiscal freedom index is an index which gets smaller as statutory taxes increase. So positive sign of its coefficient is expected.
5 The source for public investment series is World Development Indicators.
6 Although it might be viewed as an imperfect measure of the level of "development", throughout the section I use GDP per capita as a proxy for economic development.
7 Moreover, results would not change if I had varied ρ or $\frac{\theta_I}{\theta_F}$ separately.
8 The results are robust when we use five-year averaged data to rule out business cycle effects.

References

Acosta-Gonzalez, E., Fernandez-Rodriguez, F., Sosvilla-Riverso, S. 2014. An Empirical Examination of the Determinants of the Shadow Economy. *Applied Economics Letters*. 21 (5), 304–307.

Almeida, R., Carneiro, P. 2012. Enforcement of Labor Regulation and Informality. *American Economic Journal: Applied Economics*. 4 (3), 64–89.

Amaral, P., Quintin. E. 2006. A Competitive Model of the Informal Sector. *Journal of Monetary Economics*. 53, 1541–1553.

Anderson, T., Hsiao, W. C. 1982. Formulation and Estimation of Dynamic Models Using Panel Data. *Journal of Econometrics*. 18(1), 47–82.

Araujo, R. A., de Souza, N. A. 2010. An Evolutionary Game Theory Approach to the Dynamics of the Labour Market: A Formal and Informal Perspective. *Structural Change and Economic Dynamics*. 21 (2), 101–110.

Arellano, M., Bond, S. 1991. Some Test of Specification for Panel Data: Monte Carlo Evidence and Application to Employment Equations. *Review of Economic Studies*. 58, 277–297.

Aruoba, S. B. 2018. *Institutions, Tax Evasion and Optimal Policy*. University of Maryland, mimeo.

Aschauer, D. A. 1989. Is Public Expenditure Productive? *Journal of Monetary Economics*. 23 (2), 177–200

Bah, E. M. 2011. Structural Transformation Paths across Countries. *Emerging Markets Finance and Trade*. 47 (S2), 5–19.

Baier, S. L., Glomm, G. 2001. Long-Run Growth and Welfare Effects of Public Policies with Distortionary Taxation. *Journal of Economic Dynamics and Control*. 25, 2007–2042.

Barro, R. J., Sala-i Martin, X. 1992. Public Finance in Models of Economic Growth. *Review of Economic Studies*. 59 (4), 645–661.

Blackburn, K., Bose, N., Capasso, S. 2012. Tax Evasion, the Underground Economy and Financial Development. *Journal of Economic Behavior and Organization*. 83 (2), 243–253.

Blanchard, O., Wolfers, J. 1999. *The Role of Shocks and Institutions in the Rise of European Unemployment: The Aggregate Evidence*. NBER Working Papers No. 7282.

Bosch, M., Esteban-Pretel, J. 2012. Job Creation and Job Destruction in the Presence of Informal Markets. *Journal of Development Economics*. 98 (2), 270–286.

Bosch, M., Goni-Pacchioni, E., Maloney, W. 2012. Trade Liberalization, Labor Reforms and Formal-Informal Employment Dynamics. *Labour Economics*.19 (5), 653–667.

Brender, A., Drazen, A. 2008. How Do Budget Deficits and Economic Growth Affect Reelection Prospects? Evidence from a Large Panel of Countries. *American Economic Review*. 98 (5), 2203–2220.

Buehn, A., Lessmann, C., Markwardt, G. 2013. Decentralization and the Shadow Economy: Oates Meets Allingham–Sandmo. *Applied Economics*. 45 (18), 2567–2578.

Buehn, A., Schneider, F. 2012a. Shadow Economies around the World: Novel Insights, Accepted Knowledge, and New Estimates. *International Tax and Public Finance*. 19 (1), 139–171.

Buehn, A., Schneider, F. 2012b. Corruption and the Shadow Economy: Like Oil and Vinegar, like Water and Fire? *International Tax and Public Finance*. 19 (1), 172–194.

Busato, F., Chiarini, B. 2004. Market and Underground Activities in a Two-Sector Dynamic Equilibrium Model. *Economic Theory*. 234, 863–861.

Byiers, B. 2009. *Informality in Mozambique: Characteristics, Performance and Policy Issues*. United States Agency for International Development, mimeo.

Capasso, S., Jappelli, T. 2013. Financial Development and the Underground Economy. *Journal of Development Economics*. 101, 167–178.

Caro, L., Galindo, A. J., Melendez, M. 2012. *Credit, Labor Informality and Firm Performance in Colombia*. IDB Working Paper No. IDB-WP-325, Inter-American Development Bank, Research Department.

Charles, S. W. 2011. Institutional Quality and Economic Growth in Latin America. *Global Economy Journal*. 10 (4), 1524–1561.

Charlot, O., Malherbet, F., Terra, C. 2015. Informality in Developing Economies: Regulation and Fiscal Policies. *Journal of Economic Dynamics and Control*. 51, 1–27.

Chong, A., Gradstein, M. 2007. Inequality and Informality. *Journal of Public Economics*. 91 (1), 159–179.

Colombo, E., Onnis, L., Tirelli, P. 2016. Shadow Economies at Times of Banking Crises: Empirics and Theory. *Journal of Banking and Finance*. 62, 180–190.

Crafts, N., Kaiser, K. 2004. Long-Term Growth Prospect in Transition Economies: A Reappraisal. *Structural Change and Economic Dynamics*. 15 (1), 101–118.

Dell'Anno, R. 2010. Institutions and Human Development in the Latin American Informal Economy. *Constitutional Political Economy*. 21(3), 207–230.

Dell'Anno, R. 2016. Analyzing the Determinants of the Shadow Economy with a "Separate Approach". An Application of the Relationship between Inequality and the Shadow Economy. *World Development*. 84, 342–356.

Dessy, S., Pallage, S. 2003. Taxes, Inequality and the Size of the Informal Sector. *Journal of Development Economics*. 70 (1), 225–233.

D'Hernoncourt, J., Meon, P. G. 2012. The Not so Dark Side of Trust: Does Trust Increase the Size of the Shadow Economy? *Journal of Economic Behavior and Organization*. 81 (1), 97–121.

Dreher, A., Schneider, F. 2010. Corruption and the Shadow Economy: An Empirical Analysis. *Public Choice*. 144, 215–238.

Eicher, T., Turnovsky, S. 2000. Scale, Congestion and Growth. *Economica*. 67, 325–346.

Elgin, C. 2010. Political Turnover, Taxes and the Shadow Economy. *Bogazici University Department of Economics Working Papers*. 2010-08.

Elgin, C. 2012. Cyclicality of Shadow Economy. *Economic Papers: A Journal of Applied Economics and Policy*. 31 (4), 478–490.

Elgin, C. 2015. Informal Economy in a Dynamic Political Framework. *Macroeconomic Dynamics*. 19 (3), 578–617.

Elgin, C., Kose, A., Ohnsorge, F., Yu, S. 2019. *Shades of Grey: Measuring the Informal Economy Business Cycles*. World Bank, mimeo.

Elgin, C., Solis-Garcia, M. 2012. Public Trust, Taxes and the Informal Sector. *Bogazici Journal of Economics and Administrative Sciences*. 26 (1), 27–44.

Elgin, C., Solis-Garcia, M. 2015. Tax Enforcement, Technology and the Informal Sector. *Economic Systems*. 38, 97–120.

Elgin, C., Oyvat, C. 2013. Lurking in the Cities: Urbanization and the Informal Economy. *Structural Change and Economic Dynamics*. 27, 36–47.

Elgin, C., Oztunali, O. 2012. *Shadow Economies around the World: Model Based Estimates*. Bogazici University Department of Economics Working Papers, 2012-05.

Elgin, C., Oztunali, O. 2014. Institutions, Informal Economy, and Economic Development. *Emerging Markets Finance and Trade*. 50 (4), 145–162.

Elgin, C., Tosun, H. K. 2017. A Note on Informality and Public Trust. *Economics Bulletin*. 37 (4), 2595–2601.

Feld, L. P., Schneider, F. 2010. .Survey on the Shadow Economy and Undeclared Earnings in OECD Countries. *German Economic Review*. 11, 109–149.

Florez, L. A. 2014. *The Search and Matching Equilibrium in an Economy with an Informal Sector: A Positive Analysis of Labor Market Policies*. Banco de la Republica de Colombia, No. 011953.

Fortin, B., Marceau, N., Savard, L. 1997. Taxation, Wage Controls and the Informal Sector. *Journal of Public Economics*. 66, 293–312.

Friedman, B. A. 2014. The Relationship between Effective Governance and the Informal Economy. *International Journal of Business and Social Science*. 5 (9), 51–58.

Friedman, E., Johnson, S., Kaufman, D., Zoldo-Lobaton, P. 2000. Dodging the Grabbing Hand: The Determinants of Unofficial Activity in 69 Countries. *Journal of Public Economics*. 76 (3), 459–493.

Gatti, R., Honorati, M. 2008. *Informality among Formal Firms: Firm-Level, Cross-Country Evidence on Tax Compliance and Access to Credit*. Policy Research Working Paper Series 4476, The World Bank.

Goel, R., Nelson, M. A. 2016. Shining a Light on the Shadows: Identifying Robust Determinants of the Shadow Economy. *Economic Modelling*. 58, 351–364.

Goldberg, P. K., Pavcnik, N. 2003. The Response of the Informal Sector to Trade Liberalization. *Journal of Development Economics*. 72 (2), 463–496.

Ihrig, J., Moe, K. 2004. Lurking in the Shadows: The Informal Sector and Government Policy. *Journal of Development Economics*. 73, 541–577.

Johnson, S., Kaufmann, D., Shleifer, A. 1997. The Unofficial Economy in Transition. *Brookings Papers on Economic Activity*. 2, 159–240.

Johnson, S., Kaufmann, D. Zoido-Lobaton, P. 1998. Regulatory Discretion and the Unofficial Economy. *American Economic Review*. 88 (2), 387–392.

Klein, P., Rios-Rull, J. V. 2003. Time Consistent Optimal Fiscal Policy. *International Economic Review*. 44 (4), 1217–1246.

La Porta, R., Shleifer, A. 2014. Informality and Development. *Journal of Economic Perspectives*. 28 (3): 109–126.

Lassen, D. D. 2007. Ethnic Divisions, Trust, and the Size of the Informal Sector. *Journal of Economic Behavior and Organization*. 63 (3), 423–438.

Loayza, N. V. 1996. The Economics of the Informal Sector: A Simple Model and Some Empirical Evidence from Latin America. *Carnegie-Rochester Conf. Series Public Policy*. 45, 129–162.

Loayza, N. V., Rigolini, J. 2011. Informal Employment: Safety Net or Growth Engine? *World Development*. 39 (9), 1503–1515.

Manolas, G., Rontos, K., Sfakianakis, G., Vavouras, I. 2013. The Determinants of the Shadow Economy: The Case of Greece. *International Journal of Criminology and Sociological Theory*. 6 (1), 1036–1047.

Martin, F. 2010. Markov-Perfect Capital and Labor Taxes. *Journal of Economic Dynamics and Control*. 34 (3), 503–521.

Neck, R., Waechter, J. U., Schneider, F. 2012. Tax Avoidance versus Tax Evasion: On Some Determinants of the Shadow Economy. *International Tax and Public Finance*. 19 (1), 104–117.

Paz, L. S. 2014. The Impacts of Trade Liberalization on Informal Labor Markets: A Theoretical and Empirical Evaluation of the Brazilian Case. *Journal of International Economics*. 92 (2), 330–348.

Prado, M. 2011. Government Policy in the Formal and Informal Sectors. *European Economic Review*. 55 (8), 1120–1136.

Putnins, T. J., Sauka, A. 2011. Size and Determinants of Shadow Economies in the Baltic States. *Baltic Journal of Economics*. 11 (2), 5–25.

Raj, R. 2011. Technical Efficiency in the Informal Manufacturing Enterprises: Firm Level Evidence from an Indian State. *Journal of South Asian Development*. 6 (2), 213–232.

Rauch, J. E. 1991. Modelling the Informal Sector Formally. *Journal of Development Economics*. 35, 33–47.

Ruge, M. 2010. Determinants and Size of the Shadow Economy: A Structural Equation Model. *International Economic Journal*. 24 (4), 511–523.

Schneider, F. G., Buehn, A., Montenegro, C. E. 2010. Shadow Economies All Over the World: New Estimates for 162 Countries from 1999 to 2007. *World Bank Policy Research Working Paper*. No. 5356.

Schneider, F., Teobaldelli, D. 2012. *Beyond the Veil of Ignorance: The Influence of Direct Democracy on the Shadow Economy*. CESifo Working Paper Series 3749.

Singh, A., Jain-Chandra, S., Mohommad, A. 2012. *Inclusive Growth, Institutions, and the Underground Economy*. IMF Working Paper No. 12–47, International Monetary Fund.

Taymaz, E. 2009. *Informality and Productivity: Productivity Differentials between Formal and Informal Firms in Turkey*. ERC Working Papers 0901, ERC - Economic Research Center, Middle East Technical University.

Torgler, B., Schneider, F. 2007. *Shadow Economy, Tax Morale, Governance and Institutional Quality: A Panel Analysis*. IZA Discussion Papers, no. 2563.

Torgler, B., Schneider, F. 2009. The Impact of Tax Morale and Institutional Quality on the Shadow Economy. *Journal of Economic Psychology*. 30 (2), 228–245.

Ulyssea, G. 2010. Regulation of Entry, Labor Market Institutions and the Informal Sector. *Journal of Development Economics*. 91 (1), 87–99.

6 Effects of informality

6.1 Effects on fiscal policy

The presence and the evolution of the informal sector have drastic consequences for the design and implementation of economic policy. However, one should recognize that economic policy is a vague concept with different pillars, of which the two main ones are generally considered to be monetary and fiscal policy. However, there are several other pillars such as labor market policy, trade policy, and policy toward technology and growth. This section mainly focuses on the fiscal and monetary policy effects of informality, although I also summarize how informality might affect other aspects of economic policy.

As mentioned earlier, the informal sector literature within microeconomics initially investigated tax evasion. While this is an indicator of informality, its foremost effect is on fiscal policy. However, taxes are not the only tools of fiscal policy, whether expansionary or contractionary; rather, it can have various ingredients, including many forms of taxes, government expenditures, transfers, and public debt. These are considered in more detail below.

6.1.1 Effects on taxes

As discussed in the previous chapter, the relationship between taxes and informal sector is complicated. The previous chapter discussed taxes as a potential determinant of informal sector size. However, there is overwhelming evidence that the relationship between taxes and informality may also running in the opposite direction, from informality to taxes. In this subsection, I therefore discuss how taxes can also be affected by the informal sector.

A model with endogenous taxes

Here, I present the model constructed by Elgin and Solis-Garcia (2012). Here, we assume household-producers have access to two production technologies that allow them to produce output. In turn, each household obtains utility from the resulting profits as follows:

$$U(i)[\pi(i)] = \mathbb{E}u[\pi(i)], \quad i \in [0, 1] \qquad (6.1.1)$$

where $\mathbb{E}$ is the expected value operator, $u[\pi(i)] = \pi(i)$ is assumed to be linear for simplicity, and $\pi(i)$ represents household i's profits.

All households have identical preferences and are endowed with one unit of time that they can only use for labor. We also assume that each household draws a productivity parameter $\theta(i)$ from some known distribution Θ. The household then decides on which technology to use, in other words chooses in which sector to supply its labor input $N(i) = 1$. The production technologies, here denoted *formal* and *informal*, are as follows: The formal production technology combines each household's capital $K(i)$[1] and labor $N(i)$ to produce output $Y(i)$ and takes the following functional form:

$$\begin{aligned} Y_F(i) &= \exp[\theta(i)]\,[K(i)]^{\alpha}\,[N(i)]^{1-\alpha} \\ &= \exp[\theta(i)]\,[K(i)]^{\alpha} = z(i)\,[K(i)]^{\alpha}, \quad i \in [0, 1] \end{aligned}$$

where $\theta(i)$ is household i's productivity parameter, $\alpha \in (0, 1)$, and where we define $z(i) := \exp[\theta(i)]$. (The value of α is the same for all households.) As mentioned earlier, households can provide labor but have no capital: They need credit to produce their optimal level of output. We further assume that the only way that households can access the credit market is if they decide to become part of the formal sector. It is a simple matter to verify that a formal household's expected profits $\mathbb{E}\pi_F(i)$ are given by the following:

$$\mathbb{E}\pi_F(i) = Y_F(i) - rK(i) - \mathbb{E}T(i), \quad i \in [0, 1] \tag{6.1.2}$$

where $\mathbb{E}T(i)$ are the household's expected tax payments.

The informal production technology consists of a labor-exclusive process that provides the output to obtain a utility above a minimum subsistence level u_0. We think of this as a residual technology in the sense that households that decide to enter the informal sector are obliged to use this technology (given their inability to access capital). We assume that this technology takes the following functional form:

$$Y_I(i) = \exp[\theta(i)]\,[N_i] = z(i), \quad i \in [0, 1].$$

Consequently, the profit for an informal household is given by

$$\pi_I(i) = Y_I(i), \quad i \in [0, 1]. \tag{6.1.3}$$

This makes the household's decision simple and dichotomous, as in Elgin and Sezgin (2017): to join the formal sector or informal sector. Households that make the former choice are required to pay a rent for the capital used (assumed here to be some exogenous value r dictated by an authority external to the model, like a central bank) and are required to pay taxes. On the other hand, households in the informal sector are not subject to government taxation but also lack access to capital.

Using equations (6.1.1)–(6.1.3), it follows that the utility maximization problem of household i is given by

$$\max_{K(i)\geq 0} \{\mathbb{E}u\,[\pi_F(i)]\,,\, u\,[\pi_I(i)]\}\,, \quad i \in [0, 1]. \tag{6.1.4}$$

The model includes a government that wishes to maximize its tax revenues R. We assume that the government announces a plan to charge formal households a percentage τ of their output.

Households that decide to join the formal sector have to turn in all relevant asset and output information to the government, thereby losing all possibility of hiding any output. Another interpretation is that, in exchange, the government provides a "quality seal" that allows households to access the credit market. Furthermore, we assume here that households form an expectation regarding the government's announced tax schedule. With some probability λ, they believe that the government will commit to its announcement and impose the announced rate τ. However, with some probability, $1 - \lambda$, there is a risk of expropriation. Here, we interpret λ to some extent as a proxy variable for public trust depending on institutional quality and government commitment. For a household in the formal sector, the expected tax payments $\mathbb{E}T(i)$ take the following form:

$$\mathbb{E}T(i) = [\lambda\tau + (1 - \lambda)]\, z(i)\, [K(i)]^{\alpha}, \tag{6.1.5}$$

where τ is the government's originally announced taxation plan.

Therefore, the government solves the following problem:

$$\max_{\tau} \int_{\theta_V}^{1} Rf(i)\, di = \max_{\tau} \int_{\theta_V}^{1} \tau z(i)\, [K(i)]^{\alpha}\, f(i)\, di, \tag{6.1.6}$$

where θ_V is the potential threshold. Households whose productivity exceeds this choose to operate in the formal sector, thereby constituting the government's tax base.

The sequence of the static game is as follows. First, households receive their productivity parameter $\theta(i) \in \Theta$. Next, the government announces the tax rate it plans to charge on formal output, τ. Households observe the government's decision and, contingent on their productivity parameter $\theta(i)$ and their beliefs about the government's commitment to τ, $\mathbb{E}(\lambda)$, decide to join the formal or informal sector. Formal agents access the credit market, obtain their optimal level of $K(i)$ and produce. The government observes all formal agents and their output before taxing them according to the original plan, τ. Households achieve utility $U(i)$ $[\pi(i)]$ while informal households' profits are given by (6.1.3). The government consumes the value of the tax revenue from solving (6.1.6).

Based on this description of the model, we now can define the competitive equilibrium.

Definition 6.1.1. The **competitive equilibrium** of the environment defined earlier is given by the tax rate τ, $K(i)$, $Y_I(i)$, and $Y_F(i)$ for all $i \in [0, 1]$ such that given τ, r, and λ, $K(i)$, $Y_I(i)$, and $Y_F(i)$ solve the household producers' problem defined by (6.1.4) for all $i \in [0, 1]$.

In the competitive equilibrium, only households above some threshold level of productivity choose to stay in the formal sector. This result is stated in the proposition below:

Proposition 6.1.1. *Taking λ as given, a household i with a productivity parameter $\theta(i)$ operates in the formal sector if and only if $\theta(i) \geq \theta_V(i)$, where $\theta_V(i)$ is defined by*

$$\theta_V(i) = \left(\frac{\alpha - 1}{\alpha}\right)\left[\log(1-\tau) + \log A + \log\lambda - \left(\frac{\alpha}{1-\alpha}\right)\log r\right], \quad (6.1.7)$$

where $A := \left(\alpha^{\alpha/1-\alpha} - \alpha^{1/1-\alpha}\right)$.

Proof. Consider any household i with productivity parameter $\theta(i)$. If the household decides to enter the formal sector, its profits are given in equation (6.1.2). In that case the first-order condition with respect to capital implies that the optimal level of capital should satisfy

$$K(i) = \left[\frac{\alpha\lambda(1-\tau)z(i)}{r}\right]^{\frac{1}{1-\alpha}} \quad (6.1.8)$$

Using equation (6.1.7), and recalling that the household solves equation (6.1.4), it follows that a household is indifferent between operating in the formal or the informal sector if and only if its profits are the same in either sector, that is, if and only if $\pi_F(i) = \pi_I(i)$, or

$$A\left[\frac{\lambda(1-\tau)z(i)}{r^{\alpha}}\right]^{\frac{1}{1-\alpha}} = z(i).$$

We can apply the log function to the earlier equation and rearrange it to get the desired result.

Notice that, since we assume the existence of a unit measure of households, we can interpret $\theta_V(i)$ as a proxy for the size of the informal sector.[2]

A straightforward application of Proposition 6.1.1 is presented in Proposition 6.1.2.

Proposition 6.1.2. *If the government decides to reduce taxes τ, or if the exogenous authority (for example the central bank) decides to decrease the interest rate r, or if there is an increase in the public trust in the government, the size of the formal sector increases.*

Proof. From (6.1.7) it is straightforward to verify that

$$\frac{\partial \mathbb{E}\pi_F(i)}{\partial \tau} = -\Gamma\left[\frac{\lambda z(i)}{r^{\alpha}}\right] < 0, \quad \frac{\partial \mathbb{E}\pi_F(i)}{\partial r} = -\alpha\Gamma\left(\frac{1}{r^{\alpha+1}}\right) < 0 \text{ , and}$$

$$\frac{\partial \mathbb{E}\pi_F(i)}{\partial \lambda} = \Gamma\left[\frac{(1-\tau)z(i)}{r^{\alpha}}\right] > 0,$$

where

$$\Gamma = \left(\frac{A}{1-\alpha}\right)\left[\frac{\lambda(1-\tau)z(i)}{r^{\alpha}}\right]^{\frac{\alpha}{1-\alpha}}$$

Here, we should note that, taking taxes as exogenously given, the level of taxes and the size of the informal sector remain positively correlated. This is not surprising, given the discussion in the introduction. Our next task is to endogenize the determination of taxes.

Using the backward solution algorithm, given the announced τ and λ, the value of θ_V can be obtained from equation (6.1.8). The government can also calculate this cutoff value (which depends on τ) and then choose τ to solve

$$\max_{\tau \in [0,1]} \quad \int_{\theta_V(\tau)}^{1} A\,[1-(1-\tau)]\left[\frac{z(i)}{r^{\alpha}}\right]^{\frac{1}{1-\alpha}} f(i)\,di \qquad (6.1.9)$$
$$\text{subject to} \quad \tau \in [0,1].$$

Definition 6.1.2. A **subgame-perfect equilibrium** of the environment defined earlier is given by the tax rate τ, $K(i)$, $Y_I(i)$, and $Y_F(i)$ for $i \in [0,1]$ such that given r and λ;

1 τ solves the government's problem defined by equation (6.1.9).
2 For every possible $\tau \in [0,1]$; τ, $K(i)$, $Y_I(i)$, and $Y_F(i)$ for $i \in [0,1]$ constitute a competitive equilibrium.

Given that informal sector size $\theta_V(i)$ and the tax rate, τ, are both endogenously determined in the model, we want to obtain comparative static results with respect to λ specifically. Although the government maximization problem defined earlier does not allow us to obtain analytical results, it is straightforward to numerically simulate the model economy and characterize it through these simulations.

Numerical results

I next perform a set of numerical simulations to get a flavor of the implications of Propositions 6.1.1 and 6.1.2.[3]

We are first interested in determining how the cutoff productivity value θ_V and the government's tax revenue R are affected by varying the value of taxes τ, for a given value of λ. To do this, we create a grid (of step size 0.01) and we allow τ to move in the interval $[0.01, 0.99]$, fixing the value of λ at 0.75.[4] Average values for θ_V and R are obtained after performing 1,000 repetition and Figure 6.1 shows the results of this simulation.

Figure 6.1 shows that, keeping the level of public trust constant, tax receipts show a Laffer effect while the government's total revenue is maximized when $\tau = 0.29$. In addition, the higher the tax rate, the higher the cutoff productivity value (i.e. the value of θ_V) one needs to be in order to remain in the formal sector.

The second experiment determines how θ_V and R are affected by varying the value of λ, for a given tax rate. Following the procedure for the previous subsection, I allow λ to move in the interval $[0.01, 0.99]$ while fixing the value of τ at 0.25. Again, 1,000 repetitions are performed to obtain the average values for θ_V and R. Figure 6.2 shows the results.

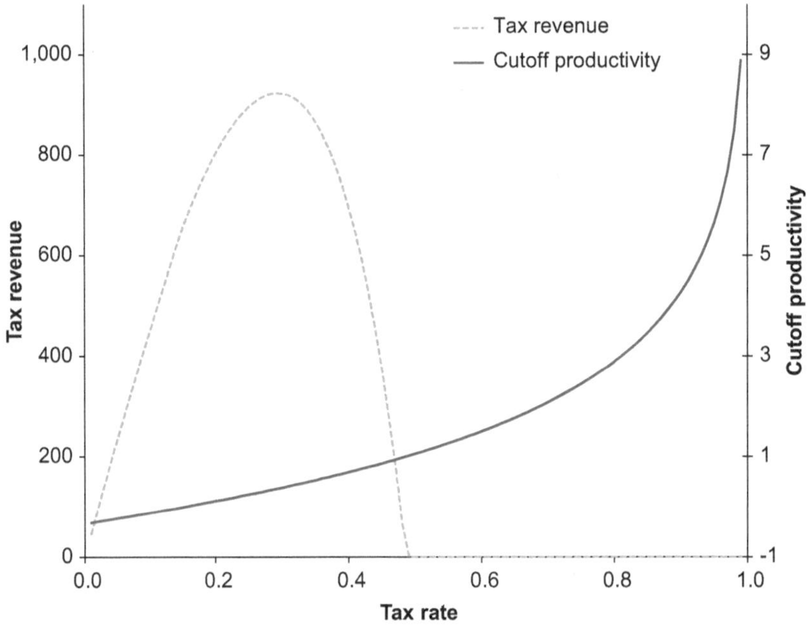

Figure 6.1 Tax revenue and cutoff productivity with varying taxes.

Figure 6.2 shows that the cutoff productivity value decreases as λ increases. Moreover, tax revenue is positive and strictly increasing in λ provided that $\lambda \geq 0.5$.

Finally, both λ and τ are allowed to vary simultaneously to get a flavor of the characterization of the subgame-perfect equilibrium.

To keep the results manageable, I perform a simulation with a grid of step size 0.1, moving λ between 0.1 and 1.0, and τ between 0.1 and 0.9. As was the case in the previous subsections, 1,000 repetitions are run to obtain the average values for θ_V and R_0.

I use the following simplification to fully characterize a result that depends on both the productivity parameter θ_V and the tax announcement τ; we use the following simplification: The values of the x-axis take the form $x = 10 \cdot \lambda + \tau$; in this way, a value of x of 4.6 has the associated parameters of $\lambda = 0.4$ and $\tau = 0.6$. Figure 6.3 shows the results of this procedure.

Figure 6.4 shows the effect of changing r to 0.02. From the two figures it is clear that, as expected, the cutoff productivity for being formal is positively related to τ but negatively to λ.

Now we can look at the numerical characterization of the subgame-perfect equilibrium in which the government chooses the optimal tax rate on the formal sector to maximize its revenue. The aim is to get comparative-statics results

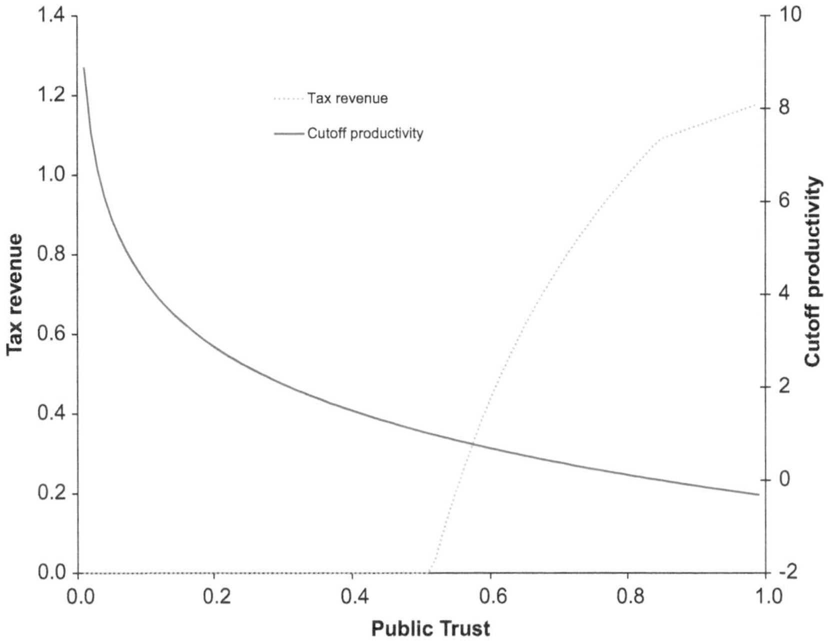

Figure 6.2 Tax revenue and cutoff productivity with varying public trust.

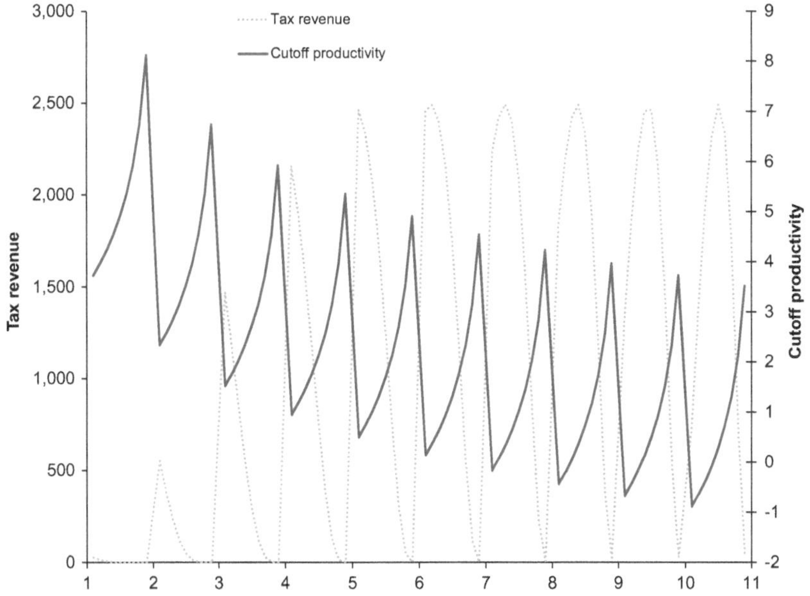

Figure 6.3 Tax revenue and cutoff productivity with varying taxes.

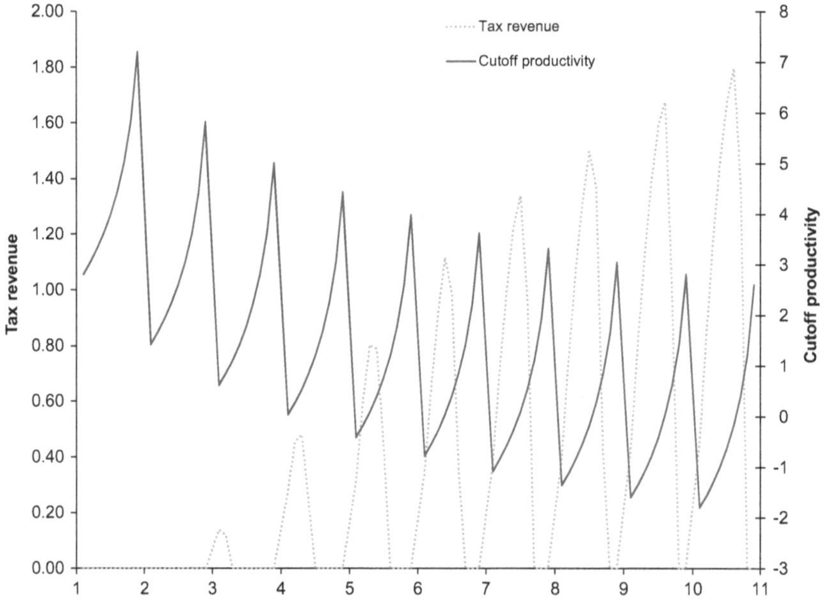

Figure 6.4 Tax revenue and cutoff productivity with varying public trust (with $r = 0.02$).

for all relevant variables including τ, with respect to λ. For this subsection I set $\alpha = 0.4$ and $r = 0.07$. I also assume $\theta(i) \sim \mathcal{N}(0, 1)$ and allow for a population of 1,000 households.

Figure 6.5 presents the behavior of the optimal tax rate τ obtained from the government's problem with respect to λ. The main finding is that higher public trust enables a government to impose a higher tax rate on the formal sector.

Figure 6.6 shows that informal sector size is a decreasing function of λ, which is a similar relationship to that shown in Figure 6.2. However, in contrast to Figure 6.2, Figure 6.6 shows that, with increasing λ, not only does the informal sector size decrease but also τ increases. In other words, increasing public trust simultaneously enables a higher tax rate while reducing informal sector size. Elgin and Solis-Garcia (2012) provide further empirical analysis that is generally in line with these model simulations.

6.1.2 Effects on public debt

Another component of fiscal policy on which informality has significant effects is public debt, as thoroughly analyzed by Elgin and Uras (2013a). Below, I borrow from this paper and report results with more up-to-date data.

It is well known that the high interest rates paid on sovereign bonds are first-order constraining factors on economic well-being in developing countries.

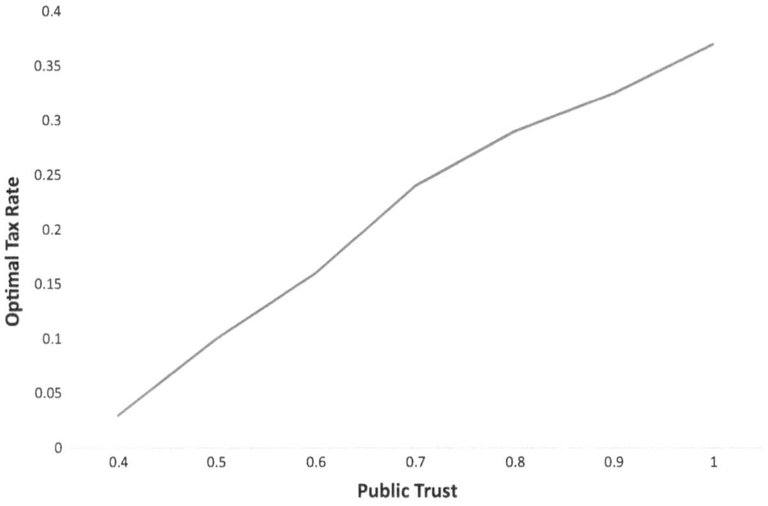

Figure 6.5 Optimal tax rate versus public trust.

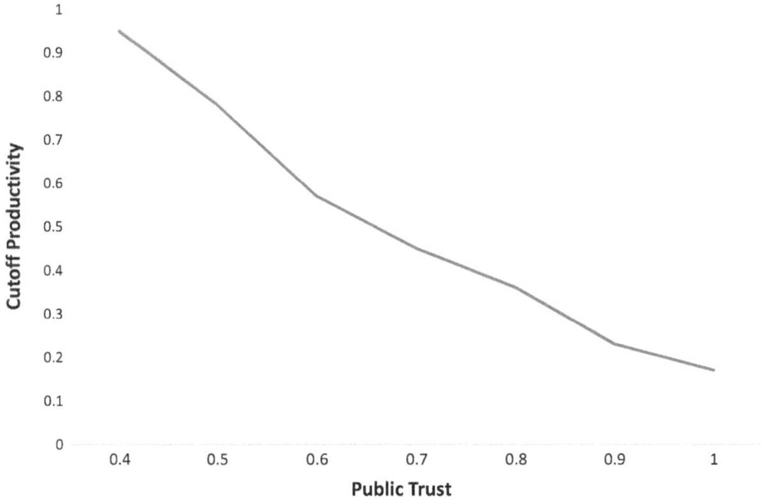

Figure 6.6 Cutoff productivity versus public trust.

Therefore, a vast literature has concentrated on understanding the determinants of sovereign debt defaults and the implied interest rates paid on such debt. Among other macroeconomic implications, the presence of a large informal economy influences the choice of fiscal policy instruments and government tax revenues, and thus affects a government's ability to repay outstanding government debt (Cicek and Elgin, 2011; Elgin and Uras, 2013a).

To see how informal sector might be related to public debt, suppose an increase in public debt leaves a country's sovereign risk premium unchanged as long as the debt-issuing government can credibly promise future contractions in public spending or increases in tax revenues that can be exploited to repay the current increase in government debt. It can then be argued that the government's ability to make such a promise using long-run fiscal policy contractions is influenced to the society's current level of tax enforcement and informal sector size. Specifically, if tax enforcement in an economy is high, the government can promise an increase in the level of future taxes or a decrease in future government purchases to repay today's public debt. In the benchmark economy, under perfect tax enforcement, an increase in future taxes or a decrease in public spending implies an increase in government surplus.

Conversely, in an economy with limited tax enforcement, the government's capacity to borrow against future increases in tax revenues is expected to be constrained. To understand this, suppose there are two sectors in the economy, denoted as informal and formal. In the formal sector, agents pay taxes and, in return, gain access to a set of institutions whereas agents in the informal sector do not pay formal taxes in full (to capture the friction associated with limited tax enforcement). In return, they only gain limited access to the institutions of the formal economy. In this scenario, agents choose the formal economy if the benefits from living in an environment with strong institutions outweigh the cost of taxes paid to the government. Hence, in an economy with low tax enforcement, an increase in the level of taxes (relative to an environment with high tax enforcement) may not necessarily increase overall tax revenues, even if taxation is non-distortionary, because the tax rise would stimulate some agents to switch to the informal sector. As Rauch (1991), Loayza (1997), Ihrig and Moe (2004), and Amaral and Quintin (2006) all point out, the larger the tax rise, the higher the number of agents switching from the formal to the informal sector. Therefore, with imperfect tax enforcement, an increase in government debt may not be repayable by increasing taxes since, in the presence of an informal sector, raising future taxes does not necessarily increase the government surplus. In Elgin and Uras (2013a), we defined this constrained set of alternative future fiscal policies in the presence of an informal sector as the "limited fiscal pledgeability" of a government.

A similar limited fiscal pledgeability problem arises from the perspective of public spending. Consider again a similar setting, but now suppose that the level of government purchasing affects the quality of the institutional environment and hence the benefits from formal sector production. In this setting, as Friedman et al. (2000) and Elgin (2015) argue, a decrease in government purchasing would stimulate agents to switch to the informal sector, thereby shrinking the formal sector and reducing the total taxes collected. Hence, in the presence of a large informal economy, reducing public spending does not necessarily increase the government surplus.

Following the same line of reasoning, debt is the optimal source of financing for the government of an economy with a large informal sector. A tax rise or a decrease in government purchasing would reduce the size of the formal sector whereas a rise in government indebtedness would increase formal sector production.

The government's limited fiscal pledgeability due to the informal sector is expected to increase the probability of public debt defaults, or debt restructuring, and financial stress while influencing the sovereign interest rates associated with government bonds. One would therefore expect the strength of tax enforcement and the implied size of the informal sector in an economy to affect a government's fiscal pledgeability. In turn, this affects the size of the public debt, interest rates on debt, the country's financial stress, and sovereign debt default probability. The core hypotheses tested in this section are thus as follows: Ceteris paribus,

1 A large informal sector size (IS) is associated with high public indebtedness (PD), $(\partial PD/\partial IS > 0)$,
2 A large informal sector size is associated with high interest rates charged on government debt (R), $(\partial R/\partial IS > 0)$,
3 A large informal sector size is associated with a higher probability of sovereign default (SD), $(\partial SD/\partial IS > 0)$.

Methodology

As outlined earlier, the main aim of this empirical analysis is to study how public indebtedness and sovereign default risk relate to the size of the informal economy. Following Elgin and Uras (2013a), I use several variables to proxy a country's default risk. In the sample some *Sovereign Default Risk* proxies are available in the form of panel data (Real Interest Rate) and cross-sectional data (the probability of sovereign default). *Public Debt* is available as a panel data. Therefore, when panel data are available (i.e. when the dependent variables are (real) interest rate and public debt), I estimate the following reduced form equations:

$$Risk_{i,t} = \beta_0 + \beta_1 IS_{i,t} + \sum_{k=3}^{2} \beta_k X_{k_{i,t}} + \theta_i + \epsilon_{i,t} \qquad (6.1.10)$$

$$Debt_{i,t} = \beta_0 + \beta_1 IS_{i,t} + \sum_{k=3}^{2} \beta_k X_{k_{i,t}} + \theta_i + \epsilon_{i,t} \qquad (6.1.11)$$

In this econometric model, $Risk_{i,t}$ proxies the Sovereign Default Risk for country i, in year t, $Debt_{i,t}$ is country i's outstanding government debt in year t, and $IS_{i,t}$ is the size of the informal sector. $X_{k_{i,t}}$ are control variables that have been highlighted in the empirical literature that may explain the variation in sovereign default risk and the country's public indebtedness while θ_i is a country fixed effect (FE). Finally, $\epsilon_{i,t}$ denotes the error term. This equation is estimated using an FE estimator.

For the cross-country regression analysis (i.e. when the left-hand side variable is the historical probability of sovereign debt default), the following linear equation is estimated using the standard ordinary least squares (OLS) estimator:

$$Risk_i = \beta_0 + \beta_1 IS_i + \sum_{k=3}^{2} \beta_k X_{k_i} + \epsilon_i.$$

In this empirical model, $Risk_i$ again proxied risk of default for country i (probability of sovereign debt default) while IS_i is the shadow economy size. X_{k_i} are other explanatory variables in addition to the informal economy while ϵ_i is the error term.

In each case, suspecting the presence of endogeneity, which may stem from the existence of reverse causality, simultaneity, omitted variable bias, or measurement errors I also run an instrumental variable (IV) regressions. For these, I instrument the size of the informal sector by using specific determinants of informality, namely the law and order index, and the capital-output ratio.

Data

I run three sets of regressions with three different dependent variables. For the panel regressions, I use the ratio of public debt to GDP and the interest rate spread as the dependent variables. For the cross-sectional OLS, the probability of default is the dependent variable. The public debt (central government debt as percentage of GDP) and interest rate series come from the World Development Indicators (WDI) of the World Bank. In the latter case, the reported results use the real interest rate. The probability of default is obtained from Reinhart and Rogoff (2009). Specifically, the default probability for each country is calculated as the number of sovereign default episodes between 1960 and 2017, divided by the number of years since 1960 (or year of independence, whichever is earliest). Notice that, as opposed to the other variables available as a panel, this series is only available as cross-sectional data. Moreover, Elgin and Uras (2013a) used the International Monetary Fund's (IMF) financial stress index as another measure of sovereign default risk. However, it is excluded here because it has not been updated recently. Finally, Elgin and Uras (2013a) used panel estimates based on MIMIC estimates of informality for 1999–2007 in Schneider et al. (2010). Here, however, I use the dynamic general equilibrium (DGE) estimates of Elgin et al. (2019).

I control for several variables highlighted in the literature as potential determinants of sovereign risk spread. These include GDP per capita, trade openness, and current account balance from Penn World Tables (PWT) 9.1, and the corruption control, bureaucratic quality, political stability, and democratic accountability indices from the International Country Risk Guide (ICRG). The latter three variables control for institutional quality, with higher values indicating better institutional development. Finally, inflation data are obtained from the WDI of the World Bank. Table 6.1 shows descriptive statistics for all variables used in this section.

Table 6.1 Summary Statistics for the Panel: 1990–2017

Variable	*Mean*	*Std. Dev.*	*Minimum*	*Maximum*
Public Debt (% GDP)	53.91	34.39	1.89	289.84
Interest Rate (%)	7.26	27.25	0.01	20.34
Default Probability (%)	15.10	19.01	0.00	58.00
Informal Sector Size (% GDP)	33.14	12.98	7.78	67.11
GDP per capita (thousand $)	7.22	11.30	0.09	57.11
Trade Openness (% GDP)	89.55	52.53	4.83	453.44
Current Account Deficit (% GDP)	−3.14	56.61	−90.00	364.47
Corruption Control	2.80	1.32	0.00	6.00
Bureaucratic Quality Index	2.32	1.20	0.00	4.00
Democratic Accountability	3.90	1.71	0.00	6.00
Political Stability	9.19	1.44	4.21	12.00
Inflation (%)	1.99	10.90	−3.11	105.21
Growth (%)	3.30	6.49	−13.85	12.37
Law and Order	3.78	1.44	0.50	6.00
Capital-Output Ratio	2.45	1.72	1.19	5.15
Income Tax Burden (% GDP)	17.71	8.11	0.82	57.89
Unemployment (%)	8.94	5.99	2.56	40.55

Results

Tables 6.2 and 6.3 present the panel data estimation results. Table 6.2 summarizes the results from the linear regressions that use the ratio of public debt to GDP as the dependent variable. Here, I run nine regressions with different independent variables added in each step. In regression 9 only, I report the IV FE regression results in which informal sector size is instrumented by several variables. For the IV estimation, I also report the Hansen test statistic for over-identifying restrictions in which the null hypotheses of valid instruments are not rejected in any of the reported results. Table 6.2 indicates that the size of the informal sector has significant explanatory power for the variation in public indebtedness (significant at 1% in all regressions). The other two variables with significant and, as expected, negative-signed regression coefficients are GDP per capita and the corruption control indices.

Table 6.3 presents the estimation results from the regressions that use the real interest rate as the dependent variable. The coefficient of the informal economy size is quite similar to that in Table 6.3. In addition to informal economy size, inflation, political stability, openness, and current account balance are significant in explaining the variation in real interest rates. Political stability decreases interest rates whereas inflation, openness, and current account deficit are associated with higher interest rates, although the coefficient for openness is insignificant in the IV estimation.

The final set of regressions reports cross-sectional estimates when I use the probability of default as the dependent variable. Here, I use averages over the period 1999–2017 for all the right-hand-side variables. In this regard,

Table 6.2 Public Debt and Informal Sector Size

Dep. Var.: Debt	*(1)*	*(2)*	*(3)*	*(4)*	*(5)*	*(6)*	*(7)*	*(8)*	*(9)*
IS	3.78*	3.79*	3.73*	3.71*	3.24*	3.18*	3.10*	3.01*	2.99*
	(0.85)	(0.88)	(0.84)	(0.93)	(0.83)	(0.69)	(0.68)	(0.70)	(0.62)
GDP per capita		−0.80	−0.86	0.99	−1.35**	−1.41**	−1.50**	−1.52**	−1.31**
		(0.59)	(0.62)	(0.70)	(0.67)	(0.68)	(0.71)	(0.71)	(0.66)
Openness			0.04	0.03	0.03	0.06	0.06	0.06	0.07
			(0.07)	(0.09)	(0.09)	(0.08)	(0.08)	(0.08)	(0.07)
Current Account				0.02	0.02	0.03	0.03	0.04	0.06
				(0.08)	(0.08)	(0.08)	(0.08)	(0.07)	(0.10)
Bureaucratic Qual.					3.10	3.30	3.49	3.64	3.78
					(4.45)	(4.79)	(4.82)	(5.00)	(5.21)
Corruption Control						−2.40**	−1.63	−1.80***	−1.11**
						(1.15)	(1.19)	(1.10)	(0.55)
Democratic Acc.							−1.12	−1.20	−1.13
							(1.13)	(1.15)	(1.20)
Political Stability							−0.80	−0.91	−0.63
							(0.73)	(0.71)	(0.70)
Inflation								0.02	0.02
								(0.08)	(0.08)
Growth								0.01	0.04
								(0.29)	(0.32)
R-squared	0.25	0.26	0.27	0.27	0.27	0.29	0.26	0.27	
Observations	1149	1149	1149	1149	1149	1149	1149	1149	1008
F-Test	0.00	0.00	0.00	0.00	0.00	0.00	0.00	0.00	0.00
Hansen Test									0.24

All panel regressions include a country fixed effect. Robust standard errors are reported in parentheses. *, **, and *** denote 1%, 5%, and 10% confidence levels, respectively. In all regressions a constant is also included but not reported. IS refers to informal sector.

Figure 6.7 provides a clear visual on the relationship between the probability of default and shadow economy size. As one can observe from the figure, the correlation between these two variables is strikingly positive.

Note that the sample size is quite small in this case as only a limited number of data observations are available for default probability. This meant that some independent variables used in the panel regressions had to be dropped to avoid collinearity issues. Table 6.4 shows that, in addition to GDP per capita, bureaucratic quality, current account deficit, corruption control, and inflation, informal sector size is significantly related to probability of default.

Elgin and Uras (2013a) suggested that, in societies where the informal sector production accounts for a substantial proportion of economic activity, this informality limits the set of credible future fiscal policy adjustments and increases the probability of debt defaults. This, in turn, affects the interest rates paid on sovereign debt. The empirical results presented in this section confirm that, even after controlling for various explanatory variables that could explain

Table 6.3 Interest Rate and Informal Sector Size

Dep. Var.: Int. Rate									
	(1)	*(2)*	*(3)*	*(4)*	*(5)*	*(6)*	*(7)*	*(8)*	*(9)*
IS	1.29*	1.21*	1.23*	1.25*	1.32*	1.33*	1.37*	1.41*	1.00*
	(0.15)	(0.12)	(0.13)	(0.14)	(0.18)	(0.19)	(0.18)	(0.19)	(0.23)
GDP per capita		−0.08	−0.11	−0.17	−0.17	−0.19	−0.20	−0.20	−0.22***
		(0.17)	(0.17)	(0.18)	(0.18)	(0.18)	(0.19)	(0.21)	(0.12)
Openness			0.03*	0.04**	0.05*	0.05*	0.06*	0.06*	0.06
			(0.01)	(0.02)	(0.02)	(0.02)	(0.02)	(0.02)	(0.04)
Current Account				0.02**	0.02**	0.02**	0.02**	0.02**	0.03***
				(0.01)	(0.01)	(0.01)	(0.01)	(0.01)	(0.02)
Bureaucratic Qual.					1.61	1.48	1.49	1.50	1.71
					(1.19)	(1.18)	(1.26)	(1.33)	(1.82)
Corruption Control						0.91*	0.58	0.57	0.20
						(0.32)	(0.40)	(0.38)	(0.32)
Democratic Acc.							0.53	0.50	0.72
							(0.40)	(0.42)	(0.44)
Political Stability							−0.36***	−0.36***	−0.64*
							(0.19)	(0.19)	(0.22)
Inflation								0.04**	0.04**
								(0.02)	(0.02)
Growth								−0.01	−0.02***
								(0.01)	(0.01)
R-squared	0.17	0.18	0.20	0.21	0.23	0.23	0.24	0.27	
Observations	1512	1512	1512	1512	1512	1512	1512	1511	1400
F-Test	0.00	0.00	0.00	0.00	0.00	0.00	0.00	0.00	0.00
Hansen Test									0.22

All panel regressions include a country fixed effect. Robust standard errors are reported in parentheses. *, **, and *** denote 1%, 5%, and 10% confidence levels, respectively. In all regressions a constant is also included but not reported. IS refers to informal sector.

the variation in debt and interest rates paid on sovereign debt, shadow economy size remains a significant determinant of a government's indebtedness, the cost of its sovereign debt, and the country's financial stress.

Elgin and Uras (2013a) also reported the results of various robustness checks with stratified and/or different data sets and specifications. I refer interested readers to the cited paper for details of these checks.

6.2 Effects on monetary policy

As I discussed in a previous chapter, one of the earlier methods, namely the money demand method for measuring the extent of informal economic activity, relies on the observation that cash usage in the informal sector is more extensive than in the formal sector. This has several implications for designing and implementing monetary policy. For example, the optimal monetary policy may be a bit more expansionary in the presence of informality as the seigniorage revenue can be used as an inflation tax, when it would otherwise be difficult

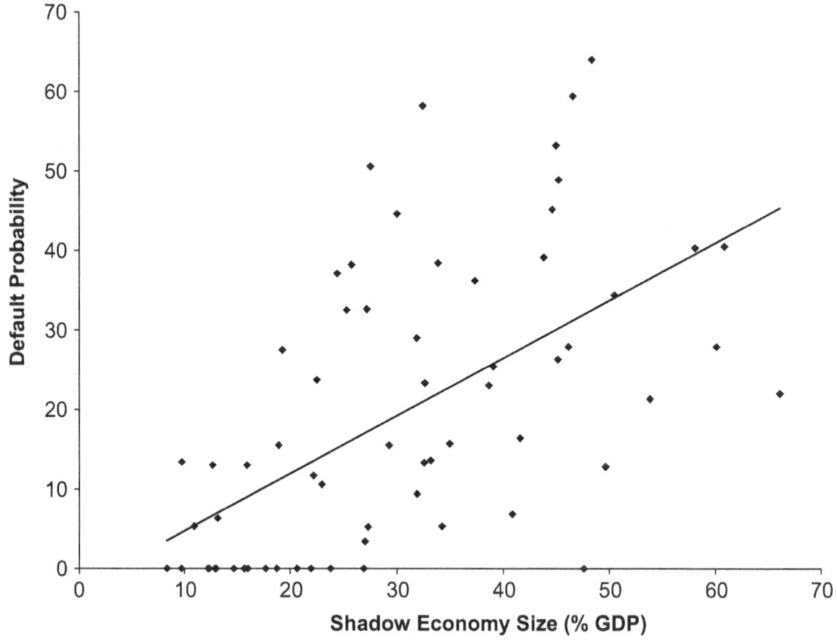

Figure 6.7 Probability of default versus informal sector size

to tax the informal sector (Roubini and Sala-i-Martin, 1995). Below, I present updated results related to this from two earlier studies: Asfuroglu and Elgin (2016), and Elgin and Uras (2014).

6.2.1 Growth effects of inflation and informal sector

The relationship between inflation and economic growth is one of the most debated and extensively investigated topics in the economic literature. From a theoretical point of view, several different mechanisms have been suggested, although most papers emphasize the negative effect of inflation on economic growth (e.g. Barro, 1991; Rebelo, 1991; Levine and Renelt, 1992; Chari et al., 1995; Bose, 2002; Blackburn and Pelloni, 2004; Varvarigos, 2010). However, as empirical tests of this adverse effect produce conflicting results, its exact nature remains far from being justified empirically (see Temple, 2000 for an excellent survey of this literature). More specifically, the strength of the relationship changes depending on the econometric specification, size of data set, number of countries, and time periods used for the empirical analysis.

Asfuroglu and Elgin (2016) used a two-sector (formal and informal) endogenous growth model with a cash-in-advance (CIA) constraint to investigate the relationship between inflation, growth, and informality.

Table 6.4 Default Probability and Informal Sector Size

Dep. Var.: Default Prob.	*(1)*	*(2)*	*(3)*	*(4)*	*(5)*	*(6)*	*(7)*	*(8)*
IS	0.61*	0.52*	0.52*	0.48*	0.46*	0.42*	0.39*	0.71*
	(0.08)	(0.08)	(0.08)	(0.09)	(0.09)	(0.09)	(0.10)	(0.07)
GDP per capita		−0.61*	−0.60*	−0.57*	−0.56*	−0.56*	−0.52*	−0.49*
		(0.09)	(0.09)	(0.09)	(0.09)	(0.09)	(0.10)	(0.08)
Openness			0.02	0.02	0.03	0.02	0.02	0.02
			(0.02)	(0.02)	(0.02)	(0.02)	(0.02)	(0.02)
Current Account				0.08*	0.08*	0.08*	0.07*	0.05***
				(0.02)	(0.02)	(0.02)	(0.02)	(0.03)
Bureaucratic Qual.					−2.97*	−2.95*	−3.06*	−4.22*
					(0.62)	(0.67)	(0.71)	(0.88)
Corruption Control						1.70*	1.93*	1.71***
						(0.59)	(0.57)	(0.91)
Inflation							0.79*	0.67**
							(0.24)	(0.34)
Growth							0.20	0.21
							(0.20)	(0.22)
R-squared	0.28	0.35	0.36	0.40	0.41	0.41	0.45	0.48
Observations	67	67	67	67	67	67	67	67
F-Test	0.00	0.00	0.00	0.00	0.00	0.00	0.00	0.00
Hansen Test								0.18

Robust standard errors are reported in parentheses. *, **, and *** denote 1%, 5%, and 10% confidence levels, respectively. In all regressions a constant is also included but not reported. IS refers to informal sector.

In this setting there is a continuum of infinitely lived households that have access to two production technologies, namely formal and informal; yet they are identical in their preferences. Time is discrete and denoted by $t = 1, 2, \ldots$. The timing of events is as follows: First, households choose their cash holdings. Then, they decide on their labor supply in formal and informal sectors and purchase goods. Finally, they get a lump sum monetary transfer after the goods market closes and arrange their portfolios for the next period.

The representative household solves the following problem:

$$\max_{\{C_t, K_{t+1}, L_{ft}, L_{it}, M_{t+1}{}^d\}} \sum_{t=0}^{\infty} \beta^t U(C_t)$$

$$\text{subject to} \quad C_t + \psi(K_{t+1} - (1-\delta)K_t) + \zeta B L_{it}{}^{\gamma} = \frac{M_t{}^d}{P_t}$$

$$C_t + K_{t+1} - (1-\delta)K_t + \frac{M_{t+1}{}^d}{P_t} = (1-\tau)AK_t L_{ft}{}^{\alpha} + (1-\rho\tau)BL_{it}{}^{\gamma} + \frac{M_t + v_t}{P_t}$$

$$L_{ft} + L_{it} = T$$
$$C_t, K_{t+1}, L_{ft}, L_{it}, M^d_{t+1} \geq 0$$
$$\lim_{t \to \infty} \beta^t \lambda_t K_{t+1} = 0$$
$$\psi, \alpha, \gamma, \delta, \zeta, \rho \in [0, 1], \beta \in (0, 1)$$

Here K_t and C_t denote physical capital stock and consumption, respectively. Physical capital depreciates at a rate $\delta \in [0, 1]$ and L_{ft} and L_{it} represent formal and informal labor supply while A and B are productivity parameters of the two sectors, respectively. The relationship of money and lump sum transfers v_t is given by $M_{t+1} = M_t + v_t$, so that M_{t+1} stands for nominal money holdings after the transfer and M^d_{t+1} denotes amount of nominal money demand for the following period.

On the production side of the economy, output can be produced both by using formal and informal technologies. To have a room for endogenous growth, the formal sector technology exhibits increasing returns to scale at the aggregate level. When written at the individual firm level, the technology still exhibits constant returns to scale with spillover effects at the aggregate level. This is the crucial driving force behind the endogeneity of growth[5] in the model. Moreover, similar to the various models presented throughout the book, the informal economy only uses labor as an input and operates using decreasing returns to scale technology. Formal output is taxed by the government at an exogenous rate $\tau \in [0, 1]$ which can only be partially enforced for informal output. Here ρ again denotes the tax enforcement parameter measuring how well taxes are enforced in the informal sector.

The representative household maximizes its discounted utility subject to three constraints: the first one is the CIA constraint, the second one denotes the resource feasibility constraint, and finally the last one is household's time constraint. In the CIA constraint, $\psi > 0$ reflects the fraction of investment that is subject to the CIA constraint. In this regard, similar to Dotsey and Sarte (2000), ψ might be interpreted as a proxy measuring how well financial (or credit) markets function, i.e. we should expect ψ to take a lower value when the level of financial development in a country is higher. Moreover, $\zeta > 0$ is a parameter governing how much output produced in the informal sector is subject to the CIA constraint. In a sense, with this parameter being positive, the informal economy absorbs some of the cash available for consumption and investment in the formal economy. Remembering that the shadow economy uses cash at a higher degree than the formal economy (see Schneider and Enste, 2000) this is not an unrealistic assumption.

We further assume that the money supply grows at a rate z_t, i.e. the government issues money at this exogenous rate z_t. Moreover, the CIA constraint always binds. For the log utility case, the condition required for this is that $z \geq \beta$.

$$M_{t+1} = z_t M_t$$

Finally, in this environment the market clearing conditions are given by the following two equations:

$$M_t{}^d = M_t$$
$$C_t + K_{t+1} - (1-\delta)K_t + G_t = AK_t L_{ft}{}^{\alpha} + BL_{it}{}^{\gamma}$$
$$G_t = \tau AK_t L_{ft}{}^{\alpha} + \rho\tau BL_{it}{}^{\gamma}$$

These represent the money market and goods market equilibria, and the government budget constraint, respectively.

The first-order conditions are given as follows:

$$C_t : \beta^t U'(C_t) - \lambda_t - \sigma_t = 0 \tag{6.2.1}$$

$$K_{t+1} : -\psi[\lambda_t - (1-\delta)\lambda_{t+1}] - \sigma_t + \sigma_{t+1}[(1-\delta + (1-\tau)AL_{ft+1}{}^{\alpha}] = 0 \tag{6.2.2}$$

$$L_{it} : -\lambda_t \zeta \gamma BL_{it}{}^{\gamma-1} + \sigma_t[\gamma(1-\rho\tau)BL_{it}{}^{\gamma-1} - \alpha(1-\tau)AK_t L_{ft}{}^{\alpha-1}] = 0 \tag{6.2.3}$$

$$M_{t+1}{}^d : -\frac{\sigma_t}{P_t} + \left[\frac{\lambda_{t+1} + \sigma_{t+1}}{P_{t+1}}\right] = 0 \tag{6.2.4}$$

By combining the household's first-order conditions, the following Euler equation is obtained, which governs the law of motion for consumption:

$$\begin{aligned}\psi U'(C_t) = &-(1-\psi)\beta U'(C_{t+1})\frac{P_t}{P_{t+1}} + \beta(1-\delta)\psi U'(C_{t+1}) \\ &+ \beta^2[(1-\delta)(1-\psi) + (1-\tau)AL^{\alpha}_{ft+1}]U'(C_{t+2})\frac{P_{t+1}}{P_{t+2}}\end{aligned}$$

It is always difficult (if not impossible) to obtain an analytical solution in two-sector models. In the present case, too, an analytical solution cannot be found to express the growth rate of the formal economy in the balanced growth-path as a function of the money growth rate, z_t, and the other parameters of the economy. I therefore rely on the numerical simulations presented in the next section.

Throughout the simulations I assume that the utility function is logarithmic while labor is supplied inelastically. I then need to choose values for various parameters of the model. For β and δ I use the standard values 0.96 and 0.08, respectively, and also normalize the time endowment T to 100 which allows L_f and L_i to be interpreted as the percentages of total time devoted to production in the formal and informal sectors, respectively. To choose a value for α I target a capital-formal output ratio of 2.75 which is the average capital-output ratio for the countries that are used in the empirical analysis of the cited paper. The calibrated value[6] of α is 0.6. As for γ I use the value reported by Roca et al. (2001). For the formal sector total factor productivity (TFP) parameter, I use the same value as Dotsey and Sarte (2000) while for the informal sector TFP, I aim to match the TFP ratio obtained from the calculations of Elgin and Oztunali (2012) and use the ratio of the informal sector TFP to the formal one as reported by Ihrig and Moe, in conjunction with the formal sector TFP value used here. Finally, the tax rate imposed on the formal sector, τ, is calibrated so that in the first numerical exercise, the size of the informal sector (as a percentage of the formal economy) matches the average size in our informal economy data set 36.54% corresponding to an average inflation rate of about 7.78%. The remaining parameters are ζ, ψ, ρ, and z and the comparative-static exercises are conducted with respect to these variables.

In the following simulations, I vary z_t such that the associated inflation rate varies between 0% and 40%. I then plot the behavior of the size of the informal economy (as a percentage of the formal economy, i.e. $\frac{BL_{it}{}^{\gamma}}{AK_t L_{ft}{}^{\alpha}}$) and growth of the formal economy (i.e. $\frac{AK_{t+1}L_{f,t+1}{}^{\alpha}}{AK_t L_{ft}{}^{\alpha}}$).

The first numerical example, shown in Figure 6.8, analyzes the growth implications of variable monetary policy for the case when the informal economy is fully subject to the CIA constraint, i.e. $\zeta = 1$.[7] In this case, a higher rate of inflation is associated with a dramatic decline in the informal sector, implying a

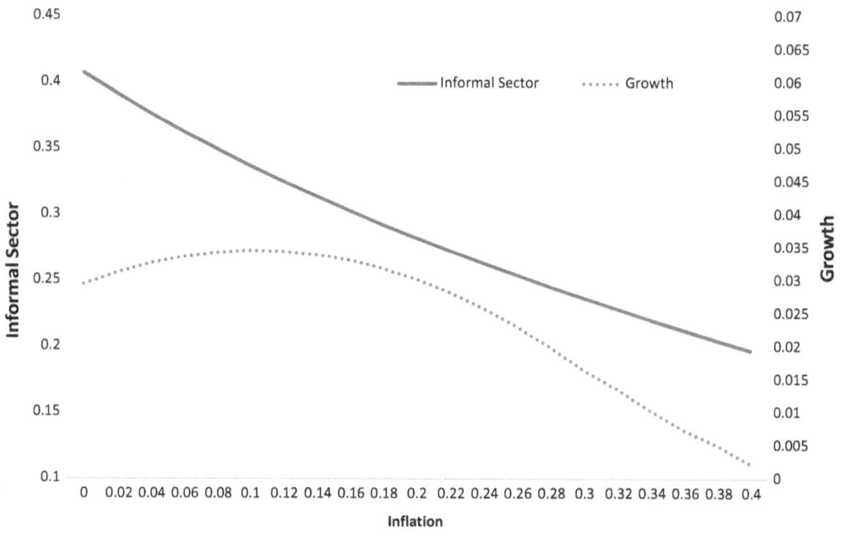

Figure 6.8 Growth versus inflation when $\zeta = 1$.

shift in the labor supply from the informal to formal economy. This offsets the growth-reducing effect of inflation (through the CIA constraint on investment) so that the growth rate increases slightly at lower levels of inflation before falling sharply. Under the specified parameter values, the growth-maximizing inflation rate is slightly above 10%.

Figure 6.9 presents the simulation results for $\zeta = 0$, that is, when the informal economy is not subject to the CIA constraint. Under this assumption, a higher rate of monetary growth (and therefore inflation) does not distort the informal economy because it is no longer subject to the liquidity constraint. In turn, it is associated with a larger informal economy and a lower growth rate in the formal economy. In this case, the growth-maximizing inflation rate is necessarily exactly equal to 0. These first two numerical simulation exercises also imply that the growth-maximizing inflation rate varies between 0% and 10% as ζ is allowed to vary between 0 and 1. That is, the more the informal economy is subject to the CIA constraint, the higher is the growth-maximizing rate of inflation in this simulated economy.

Finally, Figures 6.10 and 6.11 show the results for two further simulation exercises to check the response of the growth-inflation relationship in the presence of informality as the values of two policy parameters, ψ and ρ, are changed. Here, we assume that $\zeta = 1$, i.e. the informal economy is fully subject to the CIA constraint. This is why the inverted-U relationship between growth and inflation persists in these simulations.

Figure 6.10 shows the results from two simulations: one with $\psi = 0.35$ (denoted by weak constraint) and the other with $\psi = 0.65$. These simulations show that a stricter liquidity constraint on investment expenditure (i.e.

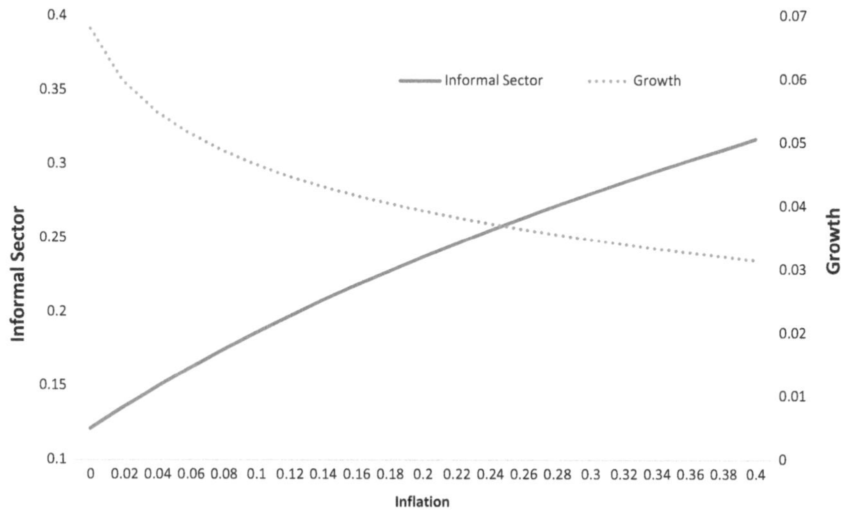

Figure 6.9 Growth versus inflation when $\zeta = 0$.

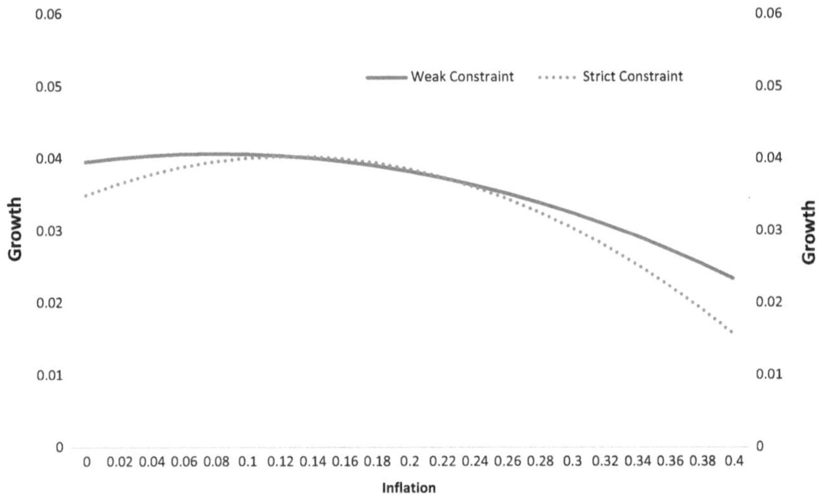

Figure 6.10 Growth versus inflation with different values of ψ.

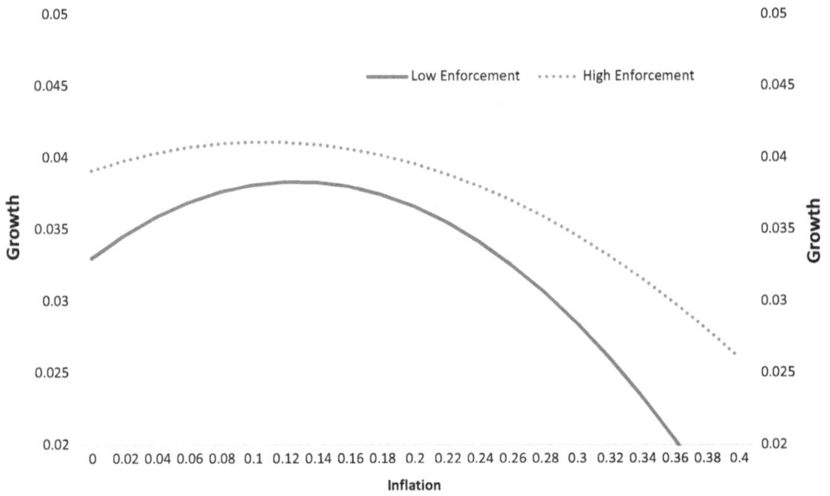

Figure 6.11 Growth versus inflation with different values of ρ.

less efficient financial markets and a less financial development) increases the volatility of output growth with respect to inflation. Moreover, the growth-maximizing inflation rate is significantly lower in the simulation with a weak constraint (8%) than that with a stricter constraint (12%).

Figure 6.11 shows comparative-static results regarding the tax enforcement parameter, ρ. In all the previous simulations, $\rho = 0.03$ whereas Figure 6.11

shows the results for $\rho = 0$ (low enforcement) and $\rho = 0.75$ (high enforcement). Under stricter tax enforcement on the informal sector, the growth rate is significantly larger for all levels of inflation while the growth-maximizing inflation rate is lower. This indicates that stricter tax enforcement on informal sector income further distorts households' intra-temporal decision-making. That is, increasing inflation incentivizes the household to devote more time to the formal sector, thereby increasing growth in formal sector output.

Informality in the CIA constraint

A quick comparison of Figures 6.8 and 6.9 reveals that the contribution of this model would be limited if the level at which the informal sector is subject to the CIA constraint (i.e. ζ) is zero or very close to zero. Unfortunately, because it is not possible to find a direct counterpart of ζ in the data, I conduct a deeper analysis in the following section regarding the effects of ζ on the relationship between inflation, informality, and growth.

The first exercise is to find the growth-maximizing levels of inflation and informal sector size with increasing ζ. Table 6.5 reports the triple (informal sector size, inflation, growth) with maximized growth rates for different values of ζ, ranging from 0 to 1 in intervals of 0.2. I also report the values of the triple for $\zeta = 2$. Both the growth-maximizing level of inflation and informal sector size rise, albeit at a decreasing rate, with increasing ζ. Nevertheless, the maximized growth rate is significantly reduced, again at a decreasing rate. Notice that this exercise does not rule out an inverted-U relationship between inflation and growth as this non-linear relationship still holds for a fixed value of ζ.

Finally, I estimate the parameter ζ using Bayesian estimation[8] techniques with average informal sector size as % of GDP from the data as the observable data series. For all other parameters[9], we use the values reported as in the benchmark simulation and $\psi = 0.10$, as well as $\rho = 0.03$ as in the benchmark simulation. The estimation is only conducted for selected economies ranging from Bolivia with the largest average informal sector size to the United States with the smallest informal sector size in the data set we will use in the next section for the empirical analysis. For each country in the analysis, as

Table 6.5 Growth-Maximizing Levels of Inflation and Informal Sector Size with Varying ζ

ζ	*Inflation (%)*	*Informal Sector (% GDP)*	*Growth (%)*
0	0.00	12.24	6.72
0.2	4.25	17.50	5.64
0.4	7.50	22.39	4.80
0.6	10.25	25.30	4.20
0.8	12.75	28.75	3.65
1.0	14.75	32.10	3.45
2.0	15.25	32.45	3.00

Table 6.6 Bayesian Estimation of ζ for Few Selected Economies

	2.5%	*97.5%*	*Mean*
Bolivia	0.45	0.63	0.54
Egypt	0.34	0.60	0.47
Italy	0.19	0.25	0.22
Japan	0.07	0.15	0.11
Luxembourg	0.06	0.12	0.09
Mexico	0.30	0.44	0.37
Turkey	0.32	0.50	0.41
United Kingdom	0.13	0.21	0.17
United States	0.13	0.25	0.19
Zimbabwe	0.62	0.90	0.76

the prior distribution we use the uniform distribution[10] with lower and upper bounds of 0 and 1, respectively. Table 6.6 reports the means of the posterior distribution, as well as the Bayesian 95% intervals (2.5% and 97.5%, respectively) for the ζ estimates in different countries. What we observe from Table 6.6 is that the estimate means for all the particular countries are positive and significantly different from zero. We also observe that countries with a larger informal sector tend to have a larger estimated value for ζ. These new simulation results are generally in line with the empirical findings in Asfuroglu and Elgin (2016).

6.2.2 Effect on monetary policy through housing markets

In this subsection, I present the empirical results from Elgin and Uras (2014), which documented a cross-country empirical relationship between informal sector size and aggregate homeownership rates. In this chapter, we specifically tested the following hypotheses:

1 Informality stimulates the demand for homeownership.
2 The rate of inflation determines the sensitivity of homeownership to informality.
3 The rate of inflation strengthens the relationship between informality and homeownership in countries with developed credit markets.
4 The rate of inflation weakens the relationship between informality and homeownership in countries with less-developed credit markets.

We tested our empirical hypotheses using cross-country aggregate data. Table 6.7 presents descriptive summary statistics of all the variables used. In Elgin and Uras (2014), we used data from 2008 whereas here I use the most recently available data from 2017.

Here, I use population density, GDP per capita, government spending (percentage of GDP), young population ratio (percentage of total population), the

Table 6.7 Cross-Country Summary Statistics

Variable	*Mean*	*Std. Dev.*	*Minimum*	*Maximum*
Homeownership (%)	64.00	18.21	21.93	96.40
Informal Sector (% GDP)	28.94	11.50	7.89	61.69
Population Density	284.11	1192.51	1.45	6399.01
Government Spending (% GDP)	16.10	5.44	5.50	30.11
GDP per capita (thousand USD)	12.77	12.21	0.59	49.71
Young Population Ratio (%)	32.00	10.41	16.03	49.97
Law and Order	4.65	1.33	2.00	6.00
Gini	37.01	8.54	23.75	60.15
CRD (% of GDP)	52.58	41.34	9.44	221.11
CRBAN (% of GDP)	65.849	58.83	6.10	301.31
M2 (% of GDP)	53.11	44.39	9.70	249.55
Inflation (%)	7.11	17.01	−4.50	90.11

law and order index, and the Gini Index as control variables. I obtain the government spending and GDP per capita series from PWT 9.1 and the percentage of population under 15 and the Gini Index from the WDI. To control for quality of institutions, I use the law and order index from the ICRG. Finally, I obtain the homeownership data[11] from various sources, including Eurostat, OECD Stat, and Fisher and Jaffe (2003). To measure the development of credit markets, I use three proxies that are widely used in the literature: CRBAN, domestic credit provided by the banking sector (percentage of GDP); CRD, domestic credit to the private sector (percentage of GDP); M2, money and quasi money (percentage of GDP). All these series come from the WDI. I also use inflation series from the WDI. For the cross-country regression, in addition to the designated control variables, I also use dummies for three regional groups: Latin American and Caribbean economies; Post-Socialist Transition economies; Middle East and North African (MENA) economies. The cross-country data set includes 69 countries for 2000.

Figure 6.12 shows a striking positive correlation between aggregate homeownership rates and the size of the informal sector. Using the cross-country regressions, I then estimate the following linear model with the standard heteroskedasticity-consistent OLS estimator:

$$Ownership_i = \beta_0 + \beta_1 Informal_i + \sum_{k=3}^{n} \beta_k X_{k_i} + \epsilon_i.$$

In this specification, X_{k_i} denotes additional control variables with potential explanatory power on homeownership rates, including population density, GDP per capita, and government spending, while ϵ_i is the error term. Table 6.8 reports the results from these first-pass, cross-sectional regressions. As expected, the positive correlation between informal sector size and homeownership is quite robust while homeownership is also positively correlated with population density and negatively correlated with the percentage of population under 15.

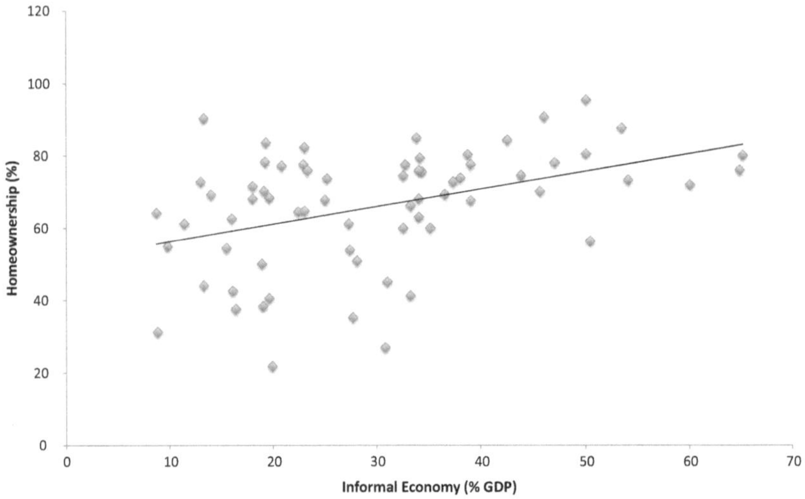

Figure 6.12 Homeownership versus informal sector size.

Table 6.8 thus provides strong support for the first hypothesis that there is an aggregate association between the size of the informal sector and homeownership rates.

To test the remaining empirical hypotheses, I estimate the following equation using the heteroskedasticity-consistent OLS estimator:

$$Ownership_i = \beta_0 + \beta_1 Informal_i + \beta_2 Inflation_i + \beta_3 (Informal_i) \cdot (Inflation_i) + \sum_{k=4}^{n} \beta_k X_{k_i} + \epsilon_i.$$

For each measure of private credit market development in Table 6.9, I split the sample and estimate the regression equation twice: first, for countries where the variable has a value less than the cross-country sample median; second, when it is larger than the median. I also report the regression results after dividing the sample into "rich" and "poor", respectively, based on GDP per capita above or equal to versus below the median GDP per capita of the original sample. This split-sample analysis captures the impact of financial development in explaining the interactions between informality, homeownership, and inflation. I also include those control variables from Table 6.8 that were significant determinants of aggregate homeownership rates, namely population density, the dummy for transition economies, and young population ratio.

The results presented in Table 6.9 confirm the hypotheses listed at the beginning of this section. The rate of inflation significantly interacts with the relationship between informal sector size and aggregate homeownership rates. That is, the inflation rate strengthens the relationship between informality and

Table 6.8 Homeownership and Informal Sector

Dep. Var.: Ownership								
	(1)	*(2)*	*(3)*	*(4)*	*(5)*	*(6)*	*(7)*	*(8)*
Informal	0.30**	0.35**	0.50*	0.49*	0.46**	0.46**	0.42**	0.42**
	(0.15)	(0.15)	(0.15)	(0.17)	(0.18)	(0.18)	(0.18)	(0.18)
Pop. Dens.		0.002**	0.002**	0.002**	0.002**	0.004***	0.004***	0.004**
		(0.001)	(0.001)	(0.001)	(0.001)	(0.002)	(0.002)	(0.002)
Latin			−6.15	−6.11	−6.07	−6.09	−6.21	−5.11
			(7.08)	(7.06)	(7.18)	(7.21)	(7.49)	(7.49)
Transition			12.33**	12.56**	12.71**	12.09**	12.41***	12.81***
			(5.69)	(5.62)	(5.67)	(5.65)	(5.69)	(5.61)
GDP per capita				−0.23	−0.22	−0.20	−0.21	−0.22
				(0.22)	(0.23)	(0.23)	(0.24)	(0.25)
Gov. Sp.					−0.22	−0.23	−0.22	−0.20
					(0.39)	(0.39)	(0.38)	(0.40)
Young Pop..						−0.04**	−0.04**	−0.04**
						(0.02)	(0.02)	(0.02)
Gini							−0.09	−0.13
							(0.50)	(0.49)
Law								2.10
								(1.70)
R-squared	0.06	0.09	0.14	0.15	0.15	0.22	0.22	0.22
Observations	69	69	69	69	69	69	69	69
F-Test	0.00	0.00	0.00	0.00	0.01	0.01	0.01	0.01

Robust standard errors are reported in parentheses. *, **, and *** denote 1%, 5%, and 10% confidence levels, respectively. In all regressions a constant is also included but not reported. Latin, and Transition refer to dummies for Latin American and Caribbean, and Post-Socialist Transition economies, respectively.

homeownership in countries with developed private credit markets whereas it weakens the relationship between informality and homeownership in countries with less-developed credit markets.

Building on this cross-country empirical evidence, Elgin and Uras (2014) developed a stylized two-sector general equilibrium model with housing markets with the following features. The model economy has two types of goods: consumption and housing. The first is produced by a continuum of households who are heterogeneous in terms of the informality of their production plants. We assume that this informality constrains the ability to invest in future consumption goods production. *Housing investment* then emerges as an alternative means of saving for the future for households with a high informal production intensity. After deriving the closed-form expressions for the equilibrium measure of households that choose to become homeowners, we showed that the more "informality intensive" households the economy includes, the larger is the aggregate homeownership rate society.

We then extended our benchmark model specification with a CIA constraint. This model allows for financial market imperfections in the form of limited access to finance. Specifically, in addition to the investment barriers

Table 6.9 Homeownership and Informality

Dep. Var.: Homeownership	*Low CRD*	*High CRD*	*Low CRBAN*	*High CRBAN*	*Low M2*	*High M2*	*Poor*	*Rich*
Informal	1.00**	0.91**	0.88**	0.79**	0.64**	0.68**	0.91*	0.54**
	(0.47)	(0.44)	(0.37)	(0.34)	(0.30)	(0.32)	(0.21)	(0.24)
Inflation	2.55**	4.98*	1.49	5.01**	2.00	5.01**	4.02**	4.09**
	(1.20)	(1.65)	(1.30)	(2.00)	(1.51)	(2.32)	(2.00)	(2.10)
Informal · Inflation	−0.06**	0.20**	−0.13***	0.21**	−0.06**	0.2***	−0.11**	0.14**
	(0.03)	(0.09)	(0.07)	(0.10)	(0.03)	(0.07)	(0.05)	(0.07)
Pop. Dens.	0.06***	0.006**	0.001	0.004*	0.001	0.003*	0.04**	0.004*
	(0.03)	(0.003)	(0.001)	(0.001)	(0.001)	(0.001)	(0.02)	(0.001)
Transition	−8.11	−23.10*	−9.42	−21.09**	−8.00	−32.11*	2.13	−11.20
	(7.01)	(5.87)	(6.79)	(10.02)	(6.49)	(8.01)	(7.23)	(8.01)
Young Pop.	−0.02**	−0.02***	−0.02**	−0.02**	−0.02**	−0.02***	−0.02**	−0.02***
	(0.01)	(0.01)	(0.01)	(0.01)	(0.01)	(0.01)	(0.01)	(0.01)
R-squared	0.22	0.24	0.20	0.32	0.22	0.35	0.30	0.21
Observations	34	35	34	35	34	35	34	35
F-Test	0.00	0.01	0.00	0.00	0.00	0.00	0.00	0.00

Robust standard errors are reported in parentheses. *, **, and *** denote 1%, 5%, and 10% confidence levels, respectively. In all regressions a constant is also included but not reported. Transition refers to a dummy variable for Post-Socialist Transition economies.

generated by the informal production delineated in the benchmark model, the CIA extension assumes that the exogenously determined fractions of housing and business investment are subject to a CIA constraint, as in Dotsey and Sarte (2000). In equilibrium, the fraction of housing and investment spending that needs to be financed by cash holdings (rather than mortgage finance and investment credit), in turn, determines the effects of inflation on homeownership rates. We showed that households with high informal production intensity increase their demand for homeownership as the rate of monetary growth (and hence the inflation rate) rises if financing housing purchases is less constrained than investment credit. Conversely, informal households decrease their demand for homeownership with rising inflation when home-purchases are subject to financing constraints.

One can draw important policy implications from these findings. Most importantly, we highlight a novel monetary transmission channel by showing that the interactions between informal sector size and homeownership rates are important determiners of the effects of monetary policy on the real economy. Specifically, our theoretical findings show that monetary growth influences housing demand and that the implications of monetary policy are non-trivial. For informally employed households, monetary growth and the demand for housing are positively related as long as mortgage markets are more developed than business credit markets. Given that housing boom-bust cycles are crucial for an economy's aggregate welfare, as the world economy experienced during the years leading up to the Great Recession, both our theoretical and empirical findings reveal an important novel interaction between monetary policy and the performance of housing markets.

6.3 Other effects of informality and policy implications

The effects of the informal sector go beyond fiscal and monetary policies. Below, based on my research, I discuss several different effects of informality on various variables.

6.3.1 Unionization

Unionization, generally defined as the proportion of workers belonging to trade unions, has experienced a secular global decline over the last 60 years (e.g. Blaschke, 2000; Kleiner, 2001; Farber and Western, 2001; Magnani and Prentice, 2003; Addison et al., 2010). However, although the trend is assumed to be global, there are few cross-country studies of unionization. Instead, the literature focuses on country-specific (or sector-level) micro-level studies (e.g. Chappell et al., 1992; Dewatripont, 1998; DiNardo and Lee, 2002; Lee and Mas, 2009). Moreover, as discussed in earlier chapters, the informal economy is generally characterized as a highly labor-intensive sector that is unaffected by most government-mandated regulations such as a minimum wage, labor standards, or unionization requirements. Thus, from the perspective of firms, the informal sector contains fewer distortions than the formal economy.

Formalizing these ideas, Zenou (2008) proposes a model in which wages in the formal economy are determined by bargaining between workers and firms that, together with search frictions, can create unemployment. In the informal sector, on the other hand, wages are paid at the marginal productivity of workers with full employment. Chaudhuri and Mukhopadhyay (2009) provide a similar model to investigate the effect of trade liberalization on wage inequality in a DGE framework.

A two-sector (formal and informal) model is also possible, in which, with the presence of labor unions in the formal sector, wages are determined following collective bargaining. We can expect that the resulting wage premium for union members in the formal sector produces a negative correlation between unionization and informal economy size. In line with this, Carneiro and Henley (1998) found that the unions' formal sector bargaining power created a negative long-run relationship between formal sector wages and the size of informal economy in Brazil between 1980 and 1993.

Motivated by the absence of any cross-country study about the relationship between unionization and informal economy size, I tested whether there was a negative correlation (Elgin, 2012). While that paper includes data up to 2009, the results here are based on the most recent data up until 2017.

Figure 6.13 illustrates the plain correlation between unionization (percentage of unionized workers) and informal economy size as a percentage of GDP

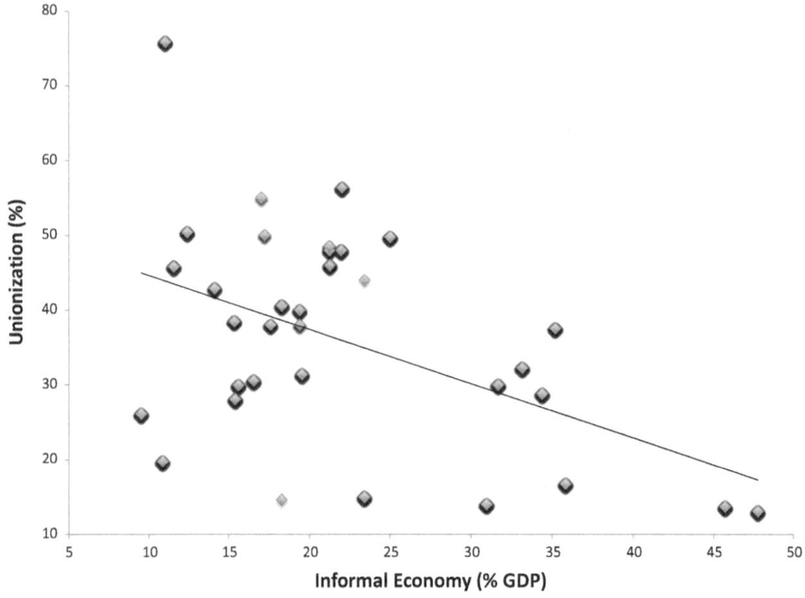

Figure 6.13 Unionization versus informal sector size.

using average data for 31 countries from 1960 to 2017. The overall data set is an unbalanced annual cross-country panel data set. While a clear negative correlation is evident from the figure, further econometric analysis is needed to check the robustness of this observation.

To see whether there is a robust correlation between the unionization and the size of the informal economy and provided that there exists one, what the sign of that correlation is, I estimate the following equation using a panel data framework:

$$Union_{i,t} = \beta_0 + \beta_1 IS_{i,t} + \sum_{k=2}^{n} \beta_k X_{k_{i,t}} + \theta_i + \gamma_t + \epsilon_{i,t}$$

In this specification, for country i in year t, $Union_{i,t}$ represents the union density (i.e. percentage of labor force belonging to a labor union), IS stands for the informal sector size as % of GDP, $X_{k_{i,t}}$ are various control variables included in the regression. These are used to control for other potential explanations made in the literature to account for the variation in unionization. θ_i and γ_i represent country and period FE, respectively. Finally, $\epsilon_{i,t}$ is the error term. Moreover, to address any potential endogeneity issues I have also run a regression using the generalized method of moments (GMM) estimator of Arellano and Bond (1991). In that case, I also include one-period lagged value of the dependent variable among the independent variables. I also used lagged values of all the independent variables as instruments.

Moreover, to identify any long-run effects, I also conduct estimations using the panel OLS estimator while the time-series averages of the cross section are estimated using an OLS estimator in a cross-sectional framework. That is, I estimate the following:

$$Union_i = \beta_0 + \beta_1 IS_i + \sum_{k=2}^{n} \beta_k X_{k_i} + \epsilon_i$$

Noticeably, in every case, the coefficient of interest in the empirical analysis will be β_1.

The regressions in this section use informal sector size as a percentage of GDP as the key independent variable I obtain from the DGE estimates of Elgin et al. (2019). Data for unionization, defined as the percentage of unionized workers, come from WDI. Unfortunately, the data set size is severely limited because unionization data are only available for Organisation for Economic Co-operation and Development (OECD) economies. One particular drawback is that it limits the cross-country variation because the data set includes so few countries. However, the relatively large time-series dimension in the data set helps offset this. The other control variables used in these regressions are GDP per worker, trade openness, government spending to GDP ratio, growth rate of GDP per worker, and urbanization (defined as the percentage of urban population), GDP per worker, growth government spending, and openness.

Table 6.10 Complete Data Set Summary Statistics: 1960–2017

	Mean	*Std. Dev.*	*Minimum*	*Maximum*
Informal Sector Size (% GDP)	23.21	9.51	8.08	47.78
Unionization (%)	35.37	14.60	13.09	75.90
GDP per worker (thousand USD)	36.99	17.20	6.29	118.45
Openness (%)	58.11	45.21	4.81	320.11
Government Exp. (% GDP)	9.41	4.01	3.55	25.89
Growth (%)	2.65	3.40	−19.93	22.89
Urbanization (%)	72.55	14.61	27.70	98.90

These are obtained from PWT 9.1 except for urbanization from WDI. This produces a well-balanced panel data set for 34 countries covering 1960–2017. Table 6.10 provides descriptive statistics of all the series used in the regressions.

Tables 6.11 and 6.12 present the estimation results. The first six columns of Table 6.11 show the results of the FE estimations while the last column (GMM) reports the results of the dynamic panel data estimation. The estimated coefficient of informal sector size is significantly and robustly negative in all cases. That is, a larger (smaller) informal economy size is associated with a smaller (larger) degree of unionization.

Table 6.11 Unionization and Informal Economy: Panel Regressions

Dep. Var.: Unionization	*(1)*	*(2)*	*(3)*	*(4)*	*(5)*	*(6)*	*GMM*
IS	−0.47*	−0.44*	−0.47*	−0.44*	−0.40**	−0.41**	−0.18**
	(0.12)	(0.13)	(0.14)	(0.14)	(0.18)	(0.19)	(0.09)
GDP per worker		−0.11*	−0.10**	−0.05	−0.02	−0.01	0.03
		(0.02)	(0.02)	(0.03)	(0.03)	(0.04)	(0.04)
Openness			−0.04**	−0.04**	−0.04**	−0.04**	−0.05**
			(0.02)	(0.02)	(0.02)	(0.02)	(0.02)
Gov. Exp.				0.35**	0.36**	0.36**	0.31**
				(0.16)	(0.16)	(0.17)	(0.15)
Growth					0.01	0.02	−0.04***
					(0.02)	(0.02)	(0.03)
Urbanization						0.38*	0.33*
						(0.12)	(0.12)
Union(−1)							0.97*
							(0.16)
R-squared	0.31	0.32	0.33	0.33	0.34	0.35	
Observations	1387	1387	1387	1387	1387	1387	1310
F-Test	0.00	0.00	0.00	0.00	0.00	0.00	
J-Test							0.14
AR(2) Test							0.17

Robust standard errors are reported in parentheses. *, **, and *** denote 1%, 5%, and 10% confidence levels, respectively.

Table 6.12 Unionization and Informal Economy: OLS Regressions

Dep. Var.: Unionization	*(1)*	*(2)*	*(3)*	*(4)*	*(5)*	*(6)*	*(7)*
IS	−0.56*	−0.59*	−0.57*	−0.53*	−0.52*	−0.48*	−0.72*
	(0.15)	(0.16)	(0.16)	(0.17)	(0.17)	(0.16)	(0.10)
GDP per worker		−0.03	−0.04*	−0.05	−0.11**	−0.12**	0.07
		(0.03)	(0.05)	(0.05)	(0.05)	(0.05)	(0.07)
Openness			−0.09*	−0.11*	−0.12*	−0.12*	−0.10*
			(0.02)	(0.02)	(0.02)	(0.02)	(0.02)
Gov. Exp.				1.74*	1.88*	1.89*	0.98*
				(0.23)	(0.23)	(0.22)	(0.18)
Growth					−0.29	−0.25	−0.07
					(0.19)	(0.18)	(0.10)
Urbanization						0.15*	0.16*
						(0.04)	(0.03)
R-squared	0.17	0.18	0.19	0.20	0.21	0.22	0.26
Observations	1387	1387	1387	1387	1387	1387	34
F-Test	0.00	0.00	0.00	0.00	0.00	0.00	0.00

Robust standard errors are reported in parentheses. * and ** denote 1% and 5% confidence levels, respectively.

Table 6.12 presents the results of the OLS regressions. In the first six columns, I use OLS with panel data whereas in the last column, I simply run a cross-sectional regression with time-series average data for 34 countries. In all cases, the estimated coefficient of informal sector size is significantly negative.

6.3.2 Effects on growth and technology

Informality affects economic growth as well as growth accounts. In Birinci and Elgin (2016), we empirically investigated the relationship between these two variables. There are two streams of literature to consider. One associates greater informality with lower growth whereas the other associates it with higher growth.

A larger informal economy can be associated with lower growth for various reasons. First, a third factor, such as excessive regulation, could lead to a larger informal sector while reducing economic growth (Sarte, 2000; Loayza et al., 2004). Second, a large informal economy could severely limit government resources to finance public goods, such as education, health, or infrastructure investment, thereby reducing potential growth. For example, Loayza (1997) presents empirical evidence for Latin American countries that an expanding informal economy hurts economic growth by reducing the availability of public services for all agents in the economy while stimulating inefficient usage of public services. Similarly, Johnson et al. (1997) present empirical evidence of a negative relationship between growth and informality for 25 transition economies.

Besides this macro-level evidence, some micro-level studies suggest that the informal economy hinders growth for several reasons. Regarding the influences of informality on economic performance, De Soto (1989) argues that the fear of detection by the authorities forces informal firms to operate on a smaller, sub-optimal scale, which prevents them from achieving efficiencies of scale, thereby reducing economic growth.

Various studies provide empirical support for this argument. Using data from 6,797 businesses from the Indian state of Kerala, Raj (2011) shows that the technological inefficiency of these manufacturing firms means they can produce only 48% of their potential output. Similarly, using data from 900 businesses in Benin, Burkina Faso, and Senegal, Benjamin and Mbaye (2010) show that formal firms are more productive than informal firms. Using survey data from 6,402 households in Mozambique, Byiers (2009) finds that formally registered, non-agricultural micro-enterprises are more productive than their informal counterparts. Using both firm-level and individual-level data from Turkey, Taymaz (2009) confirms that there is a productivity gap between formal and informal firms. He concludes that this stems from reduced access to public service, lack of infrastructure, and poor access to markets. Finally, Amin (2009) reports that formal manufacturing enterprises in Ivory Coast, Madagascar, and Mauritius are more productive than informal enterprises.

Poor access to credit is another channel that might link informality to lower growth. For example, Massenot and Straub (2011) conclude that to achieve economic growth in an open economy, it is better to have a larger formal sector because formality helps firms to collateralize their assets more efficiently. This spurs more investment and higher productivity. Similarly, using firm level-data for 49 developing countries and tax compliance as a proxy for informality, Gatti and Honorati (2008) find that tax compliance (or formality) is positively and significantly correlated with access to credit, which they identify as a fundamental source of growth. Straub (2005) also focuses on the credit market channel in identifying the negative effect of informality on growth. Caro et al. (2012) find that labor informality in Colombia is negatively and significantly correlated with access to credit, firm performance, and employment growth. Finally, for Peru, Morón et al. (2012) show that reducing self-employment and firms with fewer than ten workers increases access to credit. This increased availability, in turn, helps these small firms to grow faster.

On the other hand, some economists argue that a larger informal sector may spur economic growth. They reason that firms in the informal sector tend to be less productive (La Porta and Shleifer, 2014; Levy, 2008), employ lower-skilled workers, operate with less capital (Amaral and Quintin, 2006), and are generally less able to absorb the costs of operating in the formal sector. This adverse selection may raise productivity levels in the formal economy in countries with larger informal economies (D'Erasmo and Moscoso Boedo, 2012). However, the impact on productivity growth is unclear.

Nabi and Drine (2009), for example, conclude that a larger shadow economy may result in higher economic growth if the subsequent reduction in the size of the formal economy is offset by greater productivity in the formal sector. Eliat and Zinnes (2000) show that a large shadow economy makes recessions less severe in official GDP. They list several factors. They also provide some evidence for transition economies to show that the relationship between growth and informality may be non-linear. Finally, Elgin and Uras (2013b) show that, if the capacity constraints of formal financial institutions are binding, reducing the size of the informal sector hinders financial development, thereby harming economic growth.

To the best of my knowledge, Birinci and Elgin (2016) used the largest macroeconomic data set yet to investigate the growth effects of informality. The study makes the novel finding of a non-linear relationship between growth and informality while the interaction of growth with per capita income is also novel, with the potential to open up further lines of research. Finally, the empirical results also have serious implications for the design of economic policy to reduce informality and achieve optimal growth. The original analysis includes data up to 2009. Here, I replicate the analysis using the most recent data until 2017.

I run several regressions using different estimators. The benchmark panel FE regression I use is given by the following expression:

$$Gr_{i,t} = \beta_0 + \beta_1 is_{i,t} + \beta_1 is_{i,t}^2 + \sum_{k=3}^{n} \beta_k X_{k_{i,t}} + \theta_i + \gamma_t + \epsilon_{i,t}$$

where $Gr_{i,t}$ is the growth rate of GDP per capita in country i, in year t, and $is_{i,t}$ is the informal sector size as % of GDP. Moreover, $X_{k_{i,t}}$ are the other explanatory (control) variables in addition to informal sector and θ_i, γ_t are the country and period FE, respectively. Finally, $\epsilon_{i,t}$ denotes the error term. In these regressions, informal sector size-squared is also included among the independent variables to check for the potential existence of a non-linear relationship between informal sector size and growth.

The benchmark regressions in Birinci and Elgin (2016) used the FE estimator as well as regressions using different estimators such as the between estimator (BE), OLS in the static panel data setting, and a GMM regression in a dynamic specification. For the sake of simplicity and space, I only report the current results for the FE estimator. Interested readers are referred to Birinci and Elgin (2016).

Data

The data set is an annual cross-country panel data; however, in all the reported regressions, I use five-year averages to rule out business cycle effects, as is standard in the growth literature. In addition to growth and informal sector size, I use several control variables in the econometric analysis. The descriptive statistics for these are presented in Table 6.13. Generally, I choose control variables that have already been used in the empirical growth literature. Specifically, I control for GDP per capita, trade openness, government expenditure,

Table 6.13 Complete Data Set Summary Statistics

Acronym	*Variable*	*Mean*	*Std. Dev.*	*Minimum*	*Maximum*
Gr	Growth (%)	3.09	3.37	−4.41	12.32
IS	Informal Sector Size (in % GDP)	33.88	12.67	7.78	68.30
GDP per cap	GDP per capita (thousand USD)	12.21	13.90	0.17	76.09
Corr. Cont.	Corruption Control	2.69	1.17	0.00	6.00
Law	Law and Order	3.77	1.37	0.50	6.00
K/Y	Capital-Output Ratio	2.27	1.97	0.85	5.72
Open	Openness (% GDP)	76.86	41.10	8.29	401.09
Gov. exp.	Government exp. (% GDP)	12.11	8.09	1.29	51.10
Inf.	Inflation (%)	6.11	12.21	−9.83	152.10
Fisc. Def.	Fiscal Deficit (% GDP)	−0.79	4.34	−10.21	49.89
Fin. Dep.	Financial Depth (M2 as % GDP)	47.11	41.74	4.39	281.29
TFP	TFP Growth (%)	1.35	6.59	−27.80	64.10
Lab.	Employment (Ratio to Population)	0.43	0.10	0.18	0.68

inflation, fiscal deficit, financial depth, and two institutional quality variables: the corruption control and law and order indices.

As in Birinci and Elgin (2016), I expect trade openness, financial depth, corruption control, and law and order to be positively correlated with economic growth. Regarding the estimated coefficients of inflation, government spending, and GDP per capita, previous empirical studies have produced conflicting results, depending on the time window or sample. I also regress the three growth accounts onto informal sector size: growth in TFP, growth in capital-output ratio, and growth in labor, measured by employment. I have no definite a priori expectation regarding the estimated coefficient of growth in TFP. Nevertheless, considering that the informal sector is far more labor intensive than the formal sector, a negative coefficient of the growth in capital-output ratio and formal labor growth would not be surprising.

The informal sector data (as a percentage of GDP) in the benchmark analysis are obtained from Elgin et al. (2019). The data series for growth, GDP per capita, employment, trade openness (defined as the ratio of the sum of exports and imports to GDP), and government expenditure comes from PWT 9.1, as do the capital-output ratio and TFP series. The series for inflation, financial depth (measured by the ratio of the broad monetary aggregate M2 to GDP), and fiscal deficit comes from the WDI. Finally, the two institutional quality indices, corruption control and law and order, come from the ICRG. These are the most widely used variables in the empirical growth literature.

Finally, before discussing the estimation results, I should acknowledge that informality may also be associated with some of the control variables. For example, institutional quality variables, GDP per capita, trade openness, government spending, and inflation may all be significantly correlated with informal sector size. Furthermore, considering that informal sector size is, by definition, imperfectly measured, measurement error and possible two-way causality between informal sector size and growth, and possible missing variables may also create endogeneity in the regression analysis. Birinci and Elgin (2016) overcome these problems through several robustness checks with respect to sample size, estimation method, and data stratification. However, the tests of endogeneity and collinearity, and an analysis of the variance inflation factors calculated after the regressions did not indicate a serious issue in this respect.

Benchmark results

Table 6.14 reports the results for the benchmark estimation using the FE estimator for the whole data set. Here, every control variable is added individually to each subsequent regression. In all nine regressions, the estimated coefficient of the linear term for the informal sector is positive and the squared term is negative. This indicates a significant and robust inverted-U relationship between growth rate of GDP per capita and informal economy size. This relationship is also clearly robust after including various control variables in the regression equation. In addition to the coefficients of the informal sector size, government expenditure and trade openness also have consistently significant coefficients in all regressions. Accordingly, a lower government spending and more openness to international trade are associated with a higher growth rate of GDP per capita.

The analysis presented in Table 6.14 indicates that the growth of GDP per capita has a non-linear relationship with informal sector size. In Birinci and Elgin (2016), we took the analysis one step further by investigating the relationship between informality and several growth accounts. As is well known, the growth account exercise, which dates back to Solow (1957), measures the contribution of different factors of production to growth. Here, I present this exercise before developing it to understand how it might be linked to the presence of informality.

For conducting the growth accounting exercise using official national income statistics to determine how informality might be associated with different growth accounts, I use the basic Cobb-Douglas production function of the following form:

$$Y_{Ft} = A_{Ft}K_{Ft}^{\alpha}N_{Ft}^{1-\alpha} \tag{6.3.1}$$

This function defines formal output at the end of year t, i.e. Y_{Ft}, in terms of formal capital K_{Ft} and formal employment N_{Ft}. A_{Ft} is the formal TFP and α is defined as the capital share of formal output. (Similarly, $1 - \alpha$ is defined as the labor share of income.)

Dividing both sides of the previous equation by N_t, i.e. the population, we obtain formal output per capita, i.e. y_{Ft}, which is given by

$$\frac{Y_{Ft}}{N_t} = y_{Ft} = A_{Ft}\frac{K_{Ft}^{\alpha}N_{Ft}^{1-\alpha}}{N_t} = A_{Ft}\frac{K_{Ft}^{\alpha}N_{Ft}^{1-\alpha}}{N_t^{\alpha}N_t^{1-\alpha}} = A_{Ft}(\frac{K_{Ft}}{N_t})^{\alpha}(\frac{N_{Ft}}{N_t})^{1-\alpha}$$
$$= A_{Ft}k_{Ft}^{\alpha}n_{Ft}^{1-\alpha}. \tag{6.3.2}$$

Table 6.14 Growth and Informality: FE Estimations

Gr.									
	(1)	*(2)*	*(3)*	*(4)*	*(5)*	*(6)*	*(7)*	*(8)*	*(9)*
IS	0.72*	0.71*	0.70*	0.78*	0.74*	0.71*	0.70*	0.69*	0.66*
	(0.08)	(0.08)	(0.09)	(0.08)	(0.09)	(0.09)	(0.08)	(0.08)	(0.08)
IS^2	−0.57*	−0.56*	−0.59*	−0.61*	−0.62*	−0.65*	−0.66*	−0.68*	−0.70*
	(0.09)	(0.09)	(0.09)	(0.09)	(0.10)	(0.10)	(0.10)	(0.10)	(0.09)
Open		0.02**	0.02**	0.02**	0.02**	0.02**	0.02**	0.02**	0.03***
		(0.01)	(0.01)	(0.01)	(0.01)	(0.01)	(0.01)	(0.01)	(0.02)
Gov. exp.			−0.08**	−0.07**	−0.08**	−0.08**	−0.08**	−0.08**	−0.08**
			(0.04)	(0.04)	(0.04)	(0.04)	(0.04)	(0.04)	(0.04)
GDP per cap.				0.002**	0.002**	0.002**	0.001	0.001	0.001
				(0.001)	(0.001)	(0.001)	(0.002)	(0.002)	(0.002)
Inf.					−0.39	−0.48	−0.42	−0.41	−0.41
					(0.32)	(0.33)	(0.34)	(0.34)	(0.35)
Corr. Cont.						0.51	0.50	0.47	0.45
						(0.40)	(0.41)	(0.41)	(0.40)
Law							1.02	1.03	1.04
							(0.90)	(0.86)	(0.85)
Fisc. Def.								−0.30**	−0.31**
								(0.15)	(0.16)
Fin. Dep.									0.19
									(1.00)
R-squared	0.17	0.17	0.18	0.19	0.19	0.19	0.20	0.21	0.22
Observations	1576	1576	1576	1576	1408	1030	1030	1030	1027
F-Test	0.00	0.00	0.00	0.00	0.00	0.00	0.00	0.00	0.00

All panel regressions include a country fixed effect and year dummies. Robust standard errors are reported in parentheses. *, **, and *** denote 1%, 5%, and 10% confidence levels, respectively. In all regressions a constant is also included but not reported.

where k_{Ft} and n_{Ft} are per capita formal capital stock and employment, respectively. Next, taking the natural logarithm and manipulating the earlier equation, I obtain:

$$ln(y_{Ft}) = ln(n_{Ft}) + \frac{\alpha}{1-\alpha} ln(\frac{k_{Ft}}{y_{Ft}}) + \frac{1}{1-\alpha} ln(A_{Ft}) \quad (6.3.3)$$

Considering that I have data on y_{Ft}, n_{Ft}, and k_{Ft} I can calculate A_{Ft} using this equation. What remains to be done is to create a series for k_{Ft}, or K_{Ft}. I calculate a K_{Ft} series using the perpetual inventory method using investment series from national income statistics.

As well known, the perpetual inventory method uses the following two equations to construct the capital-stock series:

$$\frac{K_{F0}}{Y_{F0}} = \frac{I/Y}{g_y + \delta} \quad (6.3.4)$$

$$K_{Ft+1} = K_{Ft}(1-\delta) + I_t \quad (6.3.5)$$

where g_y is the average growth rate of formal GDP, δ is the depreciation rate of physical capital, and I/Y is the average investment-to-GDP ratio in the period of interest. Moreover, equation (6.3.3) can also be written in growth terms as follows:

$$ln(\frac{y_{Ft+1}}{y_{Ft}}) = \frac{1}{1-\alpha}\{ln(A_{Ft+1}) - ln(A_{Ft})\} + \frac{\alpha}{1-\alpha}\{ln(k_{Ft+1}/y_{Ft+1}) - ln(k_{Ft}/y_{Ft})\} + ln(n_{Ft+1}) - ln(n_{Ft})$$

This equation decomposes the natural logarithm of the growth rate of formal GDP per capita into three different growth accounts with different coefficients: growth in formal TFP, growth in the formal capital-output ratio, and formal labor per-capita. To understand the effect of informality on growth in per capita income, one should analyze the former's separate effects on these three growth accounts.

To this end I regress these three growth accounts separately on informal sector size. Table 6.15 reports the results of the FE and OLS regressions. A larger informal economy is associated with higher growth in TFP and this association strongly interacts with GDP per capita. In other words, it is much stronger in richer than poorer countries. Simultaneously, however, a larger informal economy is also associated with lower growth in capital-output ratio, although this association does not significantly interact with GDP per capita. Similarly, informal economy size is negatively correlated with growth in employment per capita without a significant interaction with GDP per capita. These results shed more light on the inverted-U relationship between growth and informal economy size. More specifically, the difference in the relationship of informal sector size with growth between richer and poorer economies may arise from

Table 6.15 Growth Accounts and Informality

	TFP				*K/Y*				*Lab.*			
	(FE)	*(FE)*	*(OLS)*	*(OLS)*	*(FE)*	*(FE)*	*(OLS)*	*(OLS)*	*(FE)*	*(FE)*	*(OLS)*	*(OLS)*
IS	0.14*	0.29*	0.04*	0.05*	−0.20*	0.20*	−0.04*	0.19*	−0.05*	−0.09*	−0.02**	−0.02**
	(0.03)	(0.05)	(0.01)	(0.01)	(0.04)	(0.03)	(0.01)	(0.04)	(0.01)	(0.01)	(0.01)	(0.01)
IS^2		−0.17***		0.01		−0.39*		−0.24*		0.02		0.01
		(0.09)		(0.01)		(0.09)		(0.06)		0.02		(0.01)
IS · GDP-cap	0.002**	0.002**	0.003*	0.003*	0.01	−0.01***	0.001	−0.001	0.003	0.005	0.005	0.005
	(0.001)	(0.001)	(0.001)	(0.001)	(0.01)	(0.005)	(0.001)	(0.001)	(0.003)	(0.005)	(0.005)	(0.005)
Open	−0.003	−0.004	0.005*	0.005*	0.04*	0.03*	0.005**	0.003	−0.002**	−0.001	0.002	0.002
	(0.004)	(0.005)	(0.002)	(0.002)	(0.01)	(0.006)	(0.002)	(0.03)	(0.001)	(0.001)	(0.002)	(0.002)
Gov. exp.	−0.08**	−0.08**	−0.04**	−0.04**	−0.04	0.04	0.02	0.02	0.02	0.02	0.01	0.01
	(0.04)	(0.04)	(0.02)	(0.02)	(0.04)	(0.04)	(0.02)	(0.03)	(0.02)	(0.02)	(0.01)	0.01
GDP-cap	−0.0005	−0.0005	−0.0004	−0.0003	0.001**	0.002*	−0.0004	0.0005***	0.002	0.001	−0.0006	−0.0006
	(0.0005)	(0.0005)	(0.0004)		(0.0003)	(0.0005)	(0.0006)	(0.0003)	(0.002)	(0.002)	(0.007)	(0.0007)
Inf.	0.03	0.02	0.01	0.01	−0.01**	−0.01**	−0.02***	−0.02	0.02	0.02	0.02	0.02
	(0.04)	(0.03)	(0.03)	(0.03)	(0.004)	(0.004)	(0.01)	(0.01)	(0.02)	(0.02)	(0.02)	(0.02)
Corr. Cont.	0.06	0.06	0.02	0.02	0.01	0.01	0.01	0.01	0.03	0.03	0.04	0.04
	(0.04)	(0.06)	(0.03)	(0.03)	(0.04)	(0.03)	(0.02)	(0.01)	(0.04)	(0.04)	(0.03)	(0.03)
Law	0.07***	0.10*	0.04**	0.04**	0.01	0.02	0.04**	0.04**	0.03	0.04	0.04	0.05
	(0.04)	(0.03)	(0.02)	(0.02)	(0.01)	(0.02)	(0.02)	(0.02)	(0.05)	(0.05)	(0.04)	(0.05)
Fisc. Def.	0.01	0.02	0.02	0.02	−0.06	−0.05	−0.03	−0.06	0.02	0.02	0.01	0.01
	(0.01)	(0.02)	(0.02)	(0.02)	(0.05)	(0.05)	(0.05)	(0.05)	(0.05)	(0.04)	(0.04)	(0.03)
Fin. Dep.	0.02	0.03	0.01	0.01	−0.01	−0.01	0.02	0.02	−0.02	−0.03	−0.03	−0.03
	(0.03)	(0.02)	(0.01)	(0.01)	(0.01)	(0.01)	(0.02)	(0.02)	(0.02)	(0.02)	(0.03)	(0.03)
R-squared	0.17	0.17	0.08	0.08	0.17	0.18	0.07	0.09	0.12	0.13	0.15	0.14
Observations	1015	1015	1015	1015	1015	1015	1015	1015	1015	1015	1015	1015
F-Test	0.00	0.00	0.00	0.00	0.00	0.00	0.00	0.00	0.00	0.00	0.00	0.00

All panel regressions include a country fixed effect. Robust standard errors are reported in parentheses. *, **, and *** denote 1%, 5%, and 10% confidence levels, respectively. In all regressions a constant is also included but not reported.

differences in the relationship of informality with growth accounts in rich and poor economies. In other words, in developed (developing) economies, the positive relationship between informal sector size and TFP growth dominates (is dominated by) the negative relationships of growth of capital-output ratio and employment per capita with informal sector size. This might explain why the growth-informality relationship is different in developed and developing economies and why it is non-linear in the first place.

This result paves the way for future research and indicates that further examination is needed into the relationship between informality and TFP, and its interaction with GDP per capita.

6.3.3 Growth, wage-productivity gap, and informality

Drawing on the preceding empirical analysis of the relationship between growth and the informal sector, I now describe a simple demand-led growth model for understanding how informality might interact with the relationship between wages, productivity, and growth. Based on the earlier definition of informality, I model the informal sector as a highly labor-intensive, small-scale sector. Two other characteristics of informality are that it mostly produces final consumption goods and that firms heavily engaged in informal economic activities tend to be smaller. This is also one of the main reasons why many early studies used self-employment (household producers) as a proxy for informality.

The formal sector output Y_f is determined according to the following functional form:

$$Y_f = z_f K_f^{\alpha} N_f^{\beta}$$

Here, z_f denotes the TFP, K_f is the physical capital in the formal sector, and N_f is formal labor. Given perfect competition if $\alpha + \beta = 1$, these two parameters can also be interpreted as the capital and labor share of income, respectively. However, I do not impose such a restriction at this point.

The informal sector production function is given by the following expression:

$$Y_i = z_i K_i^{\eta} N_i^{\gamma}$$

Here, informal output Y_i is produced by a production function that uses physical capital K_i and informal labor N_i. Again, η and γ can be interpreted as capital and labor shares within informal sector income, respectively, provided they add up to unity. In that case, it is also safe to assume that $\eta < \alpha$ and $\gamma > \beta$, that is the informal sector is more labor intensive than the formal sector.

Finally, the model assumes that the households supplying labor to the labor market are bound by a time constraint, that is, the time devoted to both sectors in the form of the labor supply must add up to a constant given number $T > 0$.

$$N_f + N_i = T$$

Demand side

For the sake of simplicity, I assume that the model economy is a closed one. The demand side of the economy is modeled by the following equations:

$$C = C_0 + c_{wf} Y_f (1 - \pi_f) + c_{rf} Y_f \pi_f + c_{wi} Y_i (1 - \pi_i) + c_{ri} Y_i \pi_i \tag{6.3.6}$$

$$I = \phi_0 Y_f^{\phi_1} \pi_f^{\phi_2} Y_i^{\phi_3} \pi_i^{\phi_4} b^{\phi_5} \tag{6.3.7}$$

$$W_f = Y_f (1 - \pi_f) \tag{6.3.8}$$

$$W_i = Y_i (1 - \pi_i) \tag{6.3.9}$$

$$R_f = Y_f \pi_f \tag{6.3.10}$$

$$R_i = Y_i \pi_i \tag{6.3.11}$$

Here, equation (6.3.6) defines aggregate consumption C as a function of different terms. $C_0 \geq 0$ refers to autonomous consumption. c_{wf} and c_{rf} are the marginal propensities to consume by workers and capitalists in the formal sector, whereas c_{wi} and c_{ri} are the marginal propensities to consume workers and capitalists in the informal sector, respectively. All these propensities are assumed to be non-negative. Following Keynes (1936) and others cited in the introduction, we also assume that $c_{wf} > c_{rf}$ and $c_{wi} > c_{ri}$, that is the marginal propensity to consumer is larger for workers in both sectors.

Next, in equation (6.3.7) I define the investment demand function in a similar way to Naastepad and Storm (2006) and Oyvat et al. (2018). Here, $\phi_i > 0$ for $i \in \{1, 2, 3, 4, 5\}$ represent the elasticities of investment with respect to formal output, profit share in the formal sector, informal output, profit share in the informal sector, and business confidence $b > 0$, respectively.

Finally, the remaining four equations define formal and informal wage payment W_f and W_i, and formal and informal profits R_f and R_i. Here, π_f and π_i denote formal and informal profit shares, respectively. Note that the wage-productivity gaps in the formal and the informal sectors are implicitly defined by equations 6.3.8 and 6.3.9. Considering that the marginal products of formal output and informal output are both functions of the total output in these two sectors, it is obvious from these two equations that π_f and π_i determine the level of the wage-productivity gap in both sectors.

Next, assuming that total output Y is defined as $Y = Y_f + Y_i = C + I$, I can then find the following analytical expression for the impact of the profit share on the percentage change in formal output below. Notice that we define θ with respect to the formal measured output only because we argue that the measured output in the data is the formal output. This enables direct comparison against the data.

$$\theta = \frac{\partial Y_f / \partial \pi_f}{Y_f} = (c_{rf} - c_{wf}) + Y_i^{\phi_3} b^{\phi_5} \phi_0 \phi_2 \pi_f^{\phi_2 - 1} \pi_i^{\phi_4} Y_f^{\phi_1 - 1} \tag{6.3.12}$$

The first term on the right-hand side of equation (6.3.12) is negative (due to $c_{wf} > c_{rf}$). The equation entails that the economy's growth regime is profit-led if the rising profit share's negative impact through differences in marginal propensities to consume is smaller than its positive effect through investment. For positive values of θ, the growth regime is profit-led, whereas a negative θ implies a wage-led growth regime.

Given the physical capital stock of the formal and informal sectors (i.e. for a given value of K_f and K_i as well as a fixed value for T, thanks to the time constraint $N_f + N_i = T$), equation (6.3.12) can thus be rearranged as follows:

$$\theta = (c_{rf} - c_{wf}) + b^{\phi_5}\phi_0\phi_2\pi_f^{\phi_2 - 1}\pi_i^{\phi_4}f(Y_i) \tag{6.3.13}$$

The key difference between equation (6.3.12) and (6.3.13) is that the latter includes a function $f(.)$ that defines formal sector output Y_f as a function of the informal sector output Y_i, where $f'(Y_i) > 0$. More importantly, it is also clear that the sign of θ which determines the type of the growth regime significantly depends on Y_i. Taking the formal labor productivity as given (as determined by marginal product of labor (MPL) defined through the production function), it is obvious from these two equations that when the informal sector size is zero, then the first term $(c_{rf} - c_{wf})$ in the right-hand side of the equations dominates the second term and the growth regime is wage-led. However, when the informal sector size increases (absolutely or relative to the formal sector), the second term starts to increase to eventually dominate the first term. Thus, the growth regime is less likely to be wage-led or can even become profit-led. The economic mechanism behind this latter effect is that when the informal sector grows, capital stock and investment decrease because the informal sector is less capital intensive than the formal sector. This, however, increases the marginal product of capital, hence investment's positive effect on growth. Undoubtedly, how fast and when this change happens depend on the levels of the various parameters and the coefficients of the model.

To observe the model's behavior under a plausible set of parameters, we provide a simple simulation in this subsection. I need to assign specific values to the various parameters and coefficients.

Unfortunately, there are no directly available values for all the parameters of the model that are valid for all countries. Further complicating the issue, there are several measurement issues for informality while firm- and household-level micro data are needed to assign specific values to these parameters. This makes it very difficult to find values that are consistent and robust across different economies. To overcome this issue, we rely on several variables reported in PWT 9.1 as well as some cross-country panel regressions. First, we calculate the formal profit share π_f from PWT by subtracting the labor share of income from unity. 0.46 is the average formal profit share of all the economies for which labor share data are available in PWT. For the informal profit share π_i, we rely on Cantekin and Elgin (2017), who calculated these values from a firm-level survey of 1,000 representative firms in Turkey. As informal profit share data are available only from the Turkish economy, I have chosen to proceed with values from Turkey. At about 28%, Turkey, along with Mexico, has the largest informal sector as a percentage of GDP among OECD economies, which is approximately equal to the world (unweighted) average (Elgin et al., 2019). The marginal propensities are calculated from these two values using a simple panel data estimation of equation (6.3.6) while investment elasticities are calculated from equation (6.3.7). In the estimations of these two equations, Y_i values were obtained from Elgin et al. (2019) while I used the Investment Profile Index of the ICRG to calculate b. All parameter values are reported in Table 6.16.

Figure 6.14 illustrates the behavior of θ, as defined by equation (6.3.12) or (6.3.13) for different informal sector sizes. As we can see from this figure, increasing informal sector size (as a fraction of formal output) from 0 to 1

Table 6.16 Parameter Choices

Parameter	*Description*	*Value*	*Source*
c_{wf}	MPC for formal workers	0.85	Estimated
c_{rf}	MPC for formal capitalists	0.65	Estimated
ϕ_1	Formal Output Elasticity of Inv.	1.25	Estimated
ϕ_2	Formal Profit Share Elasticity of Inv.	1.15	Estimated
ϕ_3	Informal Output Elasticity of Inv.	0.45	Estimated
ϕ_4	Informal Profit Share Elasticity of Inv.	0.05	Estimated
ϕ_5	Business Confidence Elasticity of Inv.	0.11	Estimated
π_f	Formal Profit Share	0.47	Penn World Tables 9.1
π_i	Informal Profit Share	0.25	Cantekin and Elgin (2017)

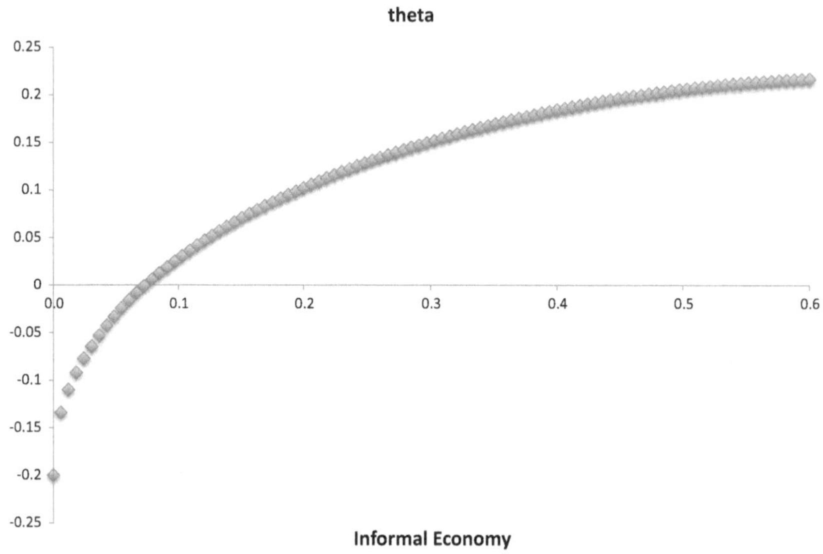

Figure 6.14 Effect of the profit share on formal output for different levels of informality.

increases the value of θ from negative (wage-led growth) to positive values (profit-led growth). The reason behind this behavior is that initially when relative informal sector size is zero, θ_i is negative, due to the fact that c_{rf} is less than c_{wf}. However, when informal sector size increases, the second term on the right-hand side of the equation (6.3.12) or (6.3.13) starts to increase and therefore θ_i increases and even becomes positive. Although a negative initial value for θ, i.e. wage-led growth, is guaranteed as long as $c_{rf} < c_{wf}$, for a different set of parameters other than the ones we used in our simulation, θ can stay negative even if informal sector size increases. Moreover, we should also notice that the range in which θ varies, from −0.20 to about +0.20, is not extremely large. However, this range very much depends on the set of parameters used in the simulation. This range varies between countries because of different country-specific parameter values.

In this section, I present the results of an econometric analysis based on annual cross-country panel data and test two hypotheses based on the results from the model constructed in the previous section:

- Ceteris paribus, a larger wage-productivity gap is associated with slower growth.
- Informal sector size significantly interacts with the relationship between the wage-productivity gap and growth. Specifically, as informal sector size increases, the correlation between the wage-productivity gap and the growth rate also increases.

I use annual cross-country (unbalanced) panel data covering 127 economies from 1950 to 2017. Informal sector size as a percentage of GDP was obtained from Elgin et al. (2019). Wage (or labor) share of income, government spending (% GDP), real GDP per capita, trade openness (defined as the ratio of the sum of exports and imports to GDP), and the dependent variable, GDP growth rate, were all acquired from PWT 9.1. Finally, the institutional quality index was constructed from the PS Group's ICRG as the sum of three sub-indices, namely corruption control, bureaucratic quality, and investment profile. Finally, I calculated the wage-productivity gap following Persky and Tsang (1974), using the ratio of MPL to real wages. MPL in the formal sector was calculated using the production function defined in the previous section along with the PWT data. Wage series was obtained by constructing the most comprehensive data series yet, using several different sources including the UNIDO, AMECO, and ILO databases.

For the benchmark regression equation I use the FE estimator with country and year FEs. In this case the regression equation is as follows:

$$Growth_{i,t} = \alpha_0 + \alpha_1 Gap_{i,t} + \alpha_2 Gap_{i,t} \cdot IS_{i,t} + \sum_{k=3}^{n} \alpha_k X_{k_{i,t}} + \mu_i + \gamma_t + \epsilon_{i,t}$$

Moreover, to check the robustness of our benchmark results and especially to address the potential existence of endogeneity, mean reversion dynamics, and two-way causality, we also run an IV regression by using lagged independent variables as instruments for the levels of the regressors. Finally, I also run a dynamic panel data regression using the GMM estimator[12] a la Arellano and Bond (1991).

In both the IV and dynamic panel data estimations, *p*-values corresponding to two tests are also provided for all tables. One of these tests is the Hansen J-test for over-identifying restrictions while the other is the AR (2) test for autocorrelation. These tests support the exogeneity of the instruments and the absence of autocorrelation in the specified order, respectively.

Estimation results and discussion

The six regression estimation results are reported in Table 6.17. The first four columns present the results of the FE estimations, the fifth column presents the IV estimation while the last column presents the GMM estimation. Overall, all the estimation results are in line with the model simulation. Specifically, even though the level of the coefficient changes significantly, especially in the last two regressions, the estimated coefficient of the wage-productivity gap (denoted by Gap in the first row of the table) is significantly negative in all regressions. The estimated coefficient of the informal sector size is significantly negative

Table 6.17 Panel Regressions

Dep. Var.: Growth						
	FE	*FE*	*FE*	*FE*	*IV*	*GMM*
Gap	−0.51***	−0.53***	−0.52***	−0.54***	−0.28**	−0.99***
	(0.19)	(0.20)	(0.20)	(0.20)	(0.22)	(0.24)
IS	−0.34*	−0.33*	−0.27	−0.25	0.07	−0.04
	(0.19)	(0.18)	(0.19)	(0.15)	(0.16)	(0.17)
IS· Gap	1.45**	1.42**	1.43**	1.49***	0.99***	2.16**
	(0.44)	(0.45)	(0.47)	(0.39)	(0.20)	(0.32)
Gov. Exp.		0.37*	0.36*	0.34	0.20	0.17*
		(0.20)	(0.19)	(0.20)	(0.18)	(0.10)
GDP-cap.			−0.05*	−0.05*	−0.02**	−0.01
			(0.03)	(0.03)	(0.01)	(0.01)
Inst. Qual.				0.07**	0.11**	0.17**
				(0.03)	(0.05)	(0.08)
Openness				0.08	−0.04*	−0.11
				(0.07)	(0.02)	(0.07)
Growth(−1)						0.88*
						(0.17)
R-Squared	0.30	0.39	0.45	0.46		
Observations	7111	7111	7111	3220	3070	2918
J-test					0.00	0.00
F-stat (*p*-value)	0.00	0.00	0.00	0.00		

All regressions include a constant as well as country and year dummies. Robust standard errors are reported in parentheses. *, **, and *** denote 10%, 5%, and 1% confidence levels, respectively.

in only the first regression. However, the coefficient of the interaction term between informal sector size and wage-productivity gap (denoted by IS · Gap in the table) is significantly positive in all regressions. This suggests that the size of the informal sector significantly affects the relationship between the wage-productivity gap and growth. That is, as the informal sector expands, the negative correlation between the gap and growth increases so that it can eventually even become positive.

Turning to the other variables, institutional quality is significantly positive in all regressions, i.e. better institutions are associated with higher GDP growth rates. The lagged dependent variable in the final dynamic panel data GMM regression also has a highly significant positive coefficient. GDP per capita is significantly negative except for the last GMM regression, offering some weak evidence in favor of convergence. Similarly, government spending (as a percentage of GDP) is significantly positive in the two FE regressions and the GMM regression. Finally, trade openness is only significant in the IV regression. This non-robust significance is generally consistent with the empirical growth literature. However, the main message arising from Table 6.17 is that the empirical analysis is largely consistent with the model presented in the previous section.

6.3.4 Pollution

It is well established in the environmental economics literature that environmental pollution highly depends on the intensity of government regulations, oversight, and enforcement of environmental standards. As Baksi and Bose (2010) argue, the presence of a large informal sector in developing countries is a serious challenge for implementing environmental regulations. It is therefore crucial to understand the links between informality and environmental performance as it would be a mistake to overlook the presence of a shadow economy when analyzing environmental policy outcomes. Elgin and Oztunali (2014b) presented panel evidence and a theoretical model to examine the effect of informality on pollution. Elgin and Oztunali (2014a) tested the same model using time-series data from Turkey while Elgin and Mazhar (2013) added the role of environmental regulation to this relationship.

There are only a few studies of the environmental impacts of the informal sector. Blackman and Bannister (1998a) claim that, in various developing countries, the informal sector, which they argue comprises low-technology, unlicensed micro-enterprises, "is a major source of pollution" and that "environmental management in this sector is exceptionally challenging". Blackman and Bannister (1998b) claim that it is virtually impossible to regulate the informal sector with conventional tools while Blackman et al. (2006) make a similar argument while focusing on the estimation of the benefits of controlling informal sector emissions. Chaudhuri (2005) builds a three-sector general equilibrium model with an informal sector and then uses this model to analyze the effects of different policies on environmental standards and the welfare of the economy. From their analysis of the effects of environmental regulation in the presence of an informal sector, Baksi and Bose (2010) find that stricter regulation can increase or reduce pollution (or have a non-linear relationship). Chattopadhyay et al. (2010) give strong support for the two effects outlined earlier.

To determine whether the relationship between pollution and informal sector size is an inverse-U, Elgin and Oztunali (2014b) estimated the following panel equation using the FE estimator:

$$E_{i,t} = \beta_0 + \beta_1 IS_{i,t} + \beta_2 IS_{i,t}^2 + \sum_{k=3}^{n} \beta_k, X_{k_{i,t}} + \theta_i + \gamma_t + \epsilon_{i,t}$$

where for country i in year t, $IS_{i,t}$ stands for the informal sector size as % of GDP, $E_{i,t}$ for the environmental pollution indicator we use as the dependent variable, and $X_{k_{i,t}}$ are various control variables included in the regression. Moreover, θ_i represents the country FE, γ_t the year dummies, and $\epsilon_{i,t}$ is the error term. In all of our static panel data regressions Hausman test points us in favor of an FE regression and Wooldridge test rejects absence of autocorrelation. Therefore, we allow for AR (1) disturbance in our regressions. In order for the inverse-U relationship to be supported by the data, we expect the signs of estimated coefficients of β_1 and β_2 to be positive and negative, respectively.

Once the inverse-U relationship is established, the next task is to empirically identify how the data give rise to such a relationship in the first place. As evident from descriptive and empirical literature on informality, the informal sector is mainly small-scale (especially compared to the formal sector) and uses highly labor-intensive and less capital-intensive production technology. The low level of capital intensity and the small scale of production make the informal sector less likely to cause environmental pollution, as noted by Antweiler et al. (2001). Following this reasoning, a larger (smaller) informal sector is expected to be associated with a better (worse) environmental performance or smaller (larger) amount of environmental pollution. Note that this is an indirect effect of informality on pollution through its effect on the intensity of capital. By the generally accepted and widely used definition of the informal sector, it does not comply with most, if not any government regulations. Given that these regulations include environmental laws, rules, regulations, and restrictions, a larger (smaller) informal sector is expected to be associated with a worse (better) environmental performance or larger (smaller) amount of environmental pollution. This can be interpreted as a direct effect of informality on pollution through an intrinsic factor of the informal sector, the absence of governmental regulation. Notice, too, that deregulation works in the opposite direction to scale. These two distinct effects of informality, working in opposite directions, may create a non-linear U or inverse-U relationship between informality and environmental pollution or performance if one effect is stronger than the other at some levels of the informal sector size but vice versa at other levels. Specifically, a hypothesized inverse-U relationship suggests that for smaller informal sectors, a marginal increase (reduction) in size is associated with an increase (reduction) in pollution. However, beyond a threshold size, this relationship is reversed. For this non-linearity to hold, we need to understand whether the relative strengths of deregulation and scale effects depend on the size of the informal sector.

To account for a possible non-linear relationship, one should first identify the factors that create variation in informal sector size such as tax levels, tax enforcement, and institutional quality. Here, I use tax enforcement, tax burden, and the bureaucratic quality and corruption control indices to explain the variation in informal sector size. If these factors create a variation in informal sector size and therefore capital intensity, then they might provide an account of a possible non-linear relationship in a multivariate framework.

I estimate the following system:

$$E_{i,t} = \beta_{1_0} + \beta_{1_1} IS_{i,t} + \beta_{1_2} K_{i,t} + \sum_{k=3}^{n} \beta_{1_k} X_{k_{i,t}} + \epsilon_{1_{i,t}}$$

$$K_{i,t} = \beta_{2_0} + \beta_{2_1} IS_{i,t} + \beta_{2_2} IS^2_{i,t} + \sum_{k=3}^{n} \beta_{2_k} Z_{k_{i,t}} + \epsilon_{2_{i,t}}$$

$$IS_{i,t} = \beta_{3_0} + \sum_{k=1}^{n} \beta_{3_k} V_{k_{i,t}} + \epsilon_{3_{i,t}}$$

where for country i in year t, E stands for the environmental pollution indicator, IS for the informal sector size as a percentage of GDP, K for capital-output ratio, $Z_{k_{i,t}}$ for exogenous variables that potentially affect capital, and $V_{k_{i,t}}$ for exogenous variables that create a variation in informal sector size.

The hypothesized deregulation and scale effects manifest themselves in the estimated coefficients of the first two equations. Specifically, keeping the deregulation effect in mind, we expect the estimated coefficient of β_{1_1} to be positive. Also, notice that this effect, if it exists, is linear. On the other hand, the scale effect will be observed in the estimated coefficients of β_{1_2}, β_{2_1}, and β_{2_1} which we expect to be positive, negative, and negative, respectively. Through the scale effect, the informal sector size is expected to reduce capital-output ratio and therefore also pollution at an increasing rate. Joint with the deregulation effect the systems has the potential to create the inverse-U relationship between informality and pollution.

In the cited paper, we used three different indicators of environmental pollution. First two of these are CO_2 and SO_2 emissions per capita which are widely used in the pollution literature. Moreover, we also use a third measure, namely the Energy Use Intensity (EUI) Index. As control variables, we use GDP per capita and its square (to control for the environmental Kuznets curve (EKC) hypothesis) and its growth rate (denoted by growth), government spending to GDP ratio (denoted by government exp.), capital-output ratio (denoted by capital), TFP (denoted by productivity) and four institutional measures, namely corruption control, bureaucratic quality, law and order, and democratic accountability indices.

Table 6.18 Complete Data Set Summary Statistics

	Mean	*Std. Deviation*	*Minimum*	*Maximum*
CO_2	4.22	6.92	0.01	101.05
SO_2	0.02	0.02	0.00	0.23
EUI	2201.84	2791.90	9.54	40710.11

Data for CO_2[13] and SO_2[14] were obtained from United Nations Statistics Division's (UNSD) Environmental Indicators while data for EUI[15] were obtained from the World Bank's WDI databases. Informal sector size data came from Buehn and Schneider (2012). In this study, I extend the analysis using up-to-date data from Elgin et al. (2019). Data for the law and order, corruption control (shortly corruption), bureaucratic quality (shortly bureaucracy), and democratic accountability (shortly democracy) indexes came from ICRG. Data for government spending and GDP per capita are obtained from PWT. Capital-output ratio is estimated with perpetual inventory method by using PWT 9.1. Finally, (total factor) productivity is estimated assuming a Cobb-Douglas production function and using PWT 9.1. Summary statistics for the environmental variables used in the regressions are given in Table 6.18. The remaining variables are the same as used in previous chapters, and were therefore not repeated here for the sake of space.

Estimation results

Using (highly) unbalanced panel data from 1960 to 2014 for 160 countries, I conduct panel regressions for the three pollution variables CO_2, SO_2 emissions per capita, and EUI as the relevant dependent variable. Tables 6.19–6.21 present the outputs of these estimations.

Table 6.19 shows that the estimated coefficients of informal sector size and squared informal sector size are significantly positive and negative, respectively. This result suggests that there is an inverted-U shaped relationship between the informal sector size and CO_2, while CO_2 is positively and significantly correlated with productivity, capital-output ratio, and government expenditure. Furthermore, CO_2 is negatively and significantly correlated with rule of law.

The relationship between SO_2 and the informal sector size has also the shape of an inverted-U. Moreover, SO_2 is positively and significantly correlated with productivity. SO_2 is also negatively and significantly correlated with democracy and GDP growth.

The relationship between EUI and the informal sector size is similar to the cases of CO_2 and SO_2. Furthermore, EUI is positively and significantly correlated with capital, GDP, and openness. EUI is also negatively and significantly correlated with law.

Overall, the positive and significant coefficient for *informal*, together with the negative and significant coefficient for informal^2, indicates the existence of an inverse-U shaped relationship between informality and environmental

Table 6.19 CO_2 Emissions and Shadow Economy

(Dependent Variable: CO_2)	*(1)*	*(2)*	*(3)*	*(4)*	*(5)*	*(6)*	*(7)*	*(8)*	*(9)*
Informal	0.49*	0.48*	0.51*	0.20**	0.22**	0.23**	0.25**	0.26*	0.33*
	(0.04)	(0.04)	(0.04)	(0.11)	(0.12)	(0.13)	(0.13)	(0.07)	(0.09)
$Informal^2$	−0.01*	−0.01*	−0.02*	−0.02*	−0.02*	−0.02*	−0.02*	−0.03*	−0.03*
	(0.00)	(0.00)	(0.00)	(0.01)	(0.01)	(0.01)	(0.01)	(0.01)	(0.01)
Law		−0.20*	−0.21*	−0.21*	−0.22*	−0.22*	−0.21*	−0.22*	−0.22*
		(0.07)	(0.07)	(0.06)	(0.06)	(0.06)	(0.06)	(0.07)	(0.07)
Democracy			0.05	0.09	0.07	0.07	0.08	0.08	0.09
			(0.29)	(0.27)	(0.27)	(0.27)	(0.25)	(0.23)	(0.23)
Productivity				0.01*	0.01*	0.01*	0.01*	0.01*	0.01*
				(0.00)	(0.00)	(0.00)	(0.00)	(0.00)	(0.00)
Capital					0.77*	0.76*	0.75*	0.79*	0.74*
					(0.08)	(0.08)	(0.07)	(0.07)	(0.09)
Growth						−0.01	−0.01	−0.01	−0.01
						(0.19)	(0.20)	(0.20)	(0.21)
Corruption							−0.08	−0.07	−0.03
							(0.10)	(0.11)	(0.12)
Bureaucracy							−0.03	−0.03	−0.01
							(0.68)	(0.67)	(0.62)
Gdp								−0.01	−0.01
								(0.12)	(0.19)
Gdp^2								0.00	0.00
								(0.44)	(0.45)
Gov. exp.									0.04*
									(0.01)
Overall R-sq	0.31	0.32	0.32	0.34	0.36	0.37	0.38	0.39	0.40
Observations	2144	2141	2141	2141	2141	2141	2141	2141	2141
F-test	0.00	0.00	0.00	0.00	0.00	0.00	0.00	0.00	0.00

Robust standard errors are reported in parentheses. ** and * denote 5% and 1% confidence levels, respectively.

Table 6.20 SO_2 Emissions and Shadow Economy

(Dependent Variable: SO_2)

	(1)	*(2)*	*(3)*	*(4)*	*(5)*	*(6)*	*(7)*	*(8)*	*(9)*
Informal	0.04*	0.04*	0.04*	0.03*	0.03*	0.03*	0.03*	0.03*	0.03*
	(0.00)	(0.01)	(0.01)	(0.01)	(0.01)	(0.01)	(0.01)	(0.01)	(0.01)
$Informal^2$	−0.01*	−0.01*	−0.01*	−0.01**	−0.01*	−0.01*	−0.01*	−0.01*	−0.01*
	(0.00)	(0.00)	(0.00)	(0.00)	(0.00)	(0.00)	(0.00)	(0.00)	(0.00)
Law		−0.01	−0.02	−0.02	−0.03	−0.04	−0.04	−0.06	−0.10
		(0.24)	(0.24)	(0.27)	(0.29)	(0.29)	(0.29)	(0.28)	(0.28)
Democracy			−0.03	−0.04	−0.06	−0.07	−0.08	−0.08	−0.09
			(0.14)	(0.15)	(0.16)	(0.17)	(0.17)	(0.17)	(0.15)
Productivity				0.02	0.01	0.02	0.02	0.03**	0.03**
				(0.02)	(0.02)	(0.02)	(0.02)	(0.02)	(0.02)
Capital					0.03	0.02	0.02	0.02	0.02
					(0.13)	(0.15)	(0.14)	(0.18)	(0.17)
Growth						0.01	0.01	0.01	0.01***
						(0.01)	(0.01)	(0.01)	(0.01)
Corruption							−0.04	−0.04	−0.04
							(0.74)	(0.72)	(0.72)
Bureaucracy							0.02	0.03	0.04
							(0.25)	(0.26)	(0.26)
Gdp								−0.01	−0.01
								(0.20)	(0.21)
Gdp^2								0.00	0.00
								(0.32)	(0.29)
Gov. exp.									0.01
									(0.47)
Overall R-sq	0.06	0.06	0.07	0.07	0.07	0.07	0.07	0.08	0.08
Observations	1839	1836	1836	1836	1836	1836	1836	1836	1836
F-test	0.00	0.00	0.00	0.00	0.00	0.00	0.00	0.00	0.00

Robust standard errors are reported in parentheses. *, **, and *** denote 1%, 5%, and 10% confidence levels, respectively.

Table 6.21 EUI Emissions and Shadow Economy

(Dependent Variable: Energy Use Intensity)	*(1)*	*(2)*	*(3)*	*(4)*	*(5)*	*(6)*	*(7)*	*(8)*	*(9)*
Informal	190.21*	326.30*	325.28*	261.81*	259.04*	259.05*	260.54*	180.17*	182.21*
	(12.21)	(12.39)	(17.12)	(15.14)	(18.69)	(21.21)	(24.18)	(20.90)	(25.12)
$Informal^2$	−2.65*	−2.76*	−2.71*	−2.92*	−2.93*	−2.90*	−2.65*	−2.39*	−2.08*
	(0.18)	(0.15)	(0.10)	(0.08)	(0.07)	(0.07)	(0.07)	(0.06)	(0.06)
Law		−19.77*	−20.01*	−21.32*	−20.19*	−20.62*	−20.35*	−22.17*	−25.30*
		(1.19)	(1.19)	(1.20)	(1.24)	(1.27)	(1.29)	(1.30)	(1.18)
Democracy			4.007	6.239	3.404	3.597	3.157	3.807	4.503
			(0.862)	(0.791)	(0.885)	(0.879)	(0.894)	(0.872)	(0.853)
Productivity				1.20*	1.18*	1.27*	1.39*	0.90**	0.84**
				(0.27)	(0.02)	(0.26)	(0.26)	(0.43)	(0.41)
Capital					232.37*	240.58*	241.72*	233.91*	200.12
					(21.38)	(21.55)	(20.89)	(20.65)	(21.20)
Growth						0.33	0.36	0.44	0.41
						(0.43)	(0.42)	(0.48)	(0.71)
Corruption							8.37	9.21	7.39
							(6.65)	(6.70)	(5.73)
Bureaucracy							1.17	1.19	1.12
							(1.02)	(0.98)	(0.96)
Gdp								0.17	0.20
								(0.03)	(0.04)
Gdp^2								−0.02	−0.03
								(0.17)	(0.16)
Gov. exp.									4.66*
									(0.79)
Overall R-sq	0.32	0.32	0.33	0.35	0.37	0.37	0.37	0.38	0.39
Observations	2173	2170	2170	2170	2170	2170	2170	2170	2170
F-test	0.00	0.00	0.00	0.00	0.00	0.00	0.00	0.00	0.00

Robust standard errors are reported in parentheses. * and ** denote 1% and 5% confidence levels, respectively.

pollution/energy use. High and low levels of informality correspond to low levels of pollution while middle levels of informality correspond to high levels of pollution. Moreover, law and order reduces pollution, and capital increases it. We should also notice that in addition to the clearly identified inverted-U relationships, we can also observe from the estimation results that the peaks of the inverted-U curves occur at around 40–55% of shadow economy size, depending on the specific regression and the dependent variable. These are the points at which the pollution and energy use are maximized with respect to the size of the informal sector.

System estimations

The results of the system estimations presented in Tables 6.22 and 6.23 show that both informal sector size and capital-output ratio (shortly capital) are

Table 6.22 CO_2, Capital and Informal Sector: Systems Estimations

	OLS			*GMM*		
Dependent Variable	*CO_2*	*Capital*	*Informal*	*CO_2*	*Capital*	*Informal*
Informal	0.70*	−0.21*		0.67*	−0.27**	
	(0.18)	(0.06)		(0.24)	(0.13)	
Informal^2		−0.02*			−0.02**	
		(0.01)			(0.01)	
Capital	1.01*			1.10*		
	(0.23)			(0.27)		
Democracy	−0.51*			−0.48**		
	(0.16)			(0.25)		
GDP	0.07*			0.08*		
	(0.02)			(0.02)		
GDP^2	−0.001*			−0.001*		
	(0.000)			(0.000)		
Pop. Density	−0.02			−0.02		
	(0.04)			(0.05)		
Growth		0.01		0.06		
		(0.08)			(0.10)	
Gov. Exp.		−0.22			−0.27	
		(0.32)			(0.19)	
Enforcement			−1.33*			−1.36*
			(0.38)			(0.25)
Corruption			−0.40			−0.30
			(0.56)			(0.36)
Bureaucracy			−5.01*			−3.12*
			(0.45)			(0.32)
Tax			0.03			−0.02
			(0.03)			(0.02)
R-squared	0.48	0.42	0.49	0.49	0.62	0.51
Observations	2141	2140	2140	2001	2001	1970

Standard errors are in parentheses. ** and * denote 5% and 1% confidence levels, respectively. In all regressions, a constant is also included but not reported.

Table 6.23 SO_2, Capital and Informal Sector: Systems Estimations

	OLS			GMM		
Dependent *Variable*	SO_2	*Capital*	*Informal*	SO_2	*Capital*	*Informal*
Informal	0.25**	−0.25***		0.31***	−0.26***	
	(0.11)	(0.05)			(0.07)	(0.06)
Informal²		−0.03***			−0.02**	
		(0.01)				(0.01)
Capital	0.78***			0.31***		
	(0.19)			(0.04)		
Democracy	−0.04**			−0.04		
	(0.02)			(0.04)		
GDP	0.01***			0.02***		
	(0.003)			(0.004)		
Openness	0.01			0.003***		
	(0.01)			(0.001)		
GDP²	−0.00007*			−0.0005***		
	(0.00001)			(0.0001)		
Pop. Density	−0.001			−0.01		
	(0.001)			(0.007)		
Growth		0.21***			0.31***	
		(0.06)			(0.12)	
Gov. Exp.		−0.16			−0.17	
		(0.16)			(0.11)	
Enforcement			−1.18***			−1.05***
			(0.39)			(0.29)
Corruption			0.35			−0.34
			(0.48)			(0.29)
Bureaucracy			−5.98***			−2.99***
			(0.75)			(0.40)
Tax			0.05			−0.04
			(0.06)			(0.04)
R-squared	0.13	0.24	0.55	0.19	0.28	0.49
Observations	1104	1588	982	953	1438	832

Standard errors are in parentheses. *, **, and *** denote 1%, 5%, and 10% confidence levels, respectively. In all regressions, a constant is also included but not reported.

positively correlated with environmental pollution while capital is negatively correlated with informal sector size, and informal sector size is negatively correlated with the level and enforcement of tax. Holding other variables constant, a decrease (increase) in tax enforcement affects environmental pollution through two channels. First, it induces an increase (decrease) in informal sector size and puts direct upward (downward) pressure on pollution levels, which I call the deregulation effect. Second, the induced increase (decrease) in informal sector size reduces (boosts) capital, which indirectly decreases (increases) pollution. I call this the scale effect. These opposing direct and indirect effects of changing informal sector size produce the non-linear, inverted-U relationship between informality and environmental pollution. Some variables (such as enforcement of taxes) may affect both informal and formal sector size or formal sector variables. However, notice that I measure the relative rather than absolute size of the informal economy, as a percentage of official GDP (i.e. the formal economy). Therefore, when a changing variable (e.g. enforcement) impacts informal sector size (as a percentage of GDP), it means that the size of the informal economy changes relative to (e.g. above and beyond) the formal economy. Thus, any potential effect of that variable (e.g. enforcement) on the formal economy is also accounted for.

Model

To account for the observations in the previous section, Elgin and Oztunali (2014b) also presented a two-sector DGE model with an informal sector and environmental pollution.

In this model, the representative household has the following utility function:

$$\max_{\{C_t, K_{t+1}, l_{ft}, l_{it}\}} \sum_{t=0}^{\infty} \beta^t U(C_t, E_t) \tag{6.3.14}$$

with $U_C(C_t, E_t) > 0$ and $U_E(C_t, E_t) < 0$, where E_t is the environmental pollution at time t. The representative household faces the following resource constraint:

$$C_t + K_{t+1} = (1 - \tau)\theta_f F(K_t, l_{ft}) + (1 - \rho\tau)\theta_i I(l_{it}) + T_t \tag{6.3.15}$$

where l_{ft} and l_{it} are the amounts of labor that are devoted to formal and informal sectors, respectively. $F(K_t, l_{ft})$ is the constant-returns-to-scale production technology of the formal sector, employing physical capital K_t and labor given the productivity parameter θ_F. $I(l_{it})$ is the production technology of the informal sector which exhibits diminishing returns to scale. T_t is lump-sum transfer. τ is the tax rate and $\rho \in [0, 1])$ is the level of tax enforcement. Notice that in this setup, the income from the informal sector (i.e. $\theta_i I(l_{it})$) is partially taxed by the government, depending on the value of the tax enforcement parameter ρ.

Environmental pollution E_t is an outcome of the production process. As there are two sectors producing output, E_t is defined as follows:

$$E_t = \mu_f \theta_f F(K_t, l_{ft}) + \mu_i \theta_i I(l_{it}) \tag{6.3.16}$$

where E_t is a linear combination of formal and informal outputs. μ_f is the pollution coefficient of the formal sector and μ_i is the pollution coefficient of the informal sector.

Given$\{K_0, \theta_f, \theta_i, \mu_f, \mu_i, \tau, \rho\}$, an equilibrium for this economy is an allocation $\{C_t^e, K_{t+1}^e, l_{ft}^e, l_{it}^e, E_t^e\}_{t=0}^{\infty}$ such that the social planner chooses $\{C_t^e, K_{t+1}^e, l_{ft}^e, l_{it}^e, E_t^e\}_{t=0}^{\infty}$ to solve the following problem:

$$\max_{\{C_t, K_{t+1}, l_{ft}, l_{it}\}} \sum_{t=0}^{\infty} \beta^t U(C_t, E_t) \tag{6.3.17}$$

$$\text{subject to} \quad \begin{aligned} & C_t + K_{t+1} = (1-\tau)\theta_f F(K_t, l_{ft}) + (1-\rho\tau)\theta_i I(l_{it}) + T_t \\ & E_t = \mu_f \theta_f F(K_t, l_{ft}) + \mu_i \theta_i I(l_{it}) \\ & l_{ft} + l_{it} = 1 \\ & \text{given } K_0, \mu_f, \mu_i \\ & C_t > 0 \end{aligned}$$

The social planner in this economy maximizes the utility function by choosing optimal consumption and capital levels, and allocating labor optimally to formal and informal sectors while taking into consideration the disutility from environmental pollution, as well as each sector's marginal pollution propensities.

For further characterization of the equilibrium, functional forms for utility and production functions have to be specified. These are presented in the next subsection.

An analytical solution to the social planner's problem can only be obtained if the problem is specified in the following form with a linear utility function:

$$\max_{\{C_t, K_{t+1}, l_{ft}, l_{it}\}} \sum_{t=0}^{\infty} \beta^t [C_t - \eta E_t] \tag{6.3.18}$$

$$\text{subject to} \quad \begin{aligned} & C_t + K_{t+1} = (1-\tau)\theta_f K_t^{\alpha}(1-l_{it})^{1-\alpha} + (1-\rho\tau)\theta_i l_{it}^{\gamma} + T_t \\ & E_t = \mu_f \theta_f K_t^{\alpha}(1-l_{it})^{1-\alpha} + \mu_i \theta_i l_{it}^{\gamma} \\ & \text{given } K_0, \mu_f, \mu_i \\ & C_t > 0 \end{aligned}$$

Imposition of steady state to the first-order conditions of the social planner's problem yields:

$$K^* = (1 - l_i^*)\Big[\beta\alpha\theta_f[(1-\tau) - \eta\mu_f]\Big]^{\frac{1}{1-\alpha}} \tag{6.3.19}$$

According to (6.3.19), the steady state capital level is negatively related to the steady state informal labor level.

Moreover, one can also obtain:

$$l_i^* = \left[\frac{\gamma\theta_i[(1-\rho\tau) - \eta\mu_i]}{[(1-\tau) - \eta\mu_f](1-\alpha)\theta_f(\beta\alpha\theta_f[(1-\tau) - \eta\mu_f])^{\frac{\alpha}{1-\alpha}}}\right]^{\frac{1}{1-\gamma}} \tag{6.3.20}$$

The steady state informal labor level is negatively related to the coefficient of tax enforcement on the informal sector ρ, the coefficient of disutility from pollution η, and informal sector's marginal pollution propensity μ_i, while it is positively related to informal sector's TFP and the decreasing return to scale parameter γ.

Finally, the steady state pollution level can be expressed as follows:

$$E^* = \mu_f\theta_f\left[\beta\alpha\theta_f[(1-\tau)-\eta\mu_f]\right]^{\frac{\alpha}{1-\alpha}}(1-l_i^*)+\mu_i\theta_i l_i^{*\gamma} \tag{6.3.21}$$

Here, the steady state environmental pollution level depends on the steady state informal labor level, both sectors' TFPs and marginal pollution propensities. Equation (6.3.21) also clearly illustrates the deregulation and scale effects of informality on pollution. The first term in this equation is simply a linear function capital stock and the second term is simply a linear function of informal output. Therefore, one can observe the deregulation effect in the second term and the scale effect in the first term.

The derivative of the steady state environmental pollution with respect to steady state informal labor is the following:

$$\frac{dE^*}{dl_i^*} = -\mu_f\theta_f\left[\beta\alpha\theta_f[(1-\tau)-\eta\mu_f]\right]^{\frac{\alpha}{1-\alpha}} + \mu_i\theta_i\gamma\left[\frac{[(1-\tau)-\eta\mu_f](1-\alpha)\theta_f(\beta\alpha\theta_f[(1-\tau)-\eta\mu_f])^{\frac{\alpha}{1-\alpha}}}{\gamma\theta_i[(1-\rho\tau)-\eta\mu_i]}\right] \tag{6.3.22}$$

As it can be observed from equation (6.3.22), the sign of dE^*/dl_i^* depends on the parameter for tax enforcement ρ since the positive second term is positively related to ρ. As a result, in a setting where dE^*/dl_i^* is initially positive, a decrease in ρ decreases dE^*/dl_i^*. After a threshold level of ρ, dE^*/dl_i^* becomes negative and this creates an inverse-U shaped relationship between E^* and l_i^*, in line with the empirical results presented earlier.

Numerical simulations

The simplified case with linear utility presented earlier can provide analytical results to help relate pollution to informal sector size. In this subsection, the aim is to obtain similar results after dropping the linear utility assumption in favor of a more general utility function that is strictly concave in both of its arguments.

Specifically, the social planner's problem now becomes the following:

$$\max_{\{C_t,K_{t+1},l_{ft},l_{it}\}} \sum_{t=0}^{\infty}\beta^t[\log(C_t)-\eta\frac{E_t^{\phi}}{\phi}] \tag{6.3.23}$$

$$\begin{aligned}\text{subject to}\quad & C_t+K_{t+1}-(1-\delta)K_t=(1-\tau)\theta_f K_t^{\alpha}(1-l_{it})^{1-\alpha}\\ & \qquad +(1-\rho\tau)\theta_i l_{it}^{\gamma}+T_t\\ & E_t=\mu_f\theta_f K_t^{\alpha}(1-l_{it})^{1-\alpha}+\mu_i\theta_i l_{it}^{\gamma}\\ & \text{given } K_0,\mu_f,\mu_i\\ & C_t>0,\eta>0,\phi>1\end{aligned}$$

Unfortunately, without further simplification, because an analytical solution to this problem is unobtainable, I have to rely on numerical simulations.

To evaluate the performance of the model we normalize μ_f to unity and experiment a set of values for μ_i. The simulation below uses the value $\mu_i = 1.98$ as we try to match the average informal sector size in the data set we use in the empirical section, i.e. we try to match $\frac{\theta_i I(l_{it})}{\theta_f F(K_t, l_{ft})}$=34.60%. The values for η and ϕ are 1 and 2, respectively. For other parameters, we use the values specified in Ihrig and Moe (2004). These are $\alpha = 0.33$, $\gamma = 0.495$, $\beta = 0.96$, $\theta_F = 2.10$, $\theta_i = 55.30$, $\tau = 0.093$, and $\delta = 0.08$.

Once we decide on these values for the parameters, we start to vary ρ from 1 to 0, i.e. reduce the tax enforcement parameter to create a variation in informal labor and hence informal sector size. The result of the simulation given in Figure 6.15 shows that there is an inverse-U relationship between steady state pollution and informal labor in the general case. Notice that this is in line with our empirical analysis in the previous section of the chapter.

The suggested non-linear relationship between the informal sector size and pollution has important policy consequences. In this section we focus on two specific policy tools which can be easily used within theoretical model presented in the previous section. These are varying the tax burden (τ) and the level of tax enforcement (ρ). Specifically, we study the behavior of steady state environmental pollution with respect to changes in tax levels and the level of tax enforcement with the parameters set earlier. Other than the fixed parameters as specified in the previous subsection, we vary τ and ρ and note the

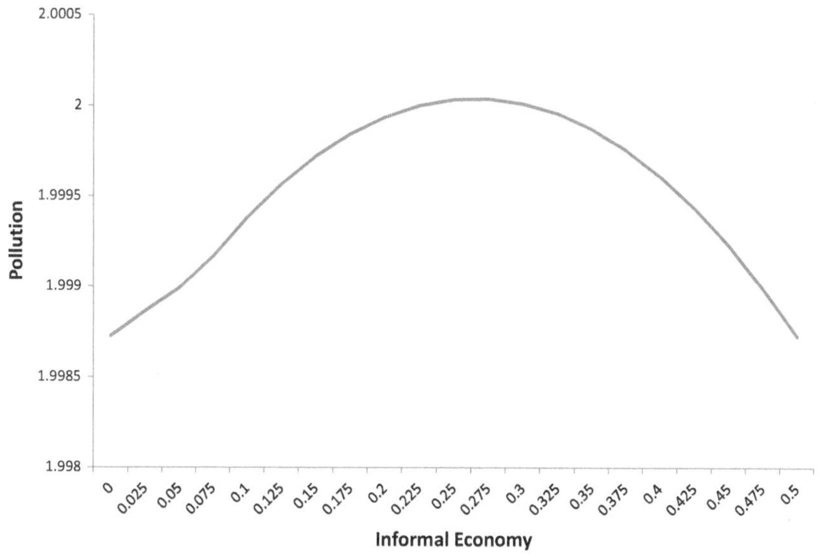

Figure 6.15 Pollution versus informality.

Table 6.24 Varying Taxes while holding enforcement constant ($\rho = 0$)

Tax rate (τ)	*0.00*	*0.10*	*0.20*	*0.30*	*0.40*
%Δ in Capital (K)	0.17	−0.05	−0.30	−0.52	−0.75
%Δ in Real GDP (Y)	0.10	−0.04	−0.19	−0.42	−0.80
%Δ in Informal Output (Y_i/Y)	−0.20	0.01	0.27	0.55	2.10
%Δ in Pollution (E)	−0.04	0.02	0.10	−0.16	−0.23

Percentage deviation from the initial steady state value.

Table 6.25 Varying Enforcement while holding taxes constant ($\tau = 0.093$)

Enforcement (ρ)	*0.05*	*0.10*	*0.25*	*0.5*	*0.75*	*2*
%Δ in Capital (K)	0.01	0.02	0.04	0.10	0.47	0.79
%Δ in Real GDP (Y)	0.01	0.02	0.04	0.06	0.08	0.11
%Δ in Informal Output (Y_i/Y)	−0.02	−0.06	−0.14	−0.27	−0.39	−0.57
%Δ in Pollution (E)	0.01	0.03	0.06	0.02	−0.01	−0.29

Percentage deviation from the initial steady state value.

behavior of various endogenous variables in percentage deviations from their steady state levels. The results of policy changes with respect to the level and enforcement of taxes are presented in Tables 6.24 and 6.25, respectively.

Table 6.24 shows the effect of varying the tax rate between 0 and 40% instead of keeping it constant at $\tau = 0.093$, as in the previous analysis. It shows how the variables differ from their steady state values with $\tau = 0.093$. Unsurprisingly, increasing τ not surprisingly reduces both capital stock and formal GDP while expanding the size of the informal sector. The effect on pollution however is non-linear. A similar result is obtained in Table 6.25 when we vary ρ. The effect is strongest if ρ is allowed to take a value greater than 1. Comparing the two policy tools, we can see that increasing tax enforcement is more effective than raising taxes. However, one should definitely consider the presence of non-linearities when using this policy to reduce pollution. For example, if tax enforcement is not sufficiently strengthened, it can actually aggravate pollution instead of reducing it. Nevertheless, in contrast to increasing the level of taxes, increasing the level of tax enforcement does not reduce real GDP or boost the informal economy. Moreover, from a policy perspective, varying enforcement is much easier than varying taxes as the latter requires a lengthier political process than the former.

6.3.5 Corporate social responsibility

Corporate social responsibility (CSR) has attracted an enormous amount of investment by the firms in the last three decades (Kolk, 2008). However, despite extensive research, the literature has so far failed to generate a consensus regarding the measurements, determinants, and effects of CSR. Several questions remain open, even such basic ones as whether or how CSR is related to firms' growth or financial performance (Lindgreen et al., 2009). Moreover, the empirical literature indicates that both the effects and determinants of CSR may be wrongly specified because relevant variables are ignored in the analysis (McWilliams and Siegel, 2000). There is extensive evidence that the CSR differs across countries (Matten and Moon, 2008). However, most CSR research has so far focused on practices in advanced economies while the CSR literature very much lacks comprehensive analyses on micro, small, and medium enterprises, which are particularly prevalent in developing economies (Spence, 1999; Utting, 2007) as they constitute a large fraction of the informal sector.

Small and medium-sized enterprises (SMEs) have specific characteristics that distinguish them from large corporations. While these vary across countries and cultures, they are generally independent, multi-tasking, cash-limited, based on personal relationships and informality (for a deep understanding of these SMEs peculiarities, see Vyakarnam et al., 1997; Spence, 1999), as well as actively managed by the owners, highly personalized, largely local in area of operation, and largely dependent on internal sources to finance growth (Vyakarnam et al., 1997). These characteristics are all expected to lead to lower CSR scores for these firms.

Investment in CSR promotes product innovation and differentiation at both product and firm levels. That is, some firms will produce goods or services with characteristics that signal to the consumer that the company is concerned about certain social issues (McWilliams et al., 2006; Thauer, 2014). Many companies will also try to establish a socially responsible corporate image. Both strategies will encourage consumers to believe that, by consuming the company's product, they are directly or indirectly supporting this image. However, it is expected that informal firms are less likely to be concerned about this image as they tend to be less open to innovation and differentiation, instead using their informality mostly to cut costs. They also tend to rely less on consumer loyalty, brand names, and reputations. Therefore, it is expected that informal firms invest significantly less in advertising and R&D as these activities are less correlated with their future performance than for formal firms. Based on the earlier discussion, I hypothesize the following:

1 The degree to which a firm is engaged in informal economic activities is negatively correlated with its CSR score.
2 A firm's expected growth (e.g. in revenue) is positively correlated with its CSR score, although this correlation significantly interacts with informality. Specifically, informality is expected to reduce the positive correlation between CSR and a firm's expected growth.
3 Advertising and R&D expenditures of a firm are positively (negatively) correlated with a firm's CSR score (tendency to engage in informal economic activities).

Country-level CSR scores are obtained for 73 countries[16] from the CSRHUB website. CSRHUB collects firm-level data for a wide cross-sectional range of

Table 6.26 Summary Statistics

	Mean	*Std. Dev.*	*Minimum*	*Maximum*
CSR	52.49	5.55	42.0	66.0
Informal Sector Size (% of GDP)	23.89	11.94	7.92	61.50
Developed Economy Dummy	0.34	0.48	0.00	1.00
GDP per capita (thousand USD)	24.85	23.83	0.61	105.86
Law and Order	4.11	1.26	1.50	6.00
Investment Profile	9.06	1.86	4.00	12.00
Latitude	33.43	16.38	1.28	64.13

economies. However, for various countries, the number of firms surveyed is quite small. In these cases, aggregate country-level CSR scores are not available, which is why the data set only includes 73 countries. The informal sector size data come from Elgin et al. (2019). For the IV regressions, I also use the following control variables: GDP per capita, a dummy for developed economies, the investment profile and law and order indices from the ICRG, latitude, a presidential regime dummy, and dummies for type of law (British, French, German, Scandinavian, or Post-Socialist). Table 6.26 presents the descriptive summary statistics of the cross-country data set.

Description of the firm-level survey

The firm-level survey was conducted in June 2018, covering 1,000 representative firms in Turkey. The surveys (via phone) were conducted with the top management representatives of each firm (owner, CEO, CFO, or general manager/director). Prior to the survey, every effort was made to ensure that the surveyed firms are generally representative of the Turkish economy across various dimensions such as geographical location, size (both in revenue and workforce), and sectoral composition.

Table 6.27 presents three categories of descriptive summary statistics of the firm-level data set, including the variables used to measure informality and the control variables. The first category is firm-specific variables not directly related to informality and CSR. The second gives information about the extent of the firms' informal tendencies while the third measures firm managers' sectoral informality.

The six variables in the first category are expected percentage growth of revenue for the next year, age of firm (in years), a dummy variable for family firms (which are quite common in Turkey), number of employees working full or part-time, and R&D and advertising expenditure as percentages of total revenue.

The second category measures the informality tendencies of each firm. Four dummies are used: whether the firm has unlimited liability, whether the firm is registered with a professional or trade chamber,[17] whether the firm has a bank account, and whether the firm pays all wages[18] to a bank account. This

Table 6.27 Descriptive Statistics

	Mean	*Std. Dev.*	*Minimum*	*Maximum*
Firm-Specific Questions				
Revenue Gr. (%)	8.99	17.65	−10.00	75.00
Firm age (years)	13.89	13.81	0.00	45.00
Family origin (dummy)	0.28	0.45	0.00	1.00
Number of employees	110.01	691.22	1.00	9500
R&D spending (% revenue)	0.03	0.03	0.00	0.15
Advertising spending (% revenue)	0.05	0.03	0.00	0.16
Firm-Level Informality Questions				
Company type: unlimited (dummy)	0.40	0.44	0.00	1.00
Registered to a chamber (dummy)	0.89	0.14	0.00	1.00
Firm's bank account (dummy)	0.94	0.10	0.00	1.00
Wage through bank (dummy)	0.45	0.48	0.00	1.00
Number. public fines	0.41	1.27	0.00	15.00
Soc. security-wage ratio (%)	0.36	0.15	0.05	0.55
Informal value added in firm (%)	22.44	22.78	0.00	90.00
Workers without insurance in firm (%)	31.80	32.11	0.00	100.00
Workers with under-insurance in firm (%)	30.71	30.01	0.00	100.00
Seasonal employment (0–10 scale)	2.74	2.27	0.00	10.00
Tax under-reporting (0–10 scale)	3.86	3.19	0.00	10.00
Fake receipts (0–10 scale)	2.99	2.27	0.00	10.00
Buy without receipt (0–10 scale)	2.16	1.71	0.00	10.00
Sell without receipt (0–10 scale)	2.02	2.16	0.00	10.00
Illegal water/electricity use (0–10 scale)	1.16	2.40	0.00	10.00
Work without overtime (0–10 scale)	4.09	3.69	0.00	10.00
Lower than min. wage (0–10 scale)	2.88	3.35	0.00	10.00
Adverse work conditions (0–10 scale)	2.65	2.04	0.00	10.00
Sectoral Informality Perceptions				
Informal value added in own sector (%)	25.81	23.30	0.00	100.00
Workers without insurance in own sector (%)	32.64	30.38	0.00	100.00
Workers with under-insurance in own sector (%)	31.57	30.13	0.00	100.00
Seasonal employment (0–10 scale)	3.66	3.37	0.00	10.00
Tax under-reporting (0–10 scale)	4.86	3.49	0.00	10.00
Fake receipts (0–10 scale)	3.14	3.03	0.00	10.00
Buy without receipt (0–10 scale)	3.46	3.11	0.00	10.00
Sell without receipt (0–10 scale)	3.44	3.17	0.00	10.00
Illegal water/electricity use (0–10 scale)	2.25	2.91	0.00	10.00
Work without overtime (0–10 scale)	4.72	3.69	0.00	10.00
Lower than min. wage (0–10 scale)	3.15	3.39	0.00	10.00
Adverse work conditions (0–10 scale)	3.85	3.42	0.00	10.00

firm-informality category includes five further variables: first, the number of fines (whether from central or local government) issued to the firm within the last calendar year; second, the ratio of the total social security payments of the firm's workers to total wage payments (which I predict is inversely proportional to informality); informal value added as a percentage of total value added in the last calendar year; and the percentages of uninsured (contrary to legal requirements) and under-insured workers. The third category has nine variables (on a 0–10 scale) to measure managerial practices that are generally seen as indicators of informality: extent of seasonal employment, underreporting taxes, issuing fake receipts, making purchases and sales without issuing formal receipts, using illegally supplied water and electricity, requiring workers to work overtime without legally required overtime payments, paying wages below the minimum wage, and having adverse work conditions.

The third category includes most of the variables in the previous category. However, the survey questions ask managers to report the extent of these informal practices in their firm's main sector. It is generally accepted that firm representatives feel more comfortable answering questions regarding their firm's sector rather than their own firm specifically. Unsurprisingly, therefore almost all the means for sectoral perception variables are higher than for firm-specific questions.

Table 6.28 reports the summary statistics of all the variables used to calculate CSR, which is assumed to have social, environmental, and economic dimensions. All variable values are based on responses from surveyed firm managers, a 10-point Likert scale (0 = total disagreement; 10 = total agreement). These measures of CSR closely follow those used by Turker (2009a, 2009b) and Gallardo-Vazquez and Sanchez-Hernandez (2014).

Using these variables, I run different SEMs to construct indices of informality and CSR. I choose to use SEM as it allows me to model the relationships of different potential predictor variables and latent dependent variables such as the CSR or informality. Although I do not exclude questions with factor loadings less than 0.60, I eliminated several questions to rule out cross-loading. Finally, to validate the proposed scales, I also test the item, construct, convergent, and discriminant validities of the indices (see Fornell and Larcker (1981) for technical details and Gallardo-Vazquez and Sanchez-Hernandez (2014) for an application of SEM to CSR).

I construct two different informality measures based on the managers' responses. The first is based on their responses about their own firm (denoted by IS1) while the second is based on their sectoral perceptions (denoted by IS2).

Cross-country regression results are reported in Table 6.29. The first five columns report the OLS regression results with heteroskedasticity-corrected standard errors. The last column reports the IV estimation results, which uses latitude, presidential regime, and type of law dummies as instruments. In line with Hypothesis 1, mentioned in the second section, for all the regressions, the estimated coefficient of informal sector size (as a percentage of GDP) is negative. Moreover, ceteris paribus, aggregate CSR scores are higher in both developed countries, and those with higher scores for law and order, and investment profile.

Table 6.28 CSR Components

	Mean	*Std. Dev.*
Social Dimensions		
Support the employment of people at risk of social exclusion	7.97	2.19
Employ disabled people beyond the legal minimum	7.71	2.58
Are aware of the employees' quality of life	7.00	2.90
Have standards of health and safety beyond the legal minimum	8.36	2.25
Invest in professional development of our employees	7.80	2.31
Follow equal opportunity guidelines in every aspect	6.66	2.69
Have mechanisms for dialogue with employees	6.88	2.91
Actively work with NGOs for volunteer activities	6.11	2.38
Empower women within the company significantly	6.00	2.38
Make sufficient monetary contributions to charities	6.05	2.99
Act legally on all matters	7.11	3.01
Environmental Dimensions		
Make every effort to minimize our environmental impact	5.89	2.49
Aim to save energy in every level of production	5.72	2.68
Engage in recycling activities	4.20	2.10
Have standards of environmental protection beyond the legal minimum	4.36	4.01
Make investments for further environmental protection	5.11	2.31
Consider alternative and environmental friendly energy sources	4.10	2.69
Target sustainable growth which considers future generations	5.90	2.55
Economic Dimensions		
Ensure quality standards for our products	7.44	2.77
Ensure quality standards for our management processes	7.02	1.99
Provide customers accurate and complete information about our products	7.00	2.33
Stable relationships of collaboration and mutual benefit with our suppliers	7.89	2.25
Respond to consumer and customer complaints	8.01	1.31
Aim to get regional or national public support	5.88	2.01
Aim to avoid unfair competition	3.88	3.91
Pay taxes and fees regularly and appropriately	7.19	2.20

Firm-level evidence

The six firm-level regressions are reported in Table 6.30. The first four use CSR as the dependent variable while the remaining two use expected percentage revenue growth. The first two regressions use the two IS measures as independent variables (in addition to sectoral and city-level dummies to control for firm sector and location). The estimated coefficient of the informality index is negative in both cases, although significantly smaller for IS2. The next two regressions add firm age, the family firm dummy, and number of employees. as additional control variables but the estimated coefficients of the informality variables remain significantly negative. In the final two regressions, the informality variables have negative estimated coefficients while the CSR index has a significantly positive coefficient but the interaction term IS·CSR is negative.

Table 6.29 Cross-Country Regressions

Dep. Var.: CSR						
	OLS	*OLS*	*OLS*	*OLS*	*OLS*	*IV*
IS	−0.27**	−0.34**	−0.37**	−0.34**	−0.39**	−0.31**
	(0.14)	(0.16)	(0.16)	(0.16)	(0.16)	(0.16)
GDP per capita		0.09*	0.04***	0.02	0.02	0.01
		(0.03)	(0.03)	(0.04)	(0.04)	(0.04)
Developed			0.07*	0.06*	0.06*	0.06*
			(0.02)	(0.02)	(0.02)	(0.02)
Law&Order.				0.36**	0.41**	0.40**
				(0.17)	(0.18)	(0.18)
Inv. Profile					0.02**	0.03*
					(0.01)	(0.01)
R-squared	0.13	0.39	0.46	0.55	0.60	
Observations	73	73	73	73	73	73
F-Test	3.12	6.12	10.49	9.02	7.44	

All regressions include continental dummies. Robust standard errors are reported in parentheses. *, **, and *** denote 1%, 5%, and 10% confidence levels, respectively.

Table 6.30 Firm-level Regressions with CSR and Revenue Growth

Dep. Var.	*CSR*	*CSR*	*CSR*	*CSR*	*Rev. Gr.*	*Rev. Gr.*
IS1	−0.66*		−0.37**		−0.39**	
	(0.20)		(0.16)		(0.16)	
IS2		−0.44*		−0.34**		−0.21**
		(0.12)		(0.16)		(0.10)
CSR					0.66*	0.68*
					(0.22)	(0.22)
IS·CSR					−0.09*	−0.12*
					(0.04)	(0.03)
Firm Age			0.05***	0.06**	0.06	0.05
			(0.03)	(0.03)	(0.04)	(0.04)
Family Firm			−0.77*	−0.74*	−0.04**	−0.05***
			(0.13)	(0.12)	(0.02)	(0.02)
No. Employees			0.02*	0.01*	0.19	0.16
			(0.00)	(0.00)	(0.13)	(0.12)
R-squared	0.23	0.24	0.53	0.57	0.38	0.34
Observations	1000	1000	1000	1000	1000	1000
F-Test	0.00	0.00	0.00	0.00	0.00	0.00

All regressions include sectoral and city-level dummies. Robust standard errors are reported in parentheses. *, **, and *** denote 1%, 5%, and 10% confidence levels, respectively.

That is, the negative correlation between informality and revenue growth nears zero as CSR rises.

Overall, the results in Table 6.30 support both the hypotheses stated earlier. That is, independent of using firm-specific IS1 or sector-specific IS2 measures,

Table 6.31 System Estimations

Dep. Var.	*CSR*	*R&D*	*CSR*	*Advertising*
IS1		−0.69*		−0.99*
		(0.20)		(0.17)
R&D	1.20**		2.19*	
	(0.65)		(0.70)	
Advertising				
Firm Age	0.05**		0.06**	
	(0.02)		(0.03)	
Family Firm	−0.73*		−0.76*	
	(0.14)		(0.13)	
No. Employees	0.02*		0.02*	
	(0.00)		(0.00)	
R-squared	0.49	0.14	0.50	0.17
Observations	1000	1000	1000	1000

All regressions include sectoral and city-level dummies. Robust standard errors are reported in parentheses. * and ** denote 1% and 5% confidence levels, respectively.

the level of informal economic activity is negatively correlated with a firm's CSR score. Moreover, expected growth (e.g. in revenue) is positively correlated with a firm's CSR score, although this correlation significantly interacts with informality. Specifically, as informality tendencies rise, the positive correlation between CSR and expected growth declines.

Finally, Table 6.31 reports the results of the two system estimations to support our third hypothesis. The first regresses CSR on R&D expenditure, along with several controls, whereas the second equation regresses R&D on informality. The second conducts a similar analysis with advertising expenditure. In general, both estimations support the hypothesis that a firm's advertising and R&D expenditure are both negatively correlated with its tendency to engage in informal economic activities. This may explain why informality is negatively correlated with CSR as both R&D and advertising expenditure are positively associated with CSR.

6.3.6 Bilateral trade effects

As world markets move closer toward interdependence, the question of what contributes to trade flows between countries has become more important. A widely used methodology for estimating trade is the gravity model. This predicts that bilateral trade between two countries is proportional to the size of their economies and inversely related to the distance between them. Although the traditional version of the gravity model, introduced by Tinbergen (1963), only incorporates GDP to measure country size and bilateral distances, recent studies also control for whether factors like a common language, border, or currency, past or current colonial ties, and involvement in trade agreements impact bilateral trade. A master's thesis that I supervised (Demirci, 2016) investigated whether the presence of an informal sector promotes exports. Here, I use up-to-date data to replicate the findings of this study.

The gravity model is one of the most widely used empirical methods in international trade due to its success in providing robust estimation results. McCallum (1995), for example, uses the gravity equation while controlling for economic size and distance with interprovincial trade data. This study, which demonstrates the usefulness of the equation, suggests a "border effect" framework, implying that trade within one country far outstrips bilateral trade between two countries, even if they have very similar legal and political environments, institutional quality, and a common language. Referring to this as the "border puzzle", Anderson and van Wincoop (2003) propose a resolution by claiming that bilateral trade depends not only on bilateral characteristics but also on a multilateral resistance term. This represents both bilateral trade barriers and country-pair trade with every possible trading partner of each country.

Despite the empirical success of gravity modeling, it lacked justified theoretical foundations for decades. Since Anderson (1979), however, the theoretical framework has been elaborated through various approaches. He justifies the model in terms of Armington trade models, in which goods are differentiated by country of origin and consumers with CES preferences. Deardorff (1995) presents derivations for the gravity equation based on the Heckscher-Ohlin model. By assuming that all firms are identical, these models can predict how a representative firm may alter its export decisions according to trade costs and the demand structure.

Eaton and Kortum (2002) propose an alternative model based on Ricardian comparative advantage with many countries, which is in line with Dornbusch et al. (1977). In the model, comparative advantages stemming from productivity differences result in international trade flows. That is, micro-level firm productivity differences have an impact on trade between countries.

The seminal work of Krugman (1980) produced a model using monopolistic competition and product differentiation to explain intra-industry trade. Melitz (2003) elaborated the idea of heterogeneous firms in international trade within the framework of the general equilibrium model. The model expands the trade model of monopolistic competition developed by Krugman (1980) while also accounting for firm heterogeneity. He also introduces the idea of reallocation of resources between exporting and non-exporting firms within a sector.

Chaney (2008) extends Melitz's model by including the decisions of firms related to export destinations, enabling more detailed estimations of the structure of bilateral trade flows. Chaney (2008), Melitz and Ottaviano (2008), and Helpman et al. (2008) have shown how this framework to investigate the micro-foundations of international trade can be used for quantitative analysis.

Throughout the empirical analysis below, I use the Correlates of War Project Dyadic Trade data set, version 4.0 (Barbieri and Keshk, 2016). This data set includes bilateral trade flows as well as total national imports and exports for 1870–2014. The dyadic trade data set provides import and export data in current US dollars for country pairs.

GDP per capita data is obtained through PWT 9.1. To incorporate other control variables in the gravity equation, I use the CEPII Gravity data set for country pairs. This includes distance between countries in each pair and dummy variables for contiguity, common language, currency, legal system origin, colonial ties, and involvement in a trade agreement.

Given the main focus of investigating how the informal sector contributes to exports, I use the data set provided by Elgin et al. (2019). Table 6.32 summarizes the two key variables used in this chapter.

Gravity models have traditionally been used to estimate trade flows between countries (Anderson, 1979). Although the gravity equation is presented in multiplicative form, it is usually estimated in a log-linear form due to the computational difficulty of exponential functions. The log-linearized version of gravity is estimated using OLS techniques while assuming constant variance for error terms (homoskedasticity) or using panel regressions assuming that the variance of error terms is constant over country pairs (Herrera, 2013). However, these estimation techniques may pose problems like loss of information due to zero trade flow or inconsistent results under heteroskedasticity.

To deal with zero trade flows problems, various censoring methods have been used in the literature such as the Tobit regression, substituting small values in zero trade values, or truncated OLS. However, eliminating zero trade flows, which are mostly distributed non-randomly, means that these estimation methods may yield biased estimates and reduce efficiency (Martin and Pham, 2015).

In addition to truncation and censoring, many scholars (e.g. Matyas, 1998; Melitz, 2007) have used panel techniques that allow heterogeneity to be captured across countries. Two main techniques have been implemented for the panel regressions: FE and random effect estimators. The panel FE estimation assumes that unobserved heterogeneous components affect each pair of countries differently and are constant over time; the random effect model assumes that the unobserved heterogeneous components are strictly exogenous (Herrera, 2013).

According to Silva and Tenreyro (2006), taking the logarithm of the gravity equation alters the characteristics of the error term. To illustrate, if data have homoskedastic error terms, then the variance of the error terms remains constant over time. However, if the error terms are heteroskedastic, then they depend on the explanatory variables. Log-linearization changes the distribution of the endogenous variables, which alters the distribution of the error terms, leading to inefficient estimations. Thus, Silva and Tenreyro (2006) argue that,

Table 6.32 Summary Statistics

	Mean	*Std. Dev.*	*Minimum*	*Maximum*
Trade Share of Exporter in Importer's Total Import	0.01	0.02	0.00	1.00
Relative Informality (% of GDP)	1.25	0.82	0.07	13.39

in the presence of heteroskedasticity, the gravity equation can be estimated in multiplicative form using a simple pseudo-maximum likelihood estimation technique. This method not only provides consistent estimations but also handles the zero trade flows problem.

This study estimates the basic form of the gravity equation augmented with a wide range of dummy variables that affect trade costs, specifically the following log-linear equation:

$$\log X_{ij} = \beta_0 + \beta_1 \log Y_j + \beta_2 \log(relinf) + \beta_3 \log(distance) + \beta_4(contiguity) + \beta_5(comlang) + \beta_6(curcol) + \beta_7(gatt_i) + \beta_8(gatt_j) + \beta_9(rta) + \beta_{10}(comleg) + \beta_{11}(comcur) + \epsilon$$

where

- β_0 is an unknown constant and β_1–β_{12} are unknown coefficients
- X_{ij} is share of exports volume from country i to country j in country j's total import
- Y_j is country j's (importer) GDP per capita
- *relinf* is relative informality measuring ratio of informal sector shares of exporter country to importer country as % of GDP
- *distance* is distance between exporter and importer in kilometer
- *contiguity* is a dummy variable of having common border
- *comlang* is a dummy variable of having common language
- *curcol* is a dummy variable of having current colonial ties
- $gatt_i$ and $gatt_j$ represents GATT or WTO membership for exporter and importer countries, respectively
- *rta* stands for the existence of regional trade agreement between trading countries
- *comleg* is a dummy of having common legal origin
- *comcur* is a dummy for having common currency

Table 6.33 presents the estimation results for the various econometric techniques. To deal with the zero trade flows problem, I use simple OLS panel regressions with both FE and random effect, censored regression (Tobit), and Pseudo Poisson Maximum Likelihood (PPML) methodologies. The dependent variable in the truncated OLS and panel regressions is the logarithm of the trade share of the exporter in the importer's total imports. In the Tobit and PPML estimations, however, the gravity equation is estimated in levels.

Although the magnitudes of the parameters in the overall estimation techniques change according to the method, their signs remain constant. In line with the literature, the importer's real GDP per capita increases exports as the distance between the two countries decreases. As expected, relative informality increases exports in an economy, with positive and statistically significant coefficients for all specifications. The coefficients for the other gravity variables are also significant. A common border, language, and legal origin, GATT or WTO membership for either trade partner, and a current regional trade agreement all

Table 6.33 Estimation Results

Dep. Var.: Log of Share of Exporter in Importer's Import	*(1) OLS*	*(2) Panel Fixed*	*(3) Panel Random*	*(4) Tobit*	*(5) PPML*
Log of GDP per capita of Importer	0.55*	0.50*	0.47*	0.06*	0.11*
	(0.07)	(0.07)	(0.08)	(0.01)	(0.01)
Log of Relative Informality	1.05*	1.10*	1.07*	0.06*	0.82*
	(0.11)	(0.10)	(0.10)	(0.00)	(0.07)
Log of Distance	−0.37*	−0.31*	−0.45*	−0.001*	−0.01*
	(0.05)	(0.04)	(0.04)	(0.00)	(0.00)
Contiguity	1.54*	1.28*	1.33*	0.07*	1.10*
	(0.09)	(0.09)	(0.11)	(0.01)	(0.14)
Common Language	0.01**	0.04**	0.04**	0.002***	0.10**
	(0.00)	(0.02)	(0.02)	(0.001)	(0.05)
Current Colonial Ties	−0.364*	0.471**	0.321*	−0.006	1.056
	(0.181)	(0.148)	(0.149)	(0.018)	(0.744)
GATT or WTO membership for Exporter	0.39*	0.20*	0.18*	0.04*	0.65*
	(0.05)	(0.04)	(0.05)	(0.00)	(0.09)
GATT or WTO membership for Importer	0.42*	0.57*	0.52*	0.010*	1.10*
	(0.06)	(0.10)	(0.12)	(0.002)	(0.10)
Regional Trade Agreement in Force	1.00*	0.99*	0.82*	0.10*	0.71*
	(0.09)	(0.10)	(0.10)	(0.02)	(0.09)
Common Legal Origin	0.11*	0.19**	0.20*	0.04*	0.09*
	(0.02)	(0.02)	(0.03)	(0.01)	(0.02)
Common Currency	0.07**	0.03	0.03	0.06	0.10
	(0.04)	(0.03)	(0.03)	(0.06)	(0.09)
Observations	482901	482901	482901	758210	571488
R-squared	0.23	0.48	50		

Note: The dependent variable is the logarithm of the trade share of the exporter in the importer's total import for specifications (1)–(3).
In the last two specifications, estimation is conducted in levels.
* All panel regressions include a country fixed effect and year dummies.
* Robust standard errors are reported in parentheses. *, **, and *** denote 1%, 5%, and 10% confidence levels, respectively.
* In all regressions, a constant is also included but not reported.

significantly increase exports. The substantial differences in the estimators are seen in the coefficient magnitudes.

Specification 1 reports the results of the simple OLS regression. As discussed earlier, because it uses the logarithm of export share as the dependent variable, it excludes country pairs with zero trade flows, which is 36% of the sample. Furthermore, it does not recognize how variables change over time by specifying time or country effects.

Specifications 2 and 3 present the results for the panel regressions with random effect and FE, respectively. The results are in accordance with the literature, with positive and statistically significant coefficients for all gravity variables (except distance), and positive coefficients for relative informality. To check the adequacy of the random effect model, I conduct the Hausman test and reject the null hypothesis. Thus, the random effect model is not consistent.

Specification 4 shows the results for the Tobit estimation that modifies the dependent variable artificially to overcome the zero trade flows problem. It yields positive and significant coefficients for the importing country's GDP per capita, relative informality, and other dummy variables, as well as a negative coefficient for distance.

Specification 5 shows the Poisson estimation results. Using a PPML estimator enables zero trade flows to be included in the estimation procedure without making any artificial data modifications as in the Tobit estimation methodology. In PPML, the dependent variable is introduced in levels rather than logarithms. Although the signs are quite similar to the OLS estimations, the magnitude of the coefficients decreases substantially with PPML. According to Silva and Tenreyro (2006), heteroskedasticity explains the difference between PPML and other estimations using only positive export values. The PPML estimates indicate that the coefficient for GDP per capita of the importer country is not close to 1, as is generally stated in the literature.

6.3.7 Implications for policy-makers

Understanding the multifaceted nature of informality has been an important focus of scholars and policy-makers alike. In this chapter, I tried to reveal the different effects of informality. The major lesson here is that the policy-makers should definitely take into account the informal sector, as well as its relationship with its determinants and its effects. Designing or implementing policy while ignoring informal sector size will always be misleading.

I have tried to demonstrate that the presence of informality influences fiscal and monetary policy as well other major macroeconomic and social variables, such as unionization, growth and technological progress, the wage-productivity gap, environmental pollution, bilateral trade, and CSR. This list is not meant to be comprehensive as I am sure that there are many more effects omitted here or are still waiting identification.

Identifying the effects of informality empirically raise two related issues. First, unfortunately, as with its determinants, informal sector size is mostly endogenous when its potential effects are regressed on itself. The issue is further complicated because finding completely or nearly exogenous instruments for the informal sector is very difficult if not impossible. Some empirical studies, including mine, have used instruments like the type of the legal system, latitude, or sociocultural variables, such as linguistic fractionalization or ethnic polarization, but these are far from ideal.

Second, as should be evident from this chapter, some of the effects of informality are simultaneously its determinants, thereby creating a reverse causality between certain variables and informal sector size. As I tried to show in several chapters, one of these variables is tax rates. From an econometric perspective, dealing with reverse causality is always hard as it is one of the primary causes of endogeneity. It is also difficult to deal with in policy terms.

Notes

1 To keep the model as simple as possible we assume that households have access to as much capital they want to employ in the production at some exogenous rate r.
2 Notice that the actual size of the informal sector as percentage of formal output is given by the following expression which obviously is an increasing function of $\theta_V(i)$:

$$\frac{\int_0^{\theta_V(i)} Y_I(i)f(i)di}{\int_{\theta_V(i)}^{1} Y_F(i)f(i)di}$$

3 In all simulations the parameter values are $\alpha = 1/3$ and $r = 0.06$ while I assume $\theta(i) \sim \mathcal{N}(0, 1)$. I allow for a population of 1,000 households.
4 Setting λ to 0.75 is only for expositional purposes and does not qualitatively change the results.
5 The use of the increasing returns to scale production function is needed to achieve perpetual growth in the economy. Notice that the Dotsey and Sarte (2000) get around this problem by assuming an AK production function.
6 As we are using increasing returns to scale function for the formal sector and decreasing returns to scale function for the informal sector, one cannot exactly interpret α and γ as the labor shares.
7 For Figures 6.8 and 6.9, we set $\psi = 0.10$ as in Dotsey and Sarte (2000) and $\rho = 0.03$ as in Busato and Chiarini (2004).
8 Following the standard practice in the literature, we run three chains each of size 150,000 Metropolis-Hastings draws and discard the first 10,000 iterations.
9 For the inflation rate z, we use the average inflation rate of the corresponding country.
10 Considering that our choice of the uniform distribution might seem somewhat arbitrary, we also have experimented estimations using the beta distributions with different means ranging from 0.25 to 0.75 with standard deviations ranging from 0.05 to 0.20 and obtained qualitatively similar results with respect to the non-negativity of the estimate of ζ as well as the ranking of the estimated values of ζ for the selected economies in Table 6.6.
11 Homeownership rate measures the average % of ownership of the house one lives in.
12 I conducted further estimations to address possible two-directional causality. I also ran regressions using the IV estimator of Anderson and Hsiao (1982). These are available upon request.
13 CO_2 emissions consist of emissions from energy industry, from transport, from fuel combustion in industry, services, households, and industrial processes such as the production of cement.
14 SO_2 emissions are calculated by using fuel combustion data and sulfur content of fossil fuels used in each country.
15 EUI refers to use of primary energy before transformation to other end-use fuels, which is equal to indigenous production plus imports and stock changes, minus exports and fuels supplied to ships and aircraft engaged in international transport.
16 The website currently reports aggregate country-level statistics only for 73 economies. See https://www.csrhub.com/CSR_ratings_by_region_and_country.

17 Turkish law requires all firms to register at least for one professional or sectoral chamber. Not being registered can therefore be interpreted as an indicator of informality.
18 Paying wages and salaries by check is very uncommon in Turkey and generally there are only two commonly used ways to pay salaries and wages. These are cash and bank deposits.

References

Addison, J. T., Bryson A., Pahnke A., Teixeira, P. 2010. *Slip Sliding Away: Further Union Decline in Germany and Britain*. CEP Discussion Papers. DP0971. Centre for Economic Performance, LSE.

Amaral, P. S., Quintin, E. 2006. A Competitive Model of the Informal Sector. *Journal of Monetary Economics*. 53 (7), 1541–1553.

Amin, M. 2009. *Labor Productivity in the Informal Sector: Necessity vs. Opportunity Firms*. The World Bank, mimeo.

Anderson, J. E. 1979. A Theoretical Foundation for the Gravity Equation. *American Economic Review*. 69 (1), 106–116.

Anderson, J. E., van Wincoop, E. 2003. Gravity with Gravitas: A Solution to the Border Puzzle. *The American Economic Review*. 93 (1), 170–192.

Anderson, T. W., Hsiao, C. 1982. Formulation and Estimation of Dynamic Models using Panel Data. *Journal of Econometrics*. 18, 67–82.

Antweiler, W., Copeland, B. R., Taylor, B. R. 2001. Is Free Trade Good for the Environment? *American Economic Review*. 91 (4), 877–908.

Arellano, M., Bond, S. R. 1991. Some Specification Tests for Panel Data: Monte Carlo Evidence and an Application to Employment Equations. *Review of Economic Studies*. 58, 277–298.

Asfuroglu, D., Elgin, C. 2016. Growth Effects of Inflation under the Presence of Informality. *Bulletin of Economic Research*. 68 (4), 311–328.

Baksi, S., Bose, P. 2010. *Environmental Regulation in the Presence of an Informal Sector*. Departmental Working Papers 2010-03, The University of Winnipeg, Department of Economics.

Barbieri, K., Keshk, O. 2016. *Correlates of War Project Trade Data Set Codebook*. Version 4.0. http://correlatesofwar.org.

Barro, R. J. 1991. Economic Growth in a Cross Section of Countries. *Quarterly Journal of Economics*. 106, 407–443.

Benjamin, N. C., Mbaye, A. A. 2010. *Informality, Productivity, and Enforcement in West Africa: A Firm Level Analysis*. IPC Working Paper Series Number 100.

Birinci, S., Elgin, C. 2016. Growth and Informality: A Comprehensive Panel Data Analysis. *Journal of Applied Economics*. 19 (2), 271–292.

Blackburn, K., Pelloni, A. 2004. On the Relationship between Growth and Volatility. *Economics Letters*. 83 (1), 123–127.

Blackman, A., Bannister, G. 1998a. Community Pressure and Clean Technology in the Informal Sector: An Econometric Analysis of the Adoption of Propane by Traditional Mexican Brickmakers. *Journal of Environmental Economics and Management*. 35 (1), 1–21.

Blackman, A., Bannister, G. 1998b. *Pollution Control in the Informal Sector: The Ciudad Juarez Brickmakers' Project*. Discussion Papers 98-15, Resources for the Future.

Blackman, A., Shih, J. S., Evans, D., Batz, M., Newbold, S., Cook, J. 2006. The Benefits and Costs of Informal Sector Pollution Control: Mexican Brick Kilns. *Environment and Development Economics*. 11 (05), 603–627.

Blaschke, S. 2000. Union Density and European Integration: Diverging Convergence. *European Journal of Industrial Relations*. 6 (2), 217–236.

Bose, N. 2002. Inflation, the Credit Market, and Economic Growth. *Oxford Economic Papers*. 54 (3), 412–434.

Buehn, A., Schneider, F. 2012. Shadow Economies around the World: Novel Insights, Accepted Knowledge, and New Estimates. *International Tax and Public Finance*. 19 (1), 139–171.

Busato, F., Chiarini, B. 2004. Market and Underground Activities in a Two-Sector Dynamic Equilibrium Model. *Economic Theory*. 234, 863–861.

Byiers, B. 2009. *Informality in Mozambique: Characteristics, Performance and Policy Issues*. USAID, mimeo.

Cantekin, K., Elgin, C. 2017. Extent and Growth Effects of Informality in Turkey: Evidence from a Firm-Level Survey. *Singapore Economic Review*. 62 (5), 1017–1038.

Carneiro, F., Henley, A. 1998. Wage Determination in Brazil: The Growth of Union Bargaining Power and Informal Employment. *Journal of Development Studies*. 34 (4), 117–138.

Caro, L., Galindo, A. J., Melendez, M. 2012. *Credit, Labor Informality and Firm Performance in Colombia*. IDB Working Paper No. IDB-WP-325.

Chaney, T. 2008. Distorted Gravity: The Intensive and Extensive Margins of International Trade. *American Economic Review*. 98 (4), 1707–1721.

Chappell, W. F., Kimenyi, M. S., Mayer, W. J. 1992. The Impact of Unionization on the Entry of Firms: Evidence from US Industries. *Journal of Labor Research*. 13 (3), 273–283.

Chari, V. V., Jones, E. L., Manuelli, R. R. 1995. The Growth Effects of Monetary Policy. *Federal Reserve Bank of Minneapolis Quarterly Review*. 19 (4), 18–32.

Chattopadhyay, S., Banerjee S., Millock, K. 2010. *Pollution Control Instruments in the Presence of an Informal Sector*. Documents de travail du Centre d'Economie de la Sorbonne 10103, Centre d'Economie de la Sorbonne, Universite Pantheon-Sorbonne (Paris 1).

Chaudhuri, S. 2005. *Pollution and Welfare in the Presence of Informal Sector: Is There Any Trade-Off*? Others 0510012, EconWPA.

Chaudhuri, S., Mukhopadhyay, U. (2009) Revisiting the Informal Sector: A General Equilibrium Approach Springer; Ch.7. 1 edition (October 26, 2009).

Cicek, D., Elgin, C. 2011. Cyclicality of Fiscal Policy and the Shadow Economy. *Empirical Economics*. 41 (3), 725–737.

Deardorff, A. V. 1995. *Determinants of Bilateral Trade: Does Gravity Work in a Neoclassical World? The Regionalization of the World Economy*. Chicago: University of Chicago Press.

Demirci, O. 2016. *International Trade and Informality*. Bogazici University Department of Economics Unpublished Master's Thesis.

D'Erasmo, P. N., Moscoso Boedo, H. J. 2012. Financial Structure, Informality and Development. *Journal of Monetary Economics*. 59 (3), 286–302.

De Soto, H. 1989. *The Other Path: The Invisible Revolution in the Third World*. New York: Harper Row.

Dewatripont, M. 1998. The Impact of Trade Unions on Incentives to Deter Entry. *The RAND Journal of Economics*. 19 (2), 191–199.

DiNardo, J., Lee, D. S. 2002. *The Impact of Unionization on Establishment Closure: A Regression Discontinuity Analysis of Representation Elections*. NBER Working Paper 8993.

Dornbusch, R., Fischer, S., Samuelson, P. A. 1977. Comparative Advantage, Trade, and Payments in a Ricardian Model with a Continuum of Goods. *American Economic Review*. 67 (5), 823–839.

Dotsey, M., Sarte, P. D. 2000. Inflation Uncertainty and Growth in a Cash-in-Advance Economy. *Journal of Monetary Economics*. 45 (3), 631–655.

Eaton, J., Kortum, S. 2002. Technology, Geography, and Trade. *Econometrica*. 70 (5), 1741–1779.

Elgin, C. 2012. Unionization and Informal Economy. *Economic Bulletin*. 32 (3), 2615–2623.

Elgin, C. 2015. Informal Economy in a Dynamic Political Framework. *Macroeconomic Dynamics*. 19 (3), 578–617.

Elgin, C., Kose, A., Ohnsorge, F., Yu, S. 2019. *Shades of Grey: Measuring the Informal Economy Business Cycles*. World Bank, mimeo.

Elgin, C., Mazhar, U. 2013. Environmental Regulation, Pollution and the Informal Economy. *SBP Research Bulletin*. 9 (1), 62–81.

Elgin, C., Oztunali, O. 2012. *Shadow Economy all around the World: Model Based Estimates*. Bogazici University Economics Department Working Paper Series, 2012-05.

Elgin, C., Oztunali, O. 2014a. Environmental Kuznets Curve for the Informal Sector of Turkey: 1950–2009. *Panoeconomicus*. 4, 471–485.

Elgin, C., Oztunali, O. 2014b. Pollution and Informal Economy. *Economic Systems*. 38 (3), 333–349.

Elgin, C., Sezgin, M. B. 2017. Sectoral Estimates of Informality: A New Method and An Application to Turkish Economy. *The Developing Economies*. 55 (4), 261–289.

Elgin, C., Solis-Garcia, M. 2012.Public Trust, Taxes, and the Informal Sector. *Bogazici Journal Review of Social, Economic and Administrative Studies*. 26 (1), 27–44.

Elgin, C., Uras, R. B. 2013a. Public Debt, Sovereign Default Risk and Shadow Economy, *Journal of Financial Stability*. 9 (4), 628–640.

Elgin, C., Uras, R. B. 2013b. Is Informality a Barrier for Financial Development? *SERIEs*. 4 (3), 309–331.

Elgin, C., Uras, R. B. 2014. Homeownership, Informality and the Transmission of Monetary Policy. *Journal of Banking and Finance*. 49, 160–168.

Eliat, Y., Zinnes, C. 2000. *The Evolution of the Shadow Economy in Transition Countries: Consequences for Economic Growth and Donor Assistance*. CAER II Discussion Paper No. 65.

Farber, H. S., Western, B. 2001. Accounting for the Decline of Unions in the Private Sector, 1973–1998. *Journal of Labor Research*. 22 (3), 459–485.

Fisher, L., Jaffe, A. 2003. Determinants of International Homeownership Rates. *Housing Finance International*. 18 (1), 34–42.

Fornell, C., Larcker, D. F. 1981. Evaluating Structural Equation Models with Unobservable Variables and Measurement Error. *Journal of Marketing Research*. 18, 39–50.

Friedman, E., Johnson, S., Kaufman, D., Zoldo-Lobaton, P. 2000. Dodging the Grabbing Hand: The Determinants of Unofficial Activity in 69 Countries. *Journal of Public Economics*. 76 (3), 459–493.

Gallardo-Vazquez, D., Sanchez-Hernandez, M. I. 2014. Structural Analysis of the Strategic Orientation to Environmental Protection in SMEs. *Business Research Quarterly*. 17 (2), 115–128.

Gatti, R., Honorati, M. 2008. *Informality among Formal Firms: Firm-Level, Cross-Country Evidence on Tax Compliance and Access to Credit*. Policy Research Working Paper Series 4476, The World Bank.

Helpman, E., Melitz, M., Rubinstein, Y. 2008. Estimating Trade Flows: Trading Partners and Trading Volumes. *Quarterly Journal of Economics*. 123 (2), 441–487.

Herrera, E. G. 2013. Comparing Alternative Methods to Estimate Gravity Models of Bilateral Trade. *Empirical Economics*. 44 (3), 1087–1111.

Ihrig, J., Moe, K. 2004. Lurking in the Shadows: The Informal Sector and Government Policy. *Journal of Development Economics*. 73, 541–77.

Johnson, S., Kaufman, D., Shleifer, A. 1997. The Unofficial Economy in Transition. *Brookings Papers on Economic Activity*. 2, 159–221.

Keynes, J. M. 1936. *The General Theory of Employment, Interest and Money*. London: MacMillan.

Kleiner, M. M. 2001. Intensity of Management Resistance: Understanding the Decline of Unionization in the Private Sector. *Journal of Labor Research*. 22 (3), 519–540.

Kolk, A. 2008. Sustainability, Accountability and Corporate Governance: Exploring Multinationals' Reporting Practices. *Business Strategy and the Environment*. 17 (1), 1–15.

Krugman, P. 1980. Scale Economies, Product Differentiation, and the Pattern of Trade. *American Economic Review*. 70, 950–959.

La Porta, R., Shleifer, A. 2014. Informality and Development. *Journal of Economic Perspectives*. 28 (3), 109–126.

Lee, D. S., Mas, A. 2009. *Long-Run Impacts of Unions on Firms New Evidence from Financial Markets, 1961–1999*. NBER Working Paper, 13709.

Levine, R., Renelt, D. 1992. A Sensitivity Analysis of Cross-Country Growth Regressions. *American Economic Review*. 82, 942–963.

Levy, S. 2008. *Good Intentions, Bad Outcomes. Social Policy, Informality and Economic Growth in Mexico*. Washington, DC: Brookings Institution Press.

Lindgreen, A., Swaen, V., Maon, F. 2009. Introduction: Corporate Social Responsibility Implementation. *Journal of Business Ethics*. 85 (2), 251–256.

Loayza, N. V. 1997. The Economics of the Informal Sector: A Simple Model and Some Empirical Evidence from Latin America. *Carnegie-Rochester Conference Series on Public Policy*. 45 (1), 129–162.

Loayza, N. V., Oviedo, A. M., Serven, L. 2004. *Regulation and Macroeconomic Performance*. World Bank Policy Research Working Paper, 3469.

Magnani, E., Prentice, D. 2003. Did Globalization Reduce Unionization? Evidence from US Manufacturing. *Labour Economics*. 10 (6), 705–726.

Martin, W., Pham, C. S. 2015. *Estimating the Gravity Model When Zero Trade Flows Are Frequent and Economically Determined*. Policy Research Working Paper Series 7308, World Bank.

Massenot, B., Straub, S. 2011. *Informal Sector and Economic Growth: The Supply of Credit Channel*. TSE Working Papers 11-254, Toulouse School of Economics (TSE).

Matten, D., Moon, J. 2008. Implicit and Explicit CSR: A Conceptual Framework for a Comparative Understanding of CSR. *Academy of Management Review*. 33 (2), 404–424.

Matyas, L. 1998. The Gravity Model: Some Econometric Considerations. *World Economy*. 21 (3), 397–401.

McCallum, J. 1995. National Borders Matter: Canada-US Regional Trade Patterns. *American Economic Review*. 85 (3), 615–623.

McWilliams, A., Siegel, D. S. 2000. Corporate Social Responsibility and Financial Performance: Correlation or Misspecification? *Strategic Management Journal*. 21 (5), 603–609.

McWilliams, A., Siegel, D. S., Wright, P. M. 2006. Corporate Social Responsibility: Strategic Implications. *Journal of Management Studies*. 43 (1), 1–18.

Melitz, M. J. 2003. The Impact of Trade on Intra Industry Reallocations and Aggregate Industry Productivity. *Econometrica*. 71 (6), 1695–1725.

Melitz, J. 2007. North, South and Distance in the Gravity Model. *European Economic Review*. 51 (4), 971–991.

Melitz, M. J., Ottaviano, G. I. 2008. Market Size, Trade, and Productivity. *Review of Economic Studies*. 75 (1), 295–316.

Morón, E., Salgado, S., Seminario, C. 2012. *Financial Dependence, Formal Credit and Firm Informality: Evidence from Peruvian Household Data*. Research Department Publications 4776, Inter-American Development Bank.

Naastepad, C. W. M., Storm, S. 2006. OECD demand regimes (1960–2000). *Journal of Post Keynesian Economics*. 29 (2), 211–246.

Nabi, M. S., Drine, I. 2009. External Debt, Informal Economy and Growth. *Economics Bulletin*. 29 (3), 1695–1707.

Oyvat, C., Oztunali, O., Elgin, C. 2018. *Wage-Led vs. Profit-Led Growth: A Comprehensive Empirical Analysis*. Greenwich Papers in Political Economy, 20951, University of Greenwich, Greenwich Political Economy Research Centre.

Persky, J., Tsang, H. 1974. Pigouvian Exploitation of Labor. *Review of Economics and Statistics*. 56 (1), 52–57.

Raj, R. 2011. Technical Efficiency in the Informal Manufacturing Enterprises: Firm Level Evidence from an Indian State. *Journal of South Asian Development*. 6 (2), 213–232.

Rauch, J. E. 1991. Modelling the Informal Sector Formally. *Journal of Development Economics*. 35, 33–47.

Rebelo, S. 1991. Long-Run Policy Analysis and Long-Run Growth. *Journal of Political Economy*. 99, 500–521.

Reinhart, C. M., Rogoff, K. S. 2009. *This Time Is Different: Eight Century of Financial Folly*. Princeton, NJ: Princeton University Press.

Roca, J. C. C., Moreno, C. D., Sanchez, J. E. G. 2001. Underground Economy and Aggregate Fluctuations. *Spanish Economic Review*. 31, 41–53.

Roubini, N., Sala-i-Martin, X. 1995. A Growth Model of Inflation, Tax Evasion, and Financial Repression. *Journal of Monetary Economics*. 35 (2), 275–301.

Sarte, P. D. G. 2000. Informality and Rent-Seeking Bureaucracies in a Model of Long-Run Growth. *Journal of Monetary Economics*. 46 (1), 173–197.

Schneider, F., Buehn, A., Montenegro, C. E. 2010. *Shadow Economies All over the World: New Estimates for 162 Countries from 1999 to 2007*. Policy Research Working Paper 5356, The World Bank.

Schneider, F., Enste, D. H. 2000. Shadow Economies: Sizes, Causes and Consequences. *Journal of Economic Perspectives*. 38, 77–114.

Silva, J. S., Tenreyro, S. 2006. The Log of Gravity. *The Review of Economics and Statistics.* 88 (4), 641–658.

Solow, R. 1957. Technical Change and the Aggregate Production Function. *Review of Economics and Statistics.* 39 (3), 312–320.

Spence, L. J. 1999. Does Size Matter? The State of the Art in Small Business Ethics. *Business Ethics: A European Review.* 8 (3), 163–174.

Straub, S. 2005. Informal Sector: The Credit Market Channel. *Journal of Development Economics.* 78 (2), 299–321.

Taymaz, E. 2009. *Informality and Productivity: Productivity Differentials between Formal and Informal Firms in Turkey.* ERC Working Papers 0901, ERC - Economic Research Center, Middle East Technical University, revised March 2009.

Temple, J. 2000. Inflation and Growth: Stories Short and Tall. *Journal of Economic Surveys.* 14 (4): 397–426.

Thauer, C. R. 2014. Goodness Comes from Within: Intra-Organizational Dynamics of Corporate Social Responsibility. *Business and Society.* 53 (4), 483–516.

Tinbergen, J. 1963. Shaping the World Economy. *The International Executive.* 5 (1), 27–30.

Turker, D. 2009a. Measuring Corporate Social Responsibility: A Scale Development Study. *Journal of Business Ethics.* 85, 411–427.

Turker, D. 2009b. How Corporate Social Responsibility Influences Organizational Commitment. *Journal of Business Ethics.* 89 (2), 189–204.

Utting, P. 2007. CSR and Equality. *Third World Quarterly.* 28 (4), 697–712.

Varvarigos, D. 2010. Inflation, Volatile Public Spending, and Endogenously Sustained Growth. *Journal of Economic Dynamics and Control.* 34 (10), 1893–1906.

Vyakarnam, S., Bailey, A., Myers, A., Burnett, D. 1997. Towards an Understanding of Ethical Behaviour in Small Firms. *Journal of Business Ethics.* 16 (15), 1625–1636.

Zenou, Y. 2008. Job Search and Mobility in Developing Countries. Theory and Policy Implications. *Journal of Development Economics.* 86 (2), 336–355.

7 Concluding remarks

In this book, I aimed to provide a comprehensive view of the literature on the economics of informality. My main goal was to investigate theoretically and empirically the measurements, determinants, and effects of informality. I sincerely hope that, in contrast to existing works on informality, this book has provided a much broader perspective to help readers understand how the informal sector is measured, and what its main determinants and effects are. Even though the literature has been developing at an exponential rate, this field remains under-explored. Consequently, none of the discussion in the book are meant to be exhaustive; nevertheless, I believe it does provide a comprehensive picture.

I never regretted working on informality during my doctoral studies; neither did I regret continuing working on it after obtaining my Ph.D. It was not always easy to convince people that studying informality is necessary and worthwhile. First, it was difficult to attract interest when presenting my findings, especially if the presentation was held in a developed economy to an audience who did not know what the informal sector means. Second, even when talking to economists in developing economies, including Turkey, it could be difficult to convince one not working on informality that this field is important. When I was looking for a position in the winter of 2010, I remember visiting a prominent university in Ankara, where the department's top macroeconomist asked me: "Why should we care about how taxes and the informal sector are related?" Although I still remember the question, I honestly don't remember what my answer was. However, I hope that it is now clear to the readers of this book.

The informal sector has become a phenomenon for both the developing and developed world over the last 60 years. Since then, it has gone through a further significant transformation. What was called the informal sector back in the 1960s or 1970s and what is called that today are not necessarily the same set of activities. That is why I believe that a new set of economic activities will be added to the informal sector in the future. As discussed in the book, the term initially referred to work by low-income and unskilled rural-urban migrants. Now, however, the informal sector includes a much wider range of economic agents and economic activities, including workers in different industries, jobs, and locations. Moreover, the rise of the internet has made temporary and freelance work quite popular, particularly in previously protected domains of white-collar urban workers in the so-called gig economy, which has become a new source for the informal sector.

After a short introduction in Chapter 1, Chapter 2 reviewed various definitions of informality from different angles as used in the research literature and by institutions. It also reviewed the recent literature and speculated about potential directions for future research. Chapter 3 presented different methods for measuring informal sector size. It reviewed the advantages and disadvantages of different definitions before highlighting the one generating the most data. Chapter 4 then used this definition to introduce the measures of informal sector size and the global trends these have revealed. It also presented forecasts of informal sector size for the next few years. Finally, Chapters 5 and 6 focused on the determinants and effects of informality, respectively, before suggesting some implications for policy-makers. Chapter 5 highlighted two major determinants, taxes and institutional quality, while not ignoring other determinants. Besides effects on monetary and fiscal policy, Chapter 6 focused on informality's effects on unionization, economic growth, wage-productivity gap, pollution and energy usage, corporate social responsibility, and bilateral trade.

I believe that the literature on informality will be transformed both by changes in the set of activities in it and through the introduction of new methods and data sets.

First, the new measurement methods and tools that I expect will be developed in the near future will mostly be based on direct methods. These will not require the simplifying and somewhat unrealistic assumptions of existing methods. The informal sector literature will definitely benefit from new methods relying on artificial intelligence, machine learning methods, and big data prediction methods in social sciences.

Second, the multiple determinants and effects of informality will be better modeled and understood through the use of computationally sophisticated models such as the heterogeneous agent-based models. While these models have already been applied to various economics subfields, they have rarely been applied to informality.

Finally, while it might seem wishful thinking, I sincerely hope that future research can benefit from the increasing availability of data from government-run audits and surveys. Such surveys are already available in several developed economies. However, they are quite rare in developing countries, which is where the informal sector is much more prevalent.

Index

ACCA 53–56
agent-based 14, 185

Bayesian estimation 127–128
bureaucratic quality index 37, 81, 117
business freedom 24, 37, 98

Cantekin, K. ix, 19, 27, 33–34, 39, 147–148, 179
capital accumulation 37–38
capital income tax 65–69
capitalists 146–148
capital share 46, 74, 141
cash-in-advance 120, 180
central government debt 116
colonial ties 171–173, 174–175
corporate social responsibility viii, 164, 181–182, 183–185
currency demand 22–23, 24

decreasing returns to scale 28, 31–33, 46, 64, 122, 177
demand-ledgrowth 12, 145
democratic accountability 37–38, 54, 60, 78, 81, 116–117, 153–154
descriptive statistics 29, 30, 47, 50–51, 79, 93, 116, 136–139
direct methods vii, 19, 20, 185
DYMIMIC 22–24, 35

econometrics 11, 39, 100, 178
education ix, 34–35, 47, 137
energy use intensity *see* EUI
ethnic fractionalization 59, 99
ethnic tensions 54
EUI 153–154, 153–157, 177
European Union 10
European Commission 4
EUROSTAT 10, 129

family firm 169, 170–171
financial depth 140
financial development 11–13, 16–17, 59, 101, 122–126, 130, 180
financial intermediation 59

GATT 174–175
generalized Euler equations 73
generalized method of moments 13, 81, 97, 135
Germany 30, 47, 178
Google 3, 11
goods market(s) 33, 121–123
Government Finance Statistics 77
gravity model(s) 171–172, 173, 181–182

hidden economy 7
housing markets viii, 128, 131–133

ICRG 46, 54, 77–78, 79, 83, 93, 116, 129, 140–148, 149, 154, 166
ILO 3, 6, 9, 10, 16, 17, 19, 20, 149
IMF 9, 39, 40, 77, 104, 116
indirect methods vii, 21
indirect taxes 37–38, 98
instrumental variable 80, 96–97, 116

International Country Risk Guide *see* ICRG
investment profile 148–149, 166–168

Kernel density 50
Keynes, J. M. 146, 181
Kuznets curve 43, 153, 180

labor demand 32
labor force participation 21–24
labor income tax 12, 61
labor market policies 58, 102
labor share 141–145, 147–149
labor supply 52, 121–122, 125, 145
Latin America(n) 14, 17, 29, 30–39, 44–47, 51, 56–58, 88, 98, 101–103, 129, 131–137, 181
linguistic fractionalization 60, 176

macroeconomic(s) viii, 11, 13, 14, 15, 16, 17, 22–24, 25–28, 38, 40, 53, 98, 102, 113, 139, 176
manufacturing 34, 103, 138, 181–182
marginal income tax 61, 77
marginal product(s) 8, 90, 146–147
marginal producitivity(ies) 8, 34, 134
MasterCard 1, 6
MENA 30, 44, 98, 129
microeconomic(s) 9, 11, 13, 14, 19, 25, 57, 105
MIMIC vii, 22–23, 24–25, 29, 35–36, 37, 38–39, 96–98, 116
minimum wage 1, 133, 168
model-based method(s) vii, 22–24
money demand 22–24, 119, 122
money supply 26, 122

numerical analysis 33–34, 66, 74, 90
numerical simulation(s) 90, 109, 123–125, 162–163

optimal fiscal policy 14, 103
optimal monetary policy 119
optimal taxation 12, 15, 74, 89
Oyvat, C. 45, 52–56, 60, 102, 146, 182

Penn World Tables 28, 46, 79, 100, 116, 148
personal income tax 37, 98
Pigouvian exploitation 182
political turnover 65, 77, 81, 102
population density 47–48, 51–52, 128–129, 130
profit-maximizing 8

Schneider, F. G. x, 5, 6, 14, 17, 19, 22–23, 24, 27–29, 36–37, 38–39, 40, 59, 60–61, 77, 87–88, 101–102, 103–104, 116, 122, 154, 179, 182
search and matching model(s) 12, 58–59
seasonal employment 167–168
self-employment 10, 20, 37, 59, 98, 138, 145
Solis-Garcia, M. 3, 4, 5, 6, 25–26, 40, 58, 61, 89, 93, 102–105, 112, 180
sovereign debt 113–115, 116–118, 119
Spearman rank 47, 48
structural equation model(s) 22, 103, 180
subgame-perfect equilibrium 109, 110
sub-Saharan 29, 30, 44
system(s) estimations 59, 158, 171

tax evasion 6, 7, 11, 12, 13, 18, 31, 57–59, 61, 100–101, 103, 105, 182
tax morale 7, 37–38, 60, 98–99, 100–104
Tobit regression 173
trade agreement(s) 171, 173–174, 175
trade barriers 58, 172
trade openness 93–94, 116–117, 135–139, 140–141, 149, 151
trade unions 133, 179
transition economies 12, 14, 30, 101, 129, 130–131, 132, 137–139
Turkish economy 39, 56, 148, 166, 180

UNCTAD 9
underground economy 10, 11, 16, 39, 40, 56, 101–104, 182
UNDP 9
unemployment (rate) 4, 12, 15, 17, 23–24, 37, 54–57, 58–59, 98–99, 101, 117, 134
United Kingdom 55, 128
United States 24, 40–47, 50–55, 75–76, 101, 127–128
utility maximization 89, 106

WTO 174–175
World Bank 4, 9, 16, 20–21, 39, 40, 54–56, 102–103, 116, 154, 178, 180–181, 182
World Development Indicators 20, 54, 77, 100, 116
World Economic Forum 20
World Values Survey 21
World Bank Enterprise Surveys 20, 21

youth population 47–48, 51–52